The DURBIN ROUTE

The GREENBRIER DIVISION *of the* **CHESAPEAKE & OHIO RAILWAY**

The Chesapeake and Ohio Railway Co.
"On Time" Circular

R. H. VAUGHAN,

**General Through Freight Agent
In Charge Solicitation and Service**

MANIFEST TIME FREIGHT TRAINS

second and third sections inclusive,
actual performance

During June, July and August, 1927

—Between—

Chicago, Ill.	Gregg, O.
Cincinnati, O.	Louisville, Ky.
Columbus, O.	Lexington, Ky.

—and—

Russell, Ky.	Durbin, W. Va.
Ashland, Ky.	Clifton Forge, Va.
Elkhorn City, Ky.	Waynesboro, (Basic) Va.
Huntington, W. Va.	Charlottesville, Va.
Charleston, W. Va.	Lynchburg, Va.
Handley, W. Va.	Richmond, Va.
Deepwater, W. Va.	Newport News, Va.
Gauley, W. Va.	Norfolk, Va.
Hinton, W. Va.	Sewell's Point, Va.
Ronceverte, W. Va.	Washington, D. C.

The Carolinas, South-East and Florida.

Issued Cincinnati, Ohio
September 3, 1927.

The DURBIN ROUTE

The GREENBRIER DIVISION *of the* CHESAPEAKE & OHIO RAILWAY

By WILLIAM PRICE McNEEL

Early Greenbrier Division passenger train crossing Greenbrier River bridge near Harter en route to Ronceverte. PCHS

Pictorial Histories Publishing Company • Charleston, West Virginia

LIBRARY OF CONGRESS
CATALOG CARD NUMBER 84-62875

ISBN 0-933126-56-5

First Printing April 1985
Second Printing April 1986

Typography: Arrow Graphics & Typography
Layout: Stan Cohen
Cover Art Work: Dolack Design Studio
Maps: George Deike

PICTORIAL HISTORIES PUBLISHING COMPANY
4103 Virginia Avenue SE
Charleston, West Virginia 25304

Introduction and Acknowledgments

THE GREENBRIER DIVISION. FROM THE CORPO-rate point of view of the Chesapeake and Ohio Railway, the Greenbrier Division was only one of many branch lines and probably thought of mainly when it was time to add up the annual balance sheet. However, in relation to those who have known this rail line, it filled a number of roles.

To several generations of railroad men, the Greenbrier was the location of their jobs, one they did well and, the author hopes, with a measure of satisfaction.

To the people of the Upper Greenbrier Valley of West Virginia, the line was for many years their vital economic lifeline to the rest of the nation.

To the nation, this branch line was for a number of years the source of a large quantity of the lumber products needed for a growing national economy. For a nation at war in 1917-1918 and 1941-1945, it was one of the transportation corridors essential for victory.

To the railfan and railroad historian, the Greenbrier Division was a branch line with not only the characteristics normally associated with branch line railroading, but also with some usually only found on main lines. Included were passenger service that ranged from parlor cars to "doodlebugs;" timed freight trains that operated between Chicago and the Eastern Seaboard; motive power from 4-4-0s to 2-6-6-2s; timetables that showed as many as eleven scheduled trains per day; and the usual assortment of wrecks and other operating problems over the years.

To the lumber industry historian, the Greenbrier was the line serving more lumber companies than any other branch line in the state, including the fabled Cass operation of the West Virginia Pulp and Paper Company.

This book is an effort to chronicle the history of this particular branch line of the Chesapeake and Ohio Railway. The area of West Virginia that was served by the Greenbrier Division is referred to by the author as the Upper Greenbrier Valley. The name comes, of course, from the Greenbrier River which has its headwaters in two forks in northern Pocahontas County. The river drains most of Pocahontas County and portions of Greenbrier and Summers Counties as it flows to a junction with the New River. For this book the Upper Greenbrier Valley is that part of the river valley in Pocahontas County and Greenbrier County north of Ronceverte.

In writing this history the author has been assisted by a number of people. In making acknowledgments and expressing thanks, there is always the risk of forgetting someone who should be mentioned, especially in a project that has spanned a number of years. However, it would be wrong to let this risk preclude expressing appreciation to those who helped. Without the contributions of many people, this book would be far less complete.

First, a word of appreciation to those of my own family who were responsible for the preservation of the files of *The Pocahontas Times* over the years. Without these papers much of the history of the Greenbrier line would have been lost.

I am greatly indebted to Thomas W. Dixon, Jr., and the Chesapeake and Ohio Historical Society. Tom spent much time going through both his own and the Society's collections of historic material to provide much valuable data on the Greenbrier Division as well as many photographs.

A special mention needs to be made of Eugene Burner. Eugene was not directly involved with this particular project, but his efforts in copying photographs for the photograph collection of the Pocahontas County Historical Society made possible many of the pictures in this book.

My thanks go to the following and their staffs for their kindness and cooperation in locating and making available to me records concerning the Greenbrier: E.C. Hostettler, Chief of the Valuation Section at the Interstate Commerce Commission, Washington, D.C.; Barry Blank, Assistant to Vice-president, and Jerry Wess, Head of the Property Accounting Office, Chessie System, with their offices in Baltimore, Maryland; and H.E. Matics, with the Westvaco Corporation in Covington, Virginia.

Richard Lehman, Midwest Corporation, Charleston, West Virginia, and Mark Hankins, Lewisburg, West Virginia, (son of Greenbrier Division engineer M.A. Hankins), made donations of track maps of the line.

Mrs. Helen Clemons Phipps kindly made available notes she had taken from her late husband, Thomas Clemons, on his career with the maintenance force of the Chesapeake and Ohio.

The National Radio Astronomy Observatory at Green Bank, West Virginia; the Monongahela National

Forest, Elkins, West Virginia; and the Westvaco Corporation, Covington, Virginia, provided photographs.

The following individuals supplied information and/or photographs: Glema L. Auldridge, Robert Auldridge, Brown Beard, Ruth S. Beebe, G.A. Brice, Charles A. Brown, Leona G. Brown, William Buckley, George Clinebell, George Deike, Harry Dolan, C.N. Dorman, J.E. Hall, Jr., Mark Hankins, Arthur B. Hedrick, Floyd Jones, Ernestine H. Keller, B.C. Kenney, John Killoran, Charles C. LaRue, Samuel Lovelace, Sydney Lovelace, James Madison, A.D. McCoy, Berl McLaughlin, Alice M. Moore, Wendell A. Scott, Ward Sharp, Earl Slavin, Mildred Slavin, Benton Smith, William R. Vivian, Harry Wanless, E.C. Whanger, and C.E. Wheeler. I am most grateful to all of these people and to others whose names I have probably forgotten to list.

My chief proofreader has been my wife, Denise, who has also been very tolerant of the time this project has taken from the family.

No claim is made that this history of the Greenbrier Division is complete or free of errors. Any mistakes are, of course, the responsibility of the author. However, I hope this book is a reasonable effort to relate the history of one of the more important and interesting branch lines of the Chesapeake and Ohio Railway. I ask my readers to please send corrections and any additional information of the Greenbrier line to me.

William P. McNeel
Marlinton, West Virginia
December 1984

For James:
He saw the last train go down the Greenbrier line when he was six months old. Perhaps this book will enable him and others of his generation to at least know the Greenbrier Division in their minds' eyes.

PHOTO CREDITS

COHS—Chesapeake and Ohio Historical Society
PCHS—Pocahontas County Historical Society
PCHS/NRP—Pocahontas County Historical Society;
        photograph taken by Dr. Norman R. Price
WPM—photograph taken by the author

Contents

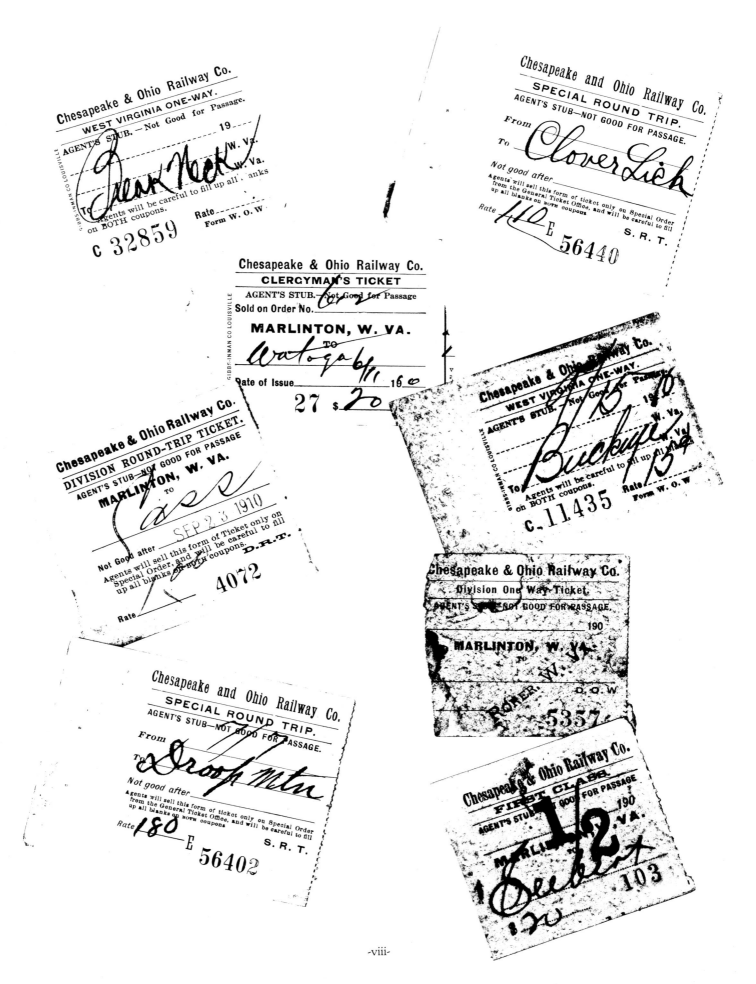

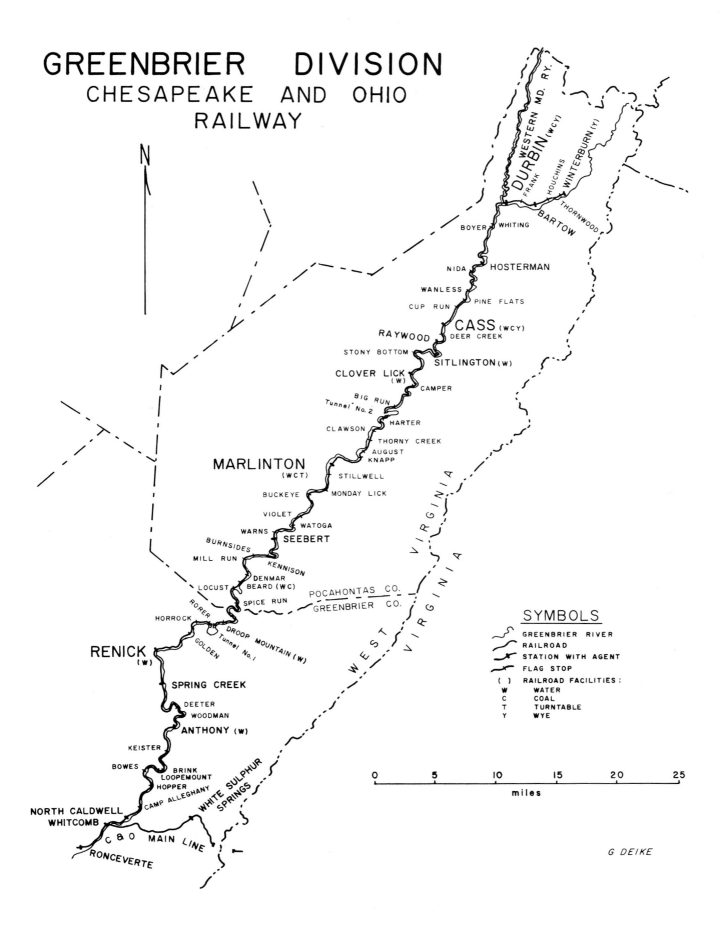

GREENBRIER DIVISION
CHESAPEAKE AND OHIO
RAILWAY

N

WESTERN MD. RY.

DURBIN (WCY)

FRANK
HOUCHINS
WINTERBURN (Y)
THORNWOOD

BARTOW

BOYER   WHITING

NIDA   HOSTERMAN

WANLESS

CUP RUN   PINE FLATS

RAYWOOD   CASS (WCY)

DEER CREEK

STONY BOTTOM   SITLINGTON (W)

CLOVER LICK
(W)

CAMPER

BIG RUN
Tunnel No. 2

HARTER

CLAWSON

THORNY CREEK
AUGUST
KNAPP

MARLINTON
(WCT)

STILLWELL

BUCKEYE   MONDAY LICK

VIOLET

WARNS   WATOGA

BURNSIDES   SEEBERT

MILL RUN
KENNISON
DENMAR
BEARD (WC)

LOCUST

SPICE RUN

POCAHONTAS CO.
GREENBRIER CO.

RORER
HORROCK
DROOP MOUNTAIN (W)
Tunnel No. 1

RENICK
(W)

GOLDEN

SPRING CREEK

DEETER
WOODMAN
ANTHONY (W)

KEISTER

BOWES

BRINK
LOOPEMOUNT
HOPPER

CAMP ALLEGHANY

WHITE SULPHUR SPRINGS

WEST   VIRGINIA

VIRGINIA

NORTH CALDWELL
WHITCOMB

C & O   MAIN LINE

RONCEVERTE

SYMBOLS

〰	GREENBRIER RIVER
∿	RAILROAD
┼	STATION WITH AGENT
┴	FLAG STOP
( )	RAILROAD FACILITIES:
W	WATER
C	COAL
T	TURNTABLE
Y	WYE

0   5   10   15   20   25
miles

G DEIKE

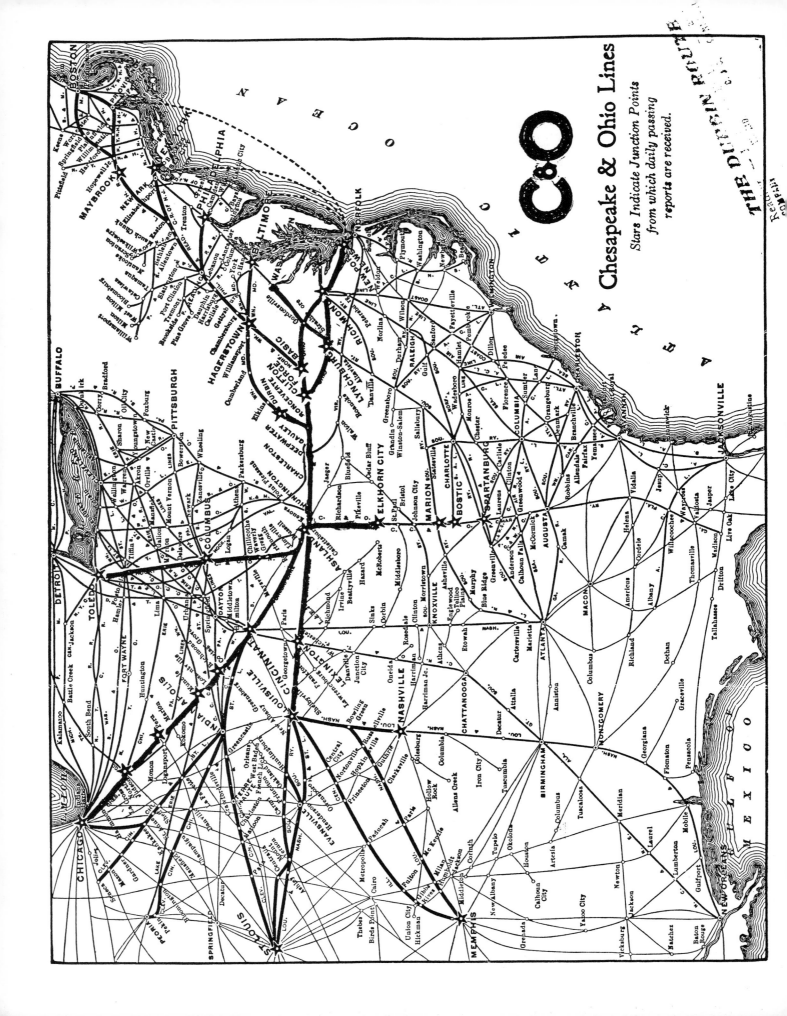

C & O

Chesapeake & Ohio Lines

Stars Indicate Junction Points from which daily passing reports are received.

THE DURGIN ROUTE

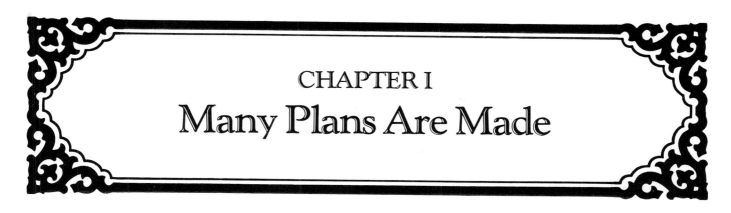

CHAPTER I
Many Plans Are Made

RAILROADS! FOLLOWING THE CIVIL WAR, A mania for the building of railroads swept the United States as the nation entered one of its periods of rapid growth. "Give us a railroad and our prosperity and successful future are assured" was the thinking of most communities of the time. And railroads were indeed needed for the economic well-being of an area, since they had become the dominant form of transportation following the Civil War. The development of the resources of any locality did depend upon being connected to the nation's rail network.

The Upper Greenbrier Valley, with its vast acreage of timber and other resources, was no exception. Many people in the valley (though not all, as we shall see) dreamed of the day when their area would join in the industrial development of other areas within the new state of West Virginia and the nation at large. However, these people would have to wait for thirty-five years after the Civil War before the nation's rail system finally ran a tentacle into the Upper Greenbrier Valley. It was not that the area and its resources were unknown, since some of the finest timber in the eastern United States was located in the Greenbrier Valley and other parts of eastern and northeastern West Virginia. The problem was the cost of building, maintaining, and operating railroads in the mountains.

At the end of the Civil War the state of West Virginia was itself largely void of railroads. Only the Baltimore and Ohio Railroad crossed the entire state and it served only a few northern counties. The Upper Greenbrier Valley had to wait its turn while the Chesapeake and Ohio Railway was built across the central part of the state and the Norfolk and Western Railroad into the southern counties. These major lines, their many branches, and other smaller railroads soon opened the many resources of the new state for development, particularly the vast coal fields of northern and southern West Virginia and the oil region in the Ohio River Valley.

Towards the end of the nineteenth century, the development of the coal and oil resources of the state was generating enough capital so that the building of railroads into the mountainous counties became possible. Also capital resources from out of West Virginia were becoming available as the depletion of the timber in other states, particularly Pennsylvania, caused men with a need for timber to look towards the vast forests of West Virginia.

However, much dreaming was done, many plans laid, numerous corporations chartered, and many miles of railroad surveyed before the first railroad crossed into the Upper Greenbrier Valley.

No serious attempt to build into this area was likely to be made until a considerably more important railroad construction project was completed—that of connecting the Chesapeake Bay region with the Ohio River. Hopes of making that connection go back into the 1700s when the method was to be a canal and road system connecting the James and Kanawha Rivers. The James River Canal Company was organized in 1785 and reorganized as the James River and Kanawha Canal Company in 1835. The canal was in operation between Richmond and Lynchburg by 1840 and later extended to Buchanan. It turned out that this was as far as the canal would be built and one of the reasons was the new, competing form of transportation, the railroad. The predecessor of today's Chesapeake and Ohio Railway was the Louisa Railroad, chartered in February 1836. In 1850 the name of the company was changed to the Virginia Central Railroad, and by the Civil War it connected Richmond with Clifton Forge. In 1853 the Covington and Ohio Railroad was chartered, but work on this line was interrupted by the Civil War. Following the war the two railroads were merged into one, the Chesapeake and Ohio Railroad. (It became the Chesapeake and Ohio Railway in 1878.) Construction took place at both ends of the route between Covington and the Ohio River. Train service to White Sulphur Springs began on July 1, 1869, and the line was completed in January 1873.

Even before the Civil War the construction of what was to become the Chesapeake and Ohio Railway involved the people in the Greenbrier Valley. In June 1850 the County Court of Pocahontas County ordered a vote to be taken on August 29 of that year on the question of subscribing to the capital stock of the Virginia Central Railroad in an amount not to exceed $10,000. No record has been found by the author of the results of that vote.

The act passed by the West Virginia Legislature on

February 26, 1867, authorizing the creation of the Chesapeake and Ohio, permitted counties to subscribe to the stock of the new company provided the subscription was approved by the voters by a three-fifths majority. As a result of this law the Pocahontas County Board of Supervisors (County Court) ordered a vote for October 24 on the question of whether the county should buy $50,000 of the preferred 8 percent stock in the Chesapeake and Ohio, to be paid for by issuing bonds. However, the proposition lost by a 132 to 17 vote.

The legislature revised the portion of the act concerning the purchase of the Chesapeake and Ohio stock by counties the next year and the Pocahontas County Board of Supervisors authorized another vote, to be taken on April 28, 1868, on the stock purchase question. This time the voters approved the purchase by a vote of 143 to 81. Although the Board appointed Cyrus Newton as agent in September 1868 to subscribe to the $50,000 in stock, no record has been found to indicate if the stock was actually purchased by the county.

The Chesapeake and Ohio was not the only railroad that came to the attention of the governing bodies in the Greenbrier Valley. Two years before the Chesapeake and Ohio stock question came up, the Pocahontas County Board of Supervisors approved in December 1865 a subscription for $10,000 of the capital stock of the Monongahela and Lewisburg Railway. The Monongahela and Lewisburg was incorporated in 1865 to build a railroad from the Pennsylvania line, through Morgantown, Fairmont, Clarksburg, and Buckhannon to an intersection with the proposed Chesapeake and Ohio. Subscribing to the stock was made conditional upon the railroad being constructed through Pocahontas County and approval by three-fifths of the voters at the next regular election. In the record of this election there is no mention of a vote having been taken on the stock issue; the railroad was never built anyway.

The question of Pocahontas County subscribing to $50,000 of the stock of a proposed railroad named the Washington, Cincinnati, and St. Louis came before the County Court several times over a two-year period in the 1870s. Votes on this issue were ordered for October 14, 1873, June 6, 1874, and September 25, 1875. Whether any of these votes were actually held and, if so, what the results were, has not been located in existing county records. The route for this railroad through the county, as described in the order for the 1875 election, was to cross the Allegheny Mountains at a gap near Frost, go down Knapps Creek to the Greenbrier River at or near Marlin's Bottom, then up Stony Creek, and down the Williams River. (This was the first of many lines proposed to go through the "Stony Creek Gap"). The proposal was for the county to issue bonds to the company and get stock in return, as the construction work actually progressed in the county. Work was to begin in two years and be completed in the county in five years. This company did lease some mineral rights in 1873 and 1874 on a number of tracts in Pocahontas County and this seems to have been the extent of its activities in the Upper Greenbrier Valley.

In 1885 and 1886 the promoters of the Chicago, Parkersburg, and Norfolk Railway urged the Pocahontas County Court to schedule a vote on the issue of buying $50,000 of stock of this railroad. This company had been incorporated in 1884 by a group of men from Parkersburg to build a railroad from Parkersburg through Wood, Wirt, Calhoun, Gilmer, Braxton, Webster, Pocahontas, and Greenbrier Counties (and we assume with plans to go on to Chicago and Norfolk). The proposed route of this road through Pocahontas County was up Elk River from Webster County, up Big Spring Fork of Elk, over the mountain to Clover Creek, and down that stream to the Greenbrier River. The line was then mapped down the west side of the river to the bend above Marlin's Bottom, crossing the river at that point, and then up Knapps Creek to Huntersville. From Huntersville the railroad was to go on to White Sulphur Springs.

Crossing the mountain from Big Spring Fork, the line was surveyed to go through a 2,850-foot tunnel and would involve 7,400 feet of trestles and bridges. Several years later, a writer in *The Pocahontas Times*, after looking over a copy of the survey filed at the Pocahontas County Court House, commented:

> . . . . but when they leave the Greenbrier and go up Clover creek to cross the divide to the waters of Elk the trouble begins. Cuts, trestles, tunnels, and fills follow each other in bewildering succession on an average grade of about two hundred feet to the mile. There are calculations for hundred thousands cubic yards of excavations of solid rock and loose earth. Thousands of cubic yards of masonry called for. We can well understand how this road struck terror to the souls of its promoters.

The buying of this stock seems to have been a controversial issue among the citizens of the county with petitions to the Court both pro and con. In July 1886 the Court decided not to call for a vote as the members felt that a majority of the people were against the proposal. Col. Henry B. Hubbard, of Wheeling, was in Pocahontas County in 1885 on business and commented on the opposition to the proposed railroad as follows:

> A few minutes after breakfast sufficed to complete our business here (Huntersville), and a look over the village satisfied us that the thing for us to do was to get away as soon as possible, and we could not help thinking it would be the best thing everyone in the town could do, for a more hopeless outlook I never saw. Still it is the county seat and a railroad or two would work wonders. A survey from Parkersburg to the Chesapeake & Ohio at White Sulphur by way of Huntersville, shows the route to be eminently practicable, as no grade over sixty feet to the mile would have to be overcome, while it would lead through a section of country abounding in timber, coal and iron ore. About fifteen miles to the west of Huntersville, on the line of the surveyed route, there is reported an abundance of the finest coking coal in the country, and twelve miles to the eastward in Beaver Creek Mountain hematite and fossiliferous ore in large quantities, with mountains of limestone between the two points to be thrown in for good measure. With these advantages it would be natural to suppose that every man, woman and child in the county would

be in favor of a railroad, but such is not the fact, as most of the solid men are reported as unfavorable to it, and to be using their influence to prevent it being built.

To us who appreciate the advantage of railroads such a state of things was almost incredible. A better understanding of the habits of this class of people, however, did much toward removing our incredulity, and to start the query whether, after all, they were not wise in their opposition so far as they are individually concerned being as they are a preeminently pastoral people with no desire for the rush, strife and turmoil of trade, but perfectly satisfied with their thousand acres covered with flocks and herds, and the comforts and influences derived from them. A tripling or quadrupling of the value of their lands would not add to their happiness nor change their occupation, but would add to the amount of their taxes without producing an extra blade of grass.

A number of other railroads made plans to bring their lines into the Upper Greenbrier Valley during the 1870s and 1880s. None of these was built and most never went beyond a paper existence. A few actually did run surveys and let us hope the surveyors actually got paid; if they were to be paid from the revenues from the running of trains, then their heirs may still have the unpaid bills.

Moorefield and South Branch Valley Railroad. Incorporated in March 1869 to begin on the Baltimore and Ohio in Hampshire County, through Romney, Moorefield, Petersburg, and hence by the most practicable route to the Ohio River at Point Pleasant. (The name was changed to the Potomac and Ohio Railway shortly after its original incorporation.) Pocahontas County was one of the counties given authority to subscribe for stock.

Cumberland, Moorefield and Broadway Railroad. Also incorporated in March 1869. This line was to be built from near Cumberland, Maryland, by way of Moorefield and Petersburg to a point on the West Virginia/Virginia line near Monterey, Virginia. Also a branch was to go from Moorefield to the state line near Broadway, Virginia. Pocahontas County was included in the counties that were authorized to subscribe for stock.

Pittsburg, Virginia, and Charleston Railroad. This company was incorporated by the Legislature in 1870 to build from the West Virginia/Pennsylvania state line, up the Monongahela River and its tributaries to some point on the Virginia and Tennessee Railroad near Salem, Virginia.

West Virginia Railroad. Planned in 1875 by men from Kanawha County to run from the mouth of the Big Sandy River in Wayne County to the mouth of the South Branch of the Potomac River on the West Virginia/Maryland line in Hampshire County, going by way of the Kanawha and Elk Rivers, through Pocahontas County and on into Pendleton County.

Potomac and Ohio Railroad. Incorporated in May 1878 to build a railroad from Charleston to the West Virginia/Virginia border in Pendleton County, passing through Pocahontas County, with two branch lines to the West Virginia/Pennsylvania line in Monongalia County and a branch line to the Ohio River in Wayne County.

Pittsburgh Southern Railway. Proposed in 1879 as a narrow gauge line with plans to build from Pittsburgh to the Chesapeake and Ohio Railway by way of Morgantown, Grafton, Tygarts Valley River, and the Greenbrier River, and possibly on into Virginia by way of the New River. In a speech to the Chamber of Commerce in Pittsburgh in March 1880, West Virginia Governor Henry M. Mathews gave a glowing account of the resources along the route of this line and how those resources would flow to Pittsburgh if the line was built. Concerning the Greenbrier Valley, the Governor waxed eloquently on the vast acreages of timber of various types and the fine agricultural land. He also told the businessmen of the Steel City of the "immense deposits" of iron ore on the Greenbrier River and several of its tributaries with a vein of brown hematite "from twelve to one hundred feet" thick as well as a deposit of "block ore" seven feet thick and "fossil ore" about forty inches.

Pittsburg and Southwest Virginia Railway. Planned in 1880 to build from the West Virginia/Pennsylvania line in Monongalia County, passing through Pocahontas and Greenbrier Counties, to the West Virginia/Virginia border in Summers, Mercer or Greenbrier County.

Grafton and Greenbrier Railroad. Planned in 1881 to build a narrow gauge line from the Baltimore and Ohio Railroad in Taylor County, through Pocahontas County, to the Chesapeake and Ohio Railway in Greenbrier County. One of the organizers was George H. Moffett, of Pocahontas County.

White Sulphur and Parkersburg Railroad. Proposed by men from Greenbrier County and Virginia in 1881 to run a railroad from White Sulphur Springs to Parkersburg, passing through Pocahontas County.

Kanawha and Chesapeake Railroad. Filed a location map and profile at the Pocahontas County Court House in October 1881, showing a route from Marlinton, up Stony Creek, and down the Williams River to Webster County. On its way up the mountain to Woodrow, a 300-foot tunnel was surveyed.

Meadow River Valley Railroad. Incorporated in 1882 to build a railroad from Cannelton, Kanawha County, by way of the Gauley and Meadow Rivers to the Greenbrier River near Renick, up the Greenbrier to its head, and then to the mouth of the South Branch of the Potomac River.

Gauley River and Pittsburg Railroad. Planned in 1882 to build from Gauley Bridge up the Gauley River to connect with the Pittsburg and West Virginia Railroad in Pocahontas County.

East River, Greenbrier, and Valley River Railroad. Proposed in 1882 to go from Mercer County, to Ronceverte, up the Greenbrier River, to the Valley River by way of the Elk River, and on to Grafton and Morgantown.

West Virginia Central Railway. Incorporated in 1883 to build a railroad from Wayne County to Charleston, up the Kanawha and Gauley Rivers, passing through Pocahontas County, and on into Virginia near Harrisonburg, and finally on to the Potomac River.

Webster Railroad. Incorporated in 1883 to build a railroad from Clarksburg to White Sulphur Springs "by the most practicable route."

Virginia, Parkersburgh, and Ohio Railway. Incorporated in 1887 to build a line from Parkersburg to the West Virginia/Virginia line in Pocahontas County with a branch from Marlin's Bottom to the Chesapeake and Ohio in Greenbrier County.

Blackwater and Greenbrier Valley Railroad. Incorporated in 1888 to build from the mouth of the Blackwater River, up either Laurel or Dry Forks (or both) to the headwaters of the Greenbrier River and on to the Chesapeake and Ohio with numerous branches.

Gauley and Eastern Railway. Incorporated in 1889 to construct a railroad from Gauley Bridge, up the Gauley River and on to Huntersville, "by the most practicable route."

Elk Valley and Tide Water Railroad. Incorporated in 1889 to build from Charleston to Braxton Court House (Sutton) and on to the West Virginia/Virginia border near Frost.

Ohio and West Virginia Southern Railway. Incorporated in 1889 to build a railroad from Williamstown in Wood County to Huntersville by the usual "most practicable route" and then to the West Virginia/Virginia state line.

West Virginia Midland Railway. Incorporated in 1890 to construct a line from Tucker County to Ronceverte "by the most practicable route."

Ronceverte, Lewisburg, and Coal Knob Railroad. Incorporated in 1890 to build from Ronceverte to Grafton "by the most practicable route."

Grafton and Kanawha Railroad. Incorporated in 1890 to build a line from Grafton to Beverly in Randolph County and then on to Charleston passing through Pocahontas County enroute. One of the incorporators was John T. McGraw who will appear again in the history of railroads in the Greenbrier Valley.

Potomac, Blackwater, and Greenbrier Valley Railroad. Incorporated in 1890 to build from Romney to Petersburg, up the North Fork through Pendleton County, and down the Greenbrier River to White Sulphur Springs with various branch lines enroute.

While men in far, and not so far, distant cities sat around and made paper plans to bring railroads to the Upper Greenbrier Valley, a man on the scene, faced with an immediate transportation problem, was the first to actually build a steam-powered railroad in the area. The man was Capt. A.E. Smith, a logging contractor for the St. Lawrence Boom and Manufacturing Company. The St. Lawrence Company was the major producer of the white pine in the region, beginning in the middle 1870s. The company's mill was located at Ronceverte on the newly constructed main line of the Chesapeake and Ohio. To move the timber it had purchased in Pocahontas and Greenbrier Counties to the mill, the company

had to make use of the Greenbrier River since there was no railroad line running to the timber. Beginning by 1876 or before and continuing for over thirty years, the annual log drives of white pine logs down the Greenbrier River to the boom at Ronceverte were an exciting and fascinating part of the history of the Upper Greenbrier Valley.

Capt. Smith got a contract in 1855 from St. Lawrence to cut the white pine on McCutcheon Tract, located in what is now Seneca State Forest. The problem he faced was that the timber was located on Thomas Run, not a large stream even in flood. To move the logs to the banks of Sitlington Creek from where they could be floated on to the Greenbrier, Smith decided on building a railroad. He purchased a seven ton saddle tank steam locomotive from the H.K. Porter Company. The engine was shipped by rail to Staunton, Virginia, and from there hauled, in pieces, by wagon to Thomas Creek. Capt. Smith named the diminutive locomotive "Little Jim" after his young son. The first railroad in the Upper Greenbrier Valley ran on Thomas Creek until the spring of 1890 and was then moved to Cummings Creek near Huntersville. "Little Jim" is believed to have been next used by Capt. Smith near Rimel. It was later used at August and the last known of it was at the lumber job of the Kidd, Kirby, and Lilly Lumber Company on Trump Run.

By 1891 the hopes of those wanting rail service into the Upper Greenbrier Valley were closer to fulfillment than they had ever been before. In February, *The Pocahontas Times* could claim, with some justification:

> Old Pocahontas County will not be without a railroad two years longer. Pocahontas County will undergo the greatest development and prosperity of any County in the State in the next five years. She will have a railroad, and the industries that will spring up from it will furnish employment to thousands of families. She has iron ore, coal and untold millions of feet of lumber, which speaks for itself.

(However, in the same issue, the correspondent from Douthards Creek, perhaps a bit cynical after the years of proposed railroads and no results, wrote, "We have been watching for the Railroad but have seen nothing of it yet. Expect the creek was too high.")

This prediction of coming rail service was based on more than vain hope as business transactions on the part of several prominent West Virginia politicians/industrialists over the preceding decade were bringing the day of the development of the resources of the Upper Greenbrier Valley closer to hand. The major actors in this drama in the 1890s were Johnson Newlon Camden and Henry Gassaway Davis. Playing important supporting roles were Davis' son-in-law, Stephen Benton Elkins, and John Thomas McGraw.

Following the Civil War the new State of West Virginia rapidly changed from one whose economy was primarily based on agriculture to an industrial one based on the development of the state's coal, oil, timber, and other natural resources. Camden, Davis, Elkins, and McGraw were among the most important of the new breed of men who combined careers in both politics and business to make the state what it is now. Today, of course, much of what they did is open to criticism for the effects it has had on the history of West Virginia, but that is not our concern in this book.

J.N. Camden was born in 1828 in Lewis County and was educated as a lawyer. He got into the banking business and in the late 1850s became one of the founders of the oil industry in West Virginia, becoming an associate of John D. Rockefeller and the Standard Oil Company. He also became a builder of railroads and a developer of coal and timber lands in various parts of the state. Active in the Democratic Party, he was a member of the United States Senate at two different times and several times an unsuccessful candidate for governor.

Henry G. Davis.   W. Va. Department of Culture and History

Johnson N. Camden.   W. Va. Department of Culture and History

H.G. Davis was a native of Maryland where he was born in 1823. He began his career as an employee of the Baltimore and Ohio Railroad, soon became a merchant, and got involved in the development of coal and timber lands and the necessary railroads in the northeastern part of West Virginia. Also a Democrat, Davis served in the West Virginia Legislature and was in the United States Senate 1871-1883. He was a candidate for Vice-president of the United States in 1904 as the running mate of the unsuccessful Democrat of that year, Alton B. Parker.

S.B. Elkins was born in 1841 in Ohio and married Hallie Davis in 1875. He joined his father-in-law in the development of the family coal and railroad empire. A Republican, he was active in the affairs of that party without letting political differences affect his business or family relationships. He was a United States Senator 1895-1911.

J.T. McGraw, like Camden, a native of western Virginia, was born in 1856 in Grafton. A lawyer by profession, he was active in the affairs of the Democratic Party at the state and national levels. He was a candidate for the United States Congress several times, but never elected. The Greenbrier Valley was one of the areas of the state where McGraw was active in land and railroad development efforts.

Senators Camden and Davis became friends and political allies soon after the Civil War and invested in each other's enterprises. For a number of years their business ventures had been in separate areas of the state but by the 1880s they both were acquiring interest in the east central mountains, including the Greenbrier Valley.

Senator Davis made his first purchase of land on the waters of the Greenbrier River in 1881, some 2000 acres on Allegheny Mountain in central Pocahontas County. In July of that year he made a camping trip of ten days into Pocahontas County and on to White Sulphur

Stephen B. Elkins.   W. Va. Department of Culture and History

John T. McGraw.   W. Va. Department of Culture and History

Springs over the proposed route (and beyond) of his West Virginia Central and Pittsburg Railroad. He was accompanied by Camden, Elkins, and four others and they passed through the Canaan Valley, up Dry Fork, Travelers Repose, and Huntersville enroute to White Sulphur.

The West Virginia Central and Pittsburg was originally the Potomac and Piedmont Coal and Railroad Company, chartered in February 1866 by the Legislature to build from the Baltimore and Ohio Railroad in Mineral County into Grant, Tucker, and Randolph Counties. Actual construction did not begin until April 1880. The company received a new charter and name in February 1881, with additional authority to build into Barbour and Pocahontas Counties. The same year the West Virginia Central acquired land and mineral rights totaling 7400 acres in Pocahontas County on Browns Mountain, Knapps Creek, and the Greenbrier River.

Under the new charter construction began in earnest and the town of Davis was reached in November 1884. The route in the Blackwater Canyon presented difficulties and the railroad was not at its next major objective, the new town of Elkins, until the summer of 1889. From here the valley of the Greenbrier was approachable by several different routes.

Meanwhile the interests of Senator Camden were also moving towards the Greenbrier Valley. In 1881 he acquired 84,000 acres of the Caperton Survey (named for United States Senator Allen T. Caperton) in Nicholas and Webster Counties. Davis and Elkins later each acquired one-fourth interest in this property at Camden's invitation. Camden obtained additional land in Nicholas and Webster Counties as well as in Pocahontas and Greenbrier Counties on the Gauley, Williams, Cherry, and Cranberry Rivers in 1889 and later years to make a total of some 135,000 acres (including the Caperton Lands). With this land and other property in Lewis, Upshur, Braxton, and Randolph Counties, the Senator was in need of a railroad to develop this property.

As the 1880s came to a close, Camden came under pressure to build a railroad into his holdings due to the threat of other railroads aiming for the same area. One was Davis and Elkins' West Virginia Central and another was a company named the Kanawha and Ohio which was planning a line up the Gauley River to a possible junction with the West Virginia Central. By June of 1887 the Kanawha and Ohio had a survey up the Gauley River to the Williams River, up the Williams and over the mountain to Marlin's Bottom, from there up Knapps Creek into Virginia, and by way of Back Creek and Jackson River to the Richmond and Allegheny Railroad.

The plan for a railroad that Camden finally devised was to consolidate two small railroads he already controlled that connected the towns of Weston and Buckhannon with the Baltimore and Ohio. A new company was formed in 1890, the West Virginia and Pittsburgh Railroad, following an agreement in December 1889 with the Baltimore and Ohio. The Baltimore and Ohio agreed to aid financially with the construction of the new railroad and to lease and operate the line for 999 years. The route finally selected was from Weston to Flatwoods, up the Elk River briefly, hence over to the Gauley River, and down the Gauley to the mouth of the Williams River. From this point several routes offered access to the Greenbrier Valley.

At least one of the threats to Camden's plans was eliminated in December 1889 when he and Davis and Elkins reached a gentleman's agreement in which they set up spheres of influence in the undeveloped areas of central and eastern West Virginia where the other would not tread. Davis also agreed to convey his interest in the Caperton lands to Camden in exchange for the interests held by Camden in the West Virginia Central and other Davis and Elkins enterprises. Elkins kept his share of the Caperton lands but agreed to cooperate with Camden.

At this point we need to back up a little and bring in the activities of John T. McGraw. He had begun to acquire land and timber rights in the Upper Greenbrier Valley in 1883 and increased his activity in land dealings in the area about 1889 when the plans of Senator Camden and others to build railroads became reasonably serious. Between 1883 and 1905 he had his name on deeds to over 145,000 acres in Pocahontas County plus considerable acreage in Webster and Randolph Counties (mostly in his own name alone, although in some early purchases the name of Jacob W. Marshall also appears). As the investments in land would not be profitable for McGraw and his associates unless a railroad were built into the Greenbrier Valley, Col. McGraw (colonel was an honorary title only) left no stone unturned in efforts to encourage Senator Camden to extend the West Virginia and Pittsburgh on into the valley.

In addition to acquiring the property already mentioned, Senator Camden was also looking at opening the iron ore fields of Pocahontas and Greenbrier Counties, West Virginia, and Allegheny and Craig Counties, Virginia, to the Pittsburgh market. In late 1890 he became a member of an iron syndicate planning for the development of the iron ore on Potts Creek near Covington, Virginia, embracing some 50,000 acres.

In extending his West Virginia and Pittsburgh Railroad to the Gauley River, Camden had in mind, from the beginning, building on to meet the Chesapeake and Ohio Railway at some point. With the acquisition of the iron ore near Covington he now had a justification for this extension and a need to locate a junction point between the two railroads. Correspondence began in December between Camden and Chesapeake and Ohio President M.E. Ingalls concerning plans for joining the two lines. Camden also invited Davis to join in by extending the West Virginia Central to Huntersville to also have a connection with the Chesapeake and Ohio.

This now gives us the background for the local optimism expressed in the quote from *The Pocahontas Times* given earlier that a railroad would soon be built through the Greenbrier Valley. Negotiations between Camden

and Chesapeake and Ohio officials continued during the early part of 1891. At first Camden planned for his railroad to join the Chesapeake and Ohio at Covington. This plan was modified when it appeared the same end could be achieved by an extension of the Hot Springs Branch of the Chesapeake and Ohio into Pocahontas County and a junction made in the Greenbrier Valley.

In an interview with a *Wheeling Register* reporter in July 1891 Camden confirmed the plan to meet in the Greenbrier Valley, probably at Marlinton (as Marlin's Bottom was now called). When asked how soon he expected to have the junction of the two railroads completed, he indicated the following summer or fall.

By late summer the two companies seem to have agreed on Marlinton as the meeting point with the Chesapeake and Ohio agreeing to ship products from the West Virginia and Pittsburgh at the same rates as it would on its own line. The West Virginia and Pittsburgh was to come into the Greenbrier Valley by building up the Williams River and down Stony Creek to Marlinton.

While Camden and the Chesapeake and Ohio were holding their discussions on the junction point for the railroads, John T. McGraw seems to have been reasonably certain that the junction would be made in the valley and began to make plans to develop a new town at the site of the village of Marlinton. McGraw and several of his associates visited Marlinton in December 1890 and took options on the farms in the area even though there was three feet of snow on the ground. The land was conveyed to McGraw by deeds in February 1891.

The Pocahontas Development Company was incorporated by the Legislature on September 26, 1891 to promote the town and two days later McGraw deeded the company a 640 acre tract at the mouth of Knapps Creek. The incorporators of the development company were John T. McGraw, J.N. Camden, Jacob W. Marshall, Francis M. Durbin, George M. Whitescarver, H.G. Davis, A.B. Fleming (Governor of West Virginia at that date), John E. Sands, J. Ed Watson, William A. Ohley, J.M. Hartley, John Blackshere, and T. Moore Jackson. Camden did not actually invest in the company but a hundred shares of stock were in his name for publicity purposes. Davis was also a "non-investing" stockholder and withdrew in early 1892. Governor Fleming was an actual investor.

To give additional prestige to their promotion, McGraw and his associates encouraged the removal of the Pocahontas County seat from Huntersville to Marlinton. (The question of removing the court house from Huntersville had cropped up periodically in the county's history.) The Pocahontas Development Company offered a free lot in the new town for a court house and $5,000 cash towards the building as an inducement. Upon the petition of 697 voters, the County Court approved presenting the removal question to a vote of the people and the change of county seats was approved on December 8, 1891, by a vote of 940 to 475.

A map issued by the Pocahontas Development Company, dated December 1, 1891, described Marlinton as the "Only Natural Outlet for Great Fields of Timber, Coking, Steam and Gas Coals, Iron Ores and Other Minerals." A grand total of six railway lines are shown converging on the new town. Besides the Chesapeake and Ohio and the West Virginia and Pittsburgh, the West Virginia Central and Pittsburgh is shown arriving from the north, a line from the Shenandoah Valley is shown coming to Marlinton from the east, a second branch of the Chesapeake and Ohio is on the map coming from White Sulphur Springs, and finally a railroad from Gauley Bridge up the Gauley and Cherry Rivers. The map shows the West Virginia and Pittsburgh coming into town from the west side of the river over a bridge at Tenth Street, continuing along that street to a junction with the Chesapeake and Ohio at about Fourth Avenue. The Chesapeake and Ohio continues up Tenth Street and up Knapps Creek, with a tunnel probably planned through Marlin Mountain to avoid the curve in the creek as it approaches town. A switch from the West Virginia and Pittsburgh leads to that railroad's yard and shops located where the tannery was later built. Yards and shops for the Chesapeake and Ohio were located between Tenth and Ninth Streets and below the present site of the Marlinton schools.

The drawing for lots in the new metropolis on the Greenbrier took place on June 1, 1892, with 191 lots drawn and assigned for a total of $42,020.

But alas, as the people of the Upper Greenbrier Valley had already learned, there is a major difference between plans for a railroad and the actual building of one. As 1891 passed into 1892, right-of-way surveys were made and rumors reported of work being let to contract but no dirt was actually moved. As early as February of 1892 doubt was being expressed by Chesapeake and Ohio Vice-president Decatur Axtell to Col. McGraw that Senator Camden would build his proposed railroad.

Also, Camden's commitment to using Marlinton as the junction point waivered even as the decision to do so was confirmed between the two railroads. His surveyors began to study the possibility of building up the Cherry River and down Spring Creek to reach the Greenbrier River as early as the late summer of 1891. He was discussing this possibility with the Chesapeake and Ohio officials by the end of the year. In August 1892 Camden reported to President Ingalls of the Chesapeake and Ohio that a survey had been made from the mouth of the Cherry to the mouth of Spring Creek with a better grade than the route via the Williams River. In December Camden wrote to Ingalls that "there is no doubt that we will want to adopt the Cherry River line."

The Chesapeake and Ohio also surveyed routes for railroads into Pocahontas County in 1892. One went from the Hot Springs Branch, up Jackson River, Back Creek, Little Back Creek, through Ryder Gap at Rimel, and down Knapps Creek to Huntersville and Marlinton. A second route went from Dunlaps, near Covington, up Ogle Creek and over Allegheny Mountain to Meadow Creek, to Anthony Creek and up either the main branch of that stream or the North Fork of Anthony Creek to Knapps Creek. A third route began at White Sulphur Springs, went up Anthony Creek, and then by either the main stream or the North Fork to Knapps Creek.

Although discussion between the two companies continued through 1892, by the end of the year it was plain that the plan of making the connection was abandoned at least for the time being.

In their letters Camden and Ingalls continued to express their desire to build the two railroads to a place of junction, but they began to make excuses for not doing so. In September 1892 Ingalls wrote, "I doubt whether the market will allow us to build much road next year, ..." and ". . . . but it is not a good time just now to build new roads." In his reply, Camden stated, "We feel very much as you do in regard to building railroads next year, that is we do not see at present that it is necessary or wise to press the building of the Greenbrier extension, ..." In an exchange of letters in December, Camden expressed some hope for building his extension to the Greenbrier in 1893, but Ingalls was not very optimistic in his reply, ". . . . but when we will commence to build our line up into that country is not so certain. The fact is, railroad bonds are not going to sell this year, and they may not next, and until they do we shall not move."

In early 1893 a correspondent to *The Pocahontas Times* from Williams River fairly well summed up the situation, "Railroad news is not so plentiful as it was, and the prospect is dull."

A number of reasons are no doubt involved in this disappointing outcome for the high hopes of the people of the Upper Greenbrier Valley held less than two years before. One of the main causes is implied in the quotes given before from the Camden and Ingalls correspondence, the economic downturn that led to the Panic of 1893 and caused the Chesapeake and Ohio to be unwilling to undertake any new enterprises. Also, the West Virginia and Pittsburgh had little surplus cash in its treasury by this time due to its massive construction projects of the preceding years and land purchases. Camden had expressed this point to Ingalls in September, "We have upon our hands a considerable amount of new road in a wilderness country and it will take some little time to develop the business so as to make the investment self-sustaining."

Other factors must have also played a role. The iron ore in the Covington area eventually proved to be of low grade and the cost of production high and suspicions of this were evident even in 1890. Also the cost of building and operating the proposed line would have been high and this must have become obvious as the surveys were made. We have noted that the Chesapeake and Ohio surveyed at least three routes and Camden had his engineers out looking for a second route, even as he was agreeing to a junction with the Chesapeake and Ohio at Marlinton by using the route up the Williams River and down Stony Creek. In their route up Anthony Creek from White Sulphur Springs the Chesapeake and Ohio had one with only a minor grade in both directions, whereas the West Virginia and Pittsburgh had major grades to contend with whether they went up the Williams River or up the Cherry River.

The West Virginia and Pittsburgh never did reach the Greenbrier River, of course. It slipped into financial trouble in the mid 1890s and was placed into receivership in 1898. In 1899 it was sold to the Baltimore and Ohio. The line was extended that year up the Cherry River to the site of the new town of Richwood. At Richwood the mill of the Cherry River Boom and Lumber Company was constructed and from this mill logging railroads were built up both the Cherry and Williams Rivers but they did not cross into the Greenbrier Valley.

As it was beginning to look as if the connection between the West Virginia and Pittsburgh and the Chesapeake and Ohio was not going to be accomplished, John T. McGraw began to look elsewhere for a railroad to come into the Greenbrier Valley. His extensive land holdings were almost worthless without a railroad in the region.

During the late summer and fall of 1892 McGraw kept Senator Davis informed of the plans of a group of New York State investors to develop some of his (McGraw's) land on the East and West Forks of the Greenbrier River, including the establishment of a sawmill, pulp mill, and tannery. In October McGraw indicated to Senator Davis that these men would like to locate their plants at Marlinton if they could get assurances that a railroad would be built to that town. Without such assurances they would abandon plans for Marlinton and locate at Ronceverte and float their timber down the Greenbrier to that point, using the boom of the St. Lawrence Boom and Manufacturing Company. As he had done in previous letters, McGraw inquired as to Davis' plans for an extension of the West Virginia Central. Mr. Davis' reply was non-committal about an extension and the most he did was to suggest a meeting of all concerned. In December the New York people incorporated the Rochester Boom and Lumber Company.

However, Senator Davis seems to have been interested and did correspond with the Chesapeake and Ohio in November on a possible connection with their railroad. McGraw wrote again in December to inform Davis that the Rochester people had received a proposition from a company in Ronceverte to handle the timber at that location, no doubt hoping to spur Davis into action on an extension into the Greenbrier Valley. He also stated his feeling that nothing was to come of Senator Camden's railroad plans and reminded Davis that the Chesapeake and Ohio had expressed an interest in making a connection with the Davis railroad.

Nothing was done at this time by either Davis or the Chesapeake and Ohio. A major reason, without much doubt, was the Panic of 1893 which had also played a role in ending Senator Camden's plans for a railroad into the Greenbrier Valley.

With improving economic conditions in 1894, McGraw approached Davis in July with the idea of the Rochester Boom and Lumber Company building its own railroad from the Forks of the Greenbrier to a connection with the Dry Fork Railroad providing arrangements could be made with that railroad and a traffic agreement made with the West Virginia Central. The West Virginia Central was involved as it was the connecting line for the Dry Fork Railroad.

The Dry Fork Railroad had been incorporated in December 1892 to build a railroad from Bretz in Tucker County, southward along the Cheat River, and then up either Glade, Laurel, or Dry Forks to the headwaters, and then down the Greenbrier River to the Chesapeake and Ohio near Caldwell. The incorporators were the owners of the Condon-Lane Boom and Lumber Company which had land on Gandy Creek. The company had been attempting to harvest the timber by floating it to a mill near Bretz (near Parsons). Work began on the Dry Fork Railroad in August 1893 at Hendricks where a junction was made with the West Virginia Central. The route up Dry Fork was selected and the line was completed to Horton on Gandy Creek by the following summer. At Horton the Condon-Lane Lumber Company erected a new saw mill.

The Dry Fork Railroad did give the citizens of Pocahontas County their first hope of a railroad since the demise of the plans for the connection of the West Virginia and Pittsburgh and the Chesapeake and Ohio. However, although there was an occasional news report that the railroad would be extended into the Greenbrier Valley as authorized by its charter, the Dry Fork never went beyond Horton. On the other hand, one of the logging lines of the Condon-Lane Lumber Company did go up Gandy Creek and over onto the East Fork of the Greenbrier River where the company had timber. This line was the first railroad to actually enter the Upper Greenbrier Valley from the outside, being in place by 1899.

But I have jumped ahead. This idea of the Rochester Lumber Company building to the Dry Fork Railroad from the Forks of the Greenbrier seems to have been premature for the economic conditions and nothing came of it. Senator Davis, however, kept an interest in a southern extension of his railroad. In November 1894 it was reported that a survey was being made for a route for a railway from Elkins to the Greenbrier River. By early summer of the following year surveys had been completed as far as southern Pocahontas County, coming to Driscol (Minnehaha Springs) and Huntersville. Additional surveying work was done in the fall of 1895.

Discussion continued between Davis, McGraw, and their various associates on conditions for building a railroad into upper Pocahontas County. The United States Leather Company was now also involved in the planning for the development of the region. These negotiations between all the parties continued through the summer and fall of 1895. Davis also kept in contact with Chesapeake and Ohio President Ingalls concerning a junction between his extension and that railroad. Interest must have also continued on the possibility of extending the Dry Fork Railroad to the Greenbrier River. However, in a letter to S.B. Elkins in September 1895, Robert Whitmer, Dry Fork President, rebuffed the former's suggestion that the Davis/Elkins interests buy a share in the Dry Fork. Whitmer insisted that Condon-Lane would retain control of their railroad although they would be happy to extend the Dry Fork if Davis and Elkins helped.

Following a meeting in New York between Col. McGraw and the United States Leather Company in late October 1895, McGraw and Davis prepared a memorandum of agreement, dated November 27, on the conditions under which a railroad would be built south from Elkins. The major points were:

1. At the Forks of the Greenbrier the United States Leather Company will construct a tannery, the Rochester Boom and Lumber Company a sawmill, and a group from Ronceverte a sawmill.

2. Davis and Elkins will take 60 percent of the stock in the new railroad, and McGraw, United States Leather Company, and their associates will take 40 percent.

3. The West Virginia Central and Pittsburg Railroad will operate the new railroad and make a liberal traffic agreement with it.

4. Other parts of the memorandum involved the issuing of bonds for construction and other financial aspects of building and operating the new line.

The negotiations between all concerned continued into the new year and included discussing the extension of the proposed railroad southward from the Forks of the Greenbrier to some point where a junction with the Chesapeake and Ohio could be arranged. Davis preferred to run to Knapps Creek at either Huntersville or Driscol, whereas McGraw naturally preferred taking the line to Marlinton. In a letter to Ingalls in late January 1896, Davis suggested the junction of Douthards and Knapps Creeks as the meeting place for the two railroads.

During this period Davis seemed to have been ready to build the new railroad. He wrote to B.M. Yeager in Pocahontas County several times in December and January encouraging him to see about getting the right-of-way through the county (free to the railroad preferably, of course) and suggesting that work on the line might begin in the spring. In his letter to Ingalls in January he stated that, if the Chesapeake and Ohio agrees, "the building of the road can be commenced in the early Spring."

However, Davis hedged his bets somewhat in his correspondence with McGraw. Several times he made mention that his associates "are not as well disposed towards building as I am," and mentioned their concern whether the resources of the area would provide the necessary traffic. In February he was not quite as optimistic in his letters to Mr. Yeager either and began to mention economic conditions being against building.

Meanwhile, McGraw and Davis came to an agreement on McGraw's contribution to the project in another memorandum, this one dated February 20, 1896. The main points were:

1. McGraw is to provide 8,000 acres of iron ore and timber lands.

2. McGraw is to obtain the right-of-way, free to the railroad, from the headwaters of the Greenbrier to Douthards Creek.

3. McGraw is to provide $50,000 in cash and will receive stock in exchange.

4. McGraw and his associates are to begin erecting a sawmill at the Forks of the Greenbrier when the railroad construction begins.

5. In return Davis is to arrange the construction of a standard gauge railroad from Elkins "as early as practicable, consistent with the conditions of the money market."

At this point it would seem from the evidence, that the construction of the long awaited railroad line into the Upper Greenbrier Valley was about to begin. And yet, within a week of the February 20 agreement between himself and McGraw, Davis wrote in a pessimistic manner about building the new line. He wrote to Yeager on February 27, "There is no certainty yet as to the building of the road." Early in March he wrote McGraw concerning a meeting with the engineer on the possible routes for the new railroad, but also commented that the Baltimore and Ohio Railroad going into receivership "will have a bad influence upon railroad investments" and stated that "I feel sure that no railroad enterprise in our region, no matter how meritorious, could be accomplished at present." In April Davis wrote to Ingalls, "I am aware that times are not suitable to commence work now."

Although Senator Davis' correspondence in the following months included an occasional letter on the proposed extension, no action was taken to start construction and 1897 arrived with no railroad for the Upper Greenbrier Valley.

No doubt tired of waiting for Davis to begin construction, in March of 1897 McGraw annulled the 1896 memorandum, as allowed by one of the clauses in that agreement. He and his associates now turned towards the Chesapeake and Ohio Railway as the most likely source of a railroad into their holdings along the Greenbrier River. This time, as will be covered in the next chapter, a railroad was actually built, although it was the actions of another group and not McGraw that finally got the Chesapeake and Ohio to move on building a branch line into the Upper Greenbrier Valley.

Davis did keep up his correspondence with various people, including McGraw, about matters in the Greenbrier Valley over the next several years. In August 1897 he seemed offended that the Chesapeake and Ohio would begin to plan on a Greenbrier Valley branch without consulting him and he wrote to President Ingalls, "I have always felt that when you were ready to build in our direction you would confer with me before concluding any definite arrangements." He also may have had surveyors in the field working on a route in late 1897 and early 1898.

In February 1898 Davis wrote to McGraw in a way that suggests he wanted to entice the latter away from the Chesapeake and Ohio and back into a project for building a railroad south from Elkins. However, Davis made no definite move on building his southern extension until the Chesapeake and Ohio had made its final commitment to building its line and actually began construction, as related in the next chapter.

During the 1890s, while our principal actors were planning and plotting to bring railroads to the Upper Greenbrier Valley, a few other proposals made at least a brief appearance on the scene.

In 1895 news of a railroad into the Greenbrier Valley from the Valley of Virginia filled newspaper space. Work on this railroad, the Chesapeake and Western, began at Harrisonburg, Virginia, in June of 1895. The company planned to build a line from the tidewater area of Virginia to Charleston, passing through Pocahontas County, according to news accounts. The route through Pocahontas County was by way of the gap in the Allegheny Mountains near Frost and down Knapps Creek.

By 1896 nothing more was being reported on the coming of the Chesapeake and Western but it would return to our history again.

Some other railroads that were proposed in the late 1890s to pass through the Greenbrier Valley were:

Chesapeake, West Virginia, and Western Railroad. Incorporated by a group of men from Charleston in 1895 to build a line from Frost to Parkersburg.

Virginia Southern and Midland Railway. John McGraw was one of the incorporators of this line which was chartered in 1895 to build from Rowlesburg, in Preston County, by way of the Cheat and Greenbrier Rivers to White Sulphur Springs.

Virginia, Fredericksburg and Western Railroad. Planned in 1895 to build a line of railroad from the Chesapeake Bay, through its namesake city, Harrisonburg, Monterey, to Sutton and hence to the Ohio River.

West Virginia Northern Railway. Chartered in 1896 with the broad authority to "construct and operate a railroad in the state of West Virginia." Its principal office was to have been in Ronceverte, the home of several of the incorporators.

1817

Engineer corps for the Chesapeake and Western Railroad at a camp on Tea Creek, a tributary of the Williams River.   PCHS

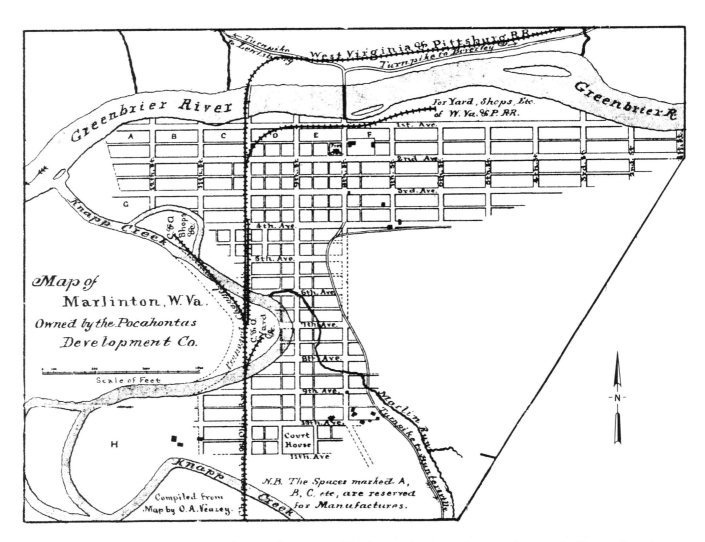

Map published by the Pocahontas Development Company in 1891 showing the proposed junction between the Chesapeake and Ohio Railway and the West Virginia and Pittsburg Railroad. See page 8.

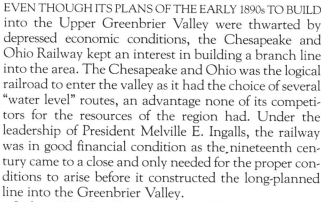

CHAPTER II
The Chesapeake & Ohio Builds a Branch Line

EVEN THOUGH ITS PLANS OF THE EARLY 1890s TO BUILD into the Upper Greenbrier Valley were thwarted by depressed economic conditions, the Chesapeake and Ohio Railway kept an interest in building a branch line into the area. The Chesapeake and Ohio was the logical railroad to enter the valley as it had the choice of several "water level" routes, an advantage none of its competitors for the resources of the region had. Under the leadership of President Melville E. Ingalls, the railway was in good financial condition as the nineteenth century came to a close and only needed for the proper conditions to arise before it constructed the long-planned line into the Greenbrier Valley.

In late 1897 the Chesapeake and Ohio organized the Greenbrier Railway Company and it was chartered on November 16, 1897, by the West Virginia Legislature. Given as incorporators were Melville E. Ingalls, Decatur Axtell, J.M. Gill, Henry C. Simms, and Frank B. Enslow. Ingalls was, as mentioned above, President of the Chesapeake and Ohio; Axtell was Vice-president of the railroad company and a member of the Board of Directors; Gill, from Huntington, was a division superintendent; and Simms and Enslow were lawyers for the railway from Huntington.

At the initial meeting of the stockholders of the Greenbrier Railway in Huntington on December 16, 1897, the following officers were elected: President—H.C. Simms; Vice-president—Decatur Axtell; Secretary—C.E. Wellford; Auditor—L.F. Sullivan; Treasurer—C.E. Potts; and Attorney—F.B. Enslow. Potts was Treasurer of the Chesapeake and Ohio, Wellford was Secretary of the railway, and Sullivan was Comptroller for the C. and O.

According to the recollections of Mr. Axtell, written a number of years later, the formation of the Greenbrier Railway came upon the recommendations of President Ingalls following conferences between Mr. Ingalls and owners of timber lands in the Greenbrier area.

One group of Greeenbrier Valley timber owners Mr. Ingalls may have conferred with was J.T. McGraw and his associates in the Rochester Boom and Lumber Company. In October of 1897 the West Virginia Legislature authorized the change of the name of the company to the Greenbrier River Lumber Company. In late September Eli Upton deeded some 35,000 acres to the Greenbrier River Lumber Company (most of which had previously been owned by Mr. McGraw) and McGraw deeded 66,900 acres to the company by a deed dated October 1, 1897. This acreage was located along the Greenbrier River from Buckley Mountain, south of Marlinton, to the head of the West Fork of the Greenbrier and into Randolph County. These tracts were mortgaged to the New York Security and Trust Company for $400,000 to provide operating capital. With this amount of money available, the Greenbrier Lumber Company could assure the Chesapeake and Ohio Railway that the lumber company's property would be developed if a railroad line was constructed. It was, of course, not long after these transactions by Col. McGraw and his associates that the chartering of the Greenbrier Railway took place.

However, no doubt the main reason causing the Chesapeake and Ohio to finally begin construction of the railroad into the Upper Greenbrier Valley was the plans of the West Virginia Pulp and Paper Company, a major producer of paper with plants located at Luke, Maryland, Davis, West Virginia, and Tyrone, Pennsylvania.

At some point in the late 1890s this company began looking towards the vast spruce forests on Cheat Mountain as a new source of the spruce wood needed for the pulp used in the manufacture of paper. In February of 1899 the West Virginia Pulp and Paper Company purchased the 66,000-acre Dewing property on the Shavers Fork of Cheat River in Pocahontas and Randolph Counties. James W. Dewing had attempted to harvest the timber on Cheat Mountain by floating the logs down the Shavers Fork to his mill at Point Marion, Pennsylvania, but, not surprisingly to anyone familar with this stream, had not been successful in his efforts. The Dewing tract was the first of land holdings by the West Virginia Pulp and Paper Company that eventually amounted to some 170,000 acres in Pocahontas, Randolph, and Webster Counties.

At the same time that the Cheat Mountain timber purchase was being considered, the paper company was making plans to construct a new paper mill to use the new source of spruce. Several locations were looked at as the possible site of the new mill.

H.G. Davis hoped to have the new paper mill located on the West Virginia Central Railroad and he corresponded in early 1899 with John G. Luke, President of the West Virginia Pulp and Paper Company, about building the mill at either Parsons or Hendricks. Upon hearing from Mr. Luke in early March about the purchase of the Dewing land and the possibility of the paper mill being located on the Chesapeake and Ohio, Sen. Davis wrote in return his opinion that the best route to the timber was by way of the Huttonsville extension of the West Virginia Central. He expressed doubt about the Chesapeake and Ohio building an extension, feeling confident that the Chesapeake and Ohio would not build "until after a conference and understanding between myself and Mr. Ingalls." Sen. Davis also wondered if there were not towns on the Greenbrier River that would object to the pollution of that river by a paper mill. He was no doubt aware that the paper company was having problems with the City of Cumberland, Maryland, over the pollution of the Potomac River from the paper mill at Luke. In this regard Sen. Davis was to be prophetic.

However, the Chesapeake and Ohio was also dealing with the paper company on the location of the new paper mill and Mr. Ingalls saw no need to reach any understanding with Sen. Davis before deciding to build branch lines. By early March the paper company made the decision to locate its new plant on the Chesapeake and Ohio main line at Caldwell in Greenbrier County. The Chesapeake and Ohio could offer a cheaper rate for shipping the paper to market and this was probably a key factor in the paper company's decision.

It was reported in the local papers in March that land had been secured at Caldwell and work was underway on the site. But then, before the people in eastern Greenbrier County had even had time to list all the economic benefits to their area that would derive from this large industry, the West Virginia Pulp and Paper Company changed its plans and the mill site was changed to Covington, Virginia.

By the last week of April there were rumors about the possible change in the mill location to Covington, although the *Greenbrier Independent* at Lewisburg hopefully believed this would not occur due to the work already done at Caldwell and the further distance of Covington from the timber on Cheat Mountain. A week later it was reported that the mill would be at Covington and work was underway at the new location before the middle of May.

The major reason discussed in the newspapers of the period for the change was the threat by the City of Hinton to bring a suit against the paper company for the pollution of the Greenbrier River (Hinton's source of water) if the mill was built. The Hinton City Council passed a resolution on April 12 which stated it would file such a suit. As noted before, the paper company had been subject to a similar problem at its Luke plant and probably did not want to be bothered with the same problem at its new mill. Some newspaper accounts stated that the mill at Luke was to be closed after the new mill was built, due to the problems with Cumberland, but this was denied

by the company. "Inducements" by Covington were also mentioned as well as the unsuitability of the ground at Caldwell for a large industry as reasons for the move. It was noted that the Jackson River at Covington was already polluted. (After hearing of the problem with Hinton, Sen. Davis wrote to John Luke at the end of April noting that Clifton Forge or Lynchburg might raise the same questions as Hinton. He reminded Mr. Luke that below Parsons on the Cheat River there were no towns of consequence.)

Location of the paper mill at Covington did not affect the need for a railroad into the Upper Greenbrier Valley, of course, as that was the location of the timber. The flurry of rumors at the time of the mill site change did include some about the possibility of a route change for the railroad, as we shall see, but not the actual construction of the new line. But we must now back up our story to 1896 and the effort to decide on a route for the Greenbrier Railway.

In late January 1896 a Chesapeake and Ohio survey crew began at Huntersville to lay out a route for a railroad from that point up Knapps Creek and did the work in a more careful manner than the hasty surveys made before. The crew members did not talk about what they were doing and a number of rumors swirled about the work. In late January *The Pocahontas Times* reported several of the more prevalent rumors:

> Some claim that it is to be a branch of the C. & O. to start from the White Sulphur. Others incline to believe that it is the extension of the Hot Springs branch destined to reach the main track again at Kanawha Falls, the purpose being to take the place of a double-track on the C. & O., which the rugged character of the New River Valley makes impracticable. It may be the consummation of the old contract with the Camden System to meet in Pocahontas, with Marlinton as the trysting place.
> The newest and best-defined plot of them all is that the C. & O. and the West Virginia Central have entered into an iron-bound contract to meet each other at Huntersville, under penalty of a large sum of money.

Following news stories reported that the survey was between White Sulphur Springs and Huntersville, to meet a surveying corps that had begun its work from the former point.

The route laid out by these surveying corps followed Howard Creek out of White Sulphur Springs, crossed to Fleming Run, joined Anthony Creek at Alvon, and followed that stream to present day Neola. From that point one survey went on up Anthony Creek, over to Cochran Creek by way of a 200 foot tunnel, and down Laurel Creek. Another survey was run from Neola up the North Fork of Anthony Creek and down Douthat Creek. The two surveys came together again near the mouth of Laurel Creek and joined Knapps Creek at Driscol.

The *Ronceverte Messenger*, however, warned the people of Pocahontas County not to get too much hope up, reminding them that "The engineering corps of the C. & O. is a salaried body, and whenever regular work is slack they are set to running sheep trails, hog tracks, concentric circles, isothermal lines, and parallels of equation, just to keep their instruments in good order, and, perhaps, to make people talk."

The *Messenger* seems to have been correct, at least for the time being, as railroad news was slim and very speculative for the remainder of 1896 and well into 1897.

That the capitalists involved in railroad building could not see the financial advantages to them of building a railroad into the Upper Greenbrier Valley was hard to believe by some local partisans. In proposing a railroad line from the east through Highland and Pocahontas Counties, Col. R.S. Turk wrote in late 1896 of the resources of these counties that would bring wealth to the railroad company tapping them. He listed iron, timber, cattle, and building stone in Highland County and timber, coal, iron ore, limestone, and marble in Pocahontas County. Col. Turk wrote that he was "astonished that so wonderful a route, into so magnificent a region has not long since been occupied by a railroad, when capital has been blowing down the Rockies Seiras (sic) and laying rusty rails over prairie and desert in the west, whilst here in the very faces and under the shadow of our great cities is more wealth than can be found in the same unoccupied expanse of territory, anywhere else in the United States."

In August 1897, however, Chesapeake and Ohio survey crews were at work again, this time starting at the Forks of the Greenbrier River and working downstream. The survey reached Marlinton about the first of October and was joined with the line run in 1896 to White Sulphur Springs by way of Driscol (Minnehaha Springs). The surveyors then went back up the Greenbrier and ran a line up Sitlington Creek, to Knapps Creek, and on to Driscol to join the line to White Sulphur. Following the incorporation of the Greenbrier Railway Company in November, described before, it seemed that now all the Chesapeake and Ohio had to do was make a decision between the two routes. (Marlinton partisans, naturally, argued for the route reaching the river at their town. They pointed out that using the route through Dunmore would miss the business of the Little Levels and Elk regions, which would probably continue to go to depots at Ronceverte and Beverly, respectively.)

According to a map and a profile sheet prepared in July 1897 by the office of the Chesapeake and Ohio's Chief Engineer, at least three more routes between Driscol and the Forks of the Greenbrier were given consideration.

Two of these routes ran north from Huntersville, up Browns Creek, and then by way of Thorny Creek and Thomas Creek to Sitlington Creek. At that point they split. One route went down Sitlington Creek to the river and up the river to the Forks. The other route went up Moore Run and Deer Creek, then through an 800 foot tunnel, crossed Brush Run, went up Laurel Run, and through a 1500 foot tunnel to reach the East Fork of the Greenbrier. It crossed the East Fork at the site of the present tannery and then went on to the Forks.

The third possible route was from Driscol by way of Knapps Creek, Shock Run, Thorny Branch, and Rosen Run to Deer Creek near Green Bank. There it joined the line through the tunnels described in the previous paragraph.

A look at the preliminary profiles of all five routes gives the probable reason for the choice of the two that were given a complete survey in the late summer and fall of 1897. As the other three go from stream to stream their profiles resemble the edge of a broken piece of glass. The tunnels would have also been a drawback on two of the routes.

However, in early 1898 the attention of the Chesapeake and Ohio was turned to the possibility of locating the new railroad along the Greenbrier River completely. It was noted that a line south of Marlinton along the river would tap the business of the existing communities and the rich agricultural areas of the Little Levels of Pocahontas County and the Big Levels of Greenbrier County.

In order to investigate this route, Capt. Bartholemew, who had been in charge of the survey work this previous summer, Mr. Hayes, an assistant engineer, B.M. Yeager, and Capt. A.E. Smith left Marlinton on February 28 by boat to examine the river below Knapps Creek. Capt. Smith knew the river extremely well, having driven logs to Ronceverte for many years. They spent four days on their inspection trip. One day was used to take a look at the possibility of using Spice Run as a way of access to the Greenbrier River from Anthony Creek. At the end of their trip downstream, it was reported that their examination of the river route showed it to be very satisfactory while the grade from Anthony Creek to Spice Run was too steep to be considered.

Another event in February was the issuing of a charter to the Greenbrier Valley Construction Company. John T. McGraw and several of his associates in the Greenbrier River Lumber Company were the incorporators. It was reported that this company was to build the new Greenbrier Railway but nothing more has been found of it in news accounts or other records.

A survey crew set up camp at the mouth of Swago Creek on April 9, 1898, and began its work on the survey of the river route south of Marlinton early the next week. The survey began at Marlinton with Mr. Bartholemew in charge of the crew. The preliminary survey to the main line near Caldwell was finished in June and the crew immediately started back up the river on the more detailed location survey. The survey work was completed back to Marlinton in the middle of October 1898.

The fact that the Chesapeake and Ohio had done a location survey was encouraging to local people, as this was the first time an operating railroad company had gone this far with their work.

With the plans of the West Virginia Pulp and Paper Company for purchasing timber land and building a new paper mill becoming finalized in early 1899, the coming of a railroad into the Upper Greenbrier Valley also finally became a reality. The work of acquiring the right-of-way was underway by March and the first deeds were recorded the following month. The date on the first deed to the Greenbrier Railway was April 11 for right-of-way in Greenbrier County at MP 13 near Anthony.

The map and profile of the route of the Greenbrier Railway from the main line at Whitcomb to Marlinton was filed in the Pocahontas County Clerk's office on April 28, having been approved by the Board of Directors of the Greenbrier Railway on April 21. William A. Hankins is listed on the documents as Engineer in Charge. The map and profile for the remainder of the route to the Forks of the Greenbrier River were filed in the Pocahontas County Clerk's office on May 17, 1899.

The first construction contract was also let in April 1899. It was for the first five miles from the main line at Whitcomb and was awarded to Lane Brothers.

In May, at the time of the decision by the West Virginia Pulp and Paper Company to change the site of its new mill to Covington there was a bit of speculation in the local papers that the route of the new railroad might be changed from the Greenbrier River to a route from the Hot Springs Branch, up the Jackson River, to Mountain Grove, through the Ryder Gap at Rimel, and then on to the Greenbrier River at Sitlington, north of Marlinton. The Chesapeake and Ohio had the route across the Allegheny Mountain re-surveyed by Engineer Hankins and it was reported in the newspapers that he found a better location than the one found in 1892 (see Chapter One).

However, when the final decision on which route to use was made at a meeting of the Chesapeake and Ohio Board of Directors on May 24, it was to use the Greenbrier River route. Arguing for the route through the Ryder Gap was Decatur Axtell, Second Vice-president at that time and in charge of surveys and construction. He felt that routing had a number of advantages over the all Greenbrier River route. According to Axtell, the

Melville E. Ingalls, president of the Chesapeake and Ohio Railway from 1888 to 1900. The Greenbrier Division was planned and construction begun while he headed the C. and O.   COHS

Decatur Axtell, vice-president of the Chesapeake and Ohio Railway from 1890 until 1918. He was in charge of survey and construction at the time the Greenbrier Division was built.   COHS

Map opposite: Section of a map prepared in May 1899 showing the two alternate routes under consideration at that time for the soon to be constructed Greenbrier Division. (Note the spelling of Sitlington Creek as Sutterlands Creek.)

The map also shows possible connections for the Greenbrier line from Camden on Gauley and Pickens on the West Virginia and Pittsburgh Railroad, from near Beverly on the West Virginia Central and Pittsburgh Railroad, and from Horton (off the map to the northeast) on the Dry Fork Railroad. The complete map shows the Greenbrier line as part of a rail link between Covington, Virginia, and Pittsburgh, Pennsylvania.   COHS

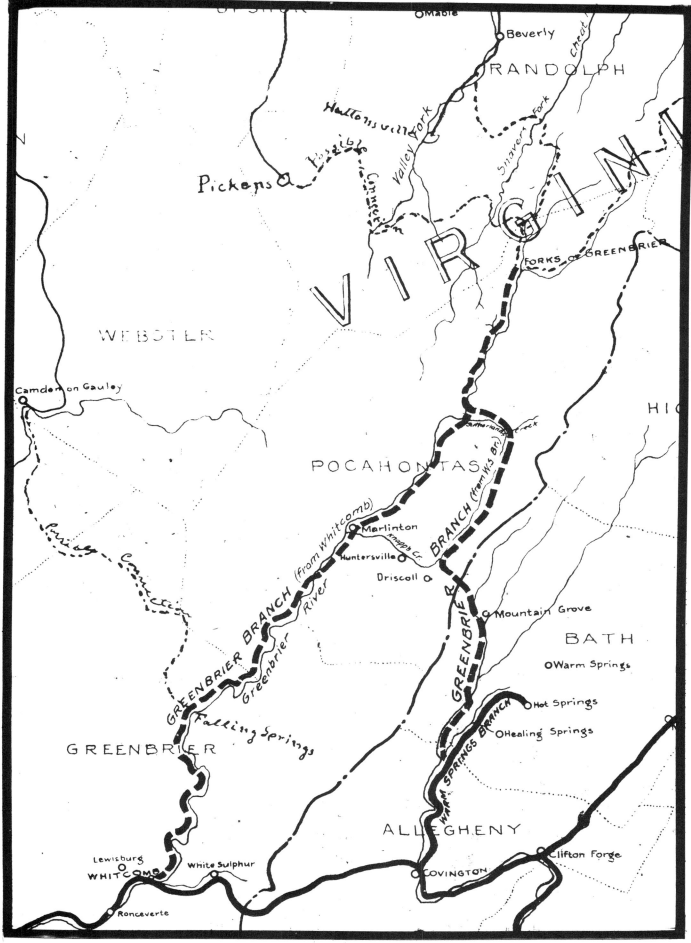

Mark O. Hankins, Chesapeake and Ohio Railway civil engineer. He and his brother William were the engineers who located and supervised the construction of the Greenbrier Division.   Mark A. Hankins

distance from the Forks of the Greenbrier to Covington via Whitcomb was 125 miles as compared to 85 miles by way of the Hot Springs Branch. Also the miles needed to be built were 95.5 by the all river route compared with 70 going through Ryder Gap. In moving traffic to Covington and the east, Axtell also gave the advantage to the Hot Springs route in the matter of grades. The line down the river was, of course, also down grade, but the main line east from Whitcomb had an ascending grade of 30 feet per mile, whereas by way of Hot Springs an ascending grade of only 20 feet per mile would be encountered. Westbound traffic would have the advantage by way of Whitcomb with an ascending grade of 60 feet per mile on the main line compared with 85 feet per mile by way of Ryder Gap. However, Axtell pointed out that the traffic westbound into the Upper Greenbrier Valley would consist mainly of returning empty cars and a small quantity of miscellaneous merchandise and supplies. He felt the cost of climbing this grade would be less than moving

trains the additional 40 miles each way. He was not impressed with the potential of the valley below Marlinton to generate traffic for the new line as were local boosters of the river route.

Credit for swinging the Board to select the river route varies depending upon the source. According to Decatur Axtell, the decision was due to the recommendation of the river route by Samuel Spencer, a member of the Board and a man who commanded the highest respect for his ability as an engineer. In this case, however, Mr. Axtell thought that perhaps Mr. Spencer failed to consider the grade on the main line when he was comparing the two routes. Given credit in the news media for helping to tilt the scale in favor of the route up the Greenbrier was a commitment by John T. McGraw to secure the right-of-way remaining to be purchased at no cost to the railroad.

Regardless of whether the effort to change the route away from the Greenbrier River below Marlinton was serious or not, the work of acquiring the right-of-way between Caldwell and Marlinton had continued during May.

Efforts were made to raise money to reimburse Col. McGraw for his expense in acquiring the right-of-way, including approaching the County Courts of Greenbrier and Pocahontas Counties. The Greenbrier County Court was asked on June 19 to appropriate $6,000 to purchase right-of-way. The Court took the matter under advisement and no record has been found that they ever approved such an appropriation. An appropriation of $1,000 was requested from the Pocahontas County Court on June 27, but it was refused on the grounds that the Court did not have the authority to expend funds in such a way.

The long drawn-out preliminaries were finally over and the long awaited railroad for the Upper Greenbrier Valley was about to become a reality.

Above Marlinton the location survey had not yet been made, so an engineer corps started this work on July 7 at Marlinton. A second corps began working south from Durbin.

Bids were received on July 10, 1899, for the construction work as far as Marlinton. The contracts for this part of the work were awarded to Shanahan, Serpell, and Company, ten miles, Lane Brothers and Company, ten miles, Douglass and Company, ten miles, C.D. Laughlin and Company, ten miles, and Luther Wright and Company, nine miles. In another source the third contract is given as fifteen miles and the fourth company is given as C.D. Langhorn and Company.

Actual construction work began in earnest almost immediately and by early August the dirt was flying at a number of places between Whitcomb and Marlinton.

Thomas E. Clemons left a construction job on the main line, where he was making 50 cents per day as a mule driver, to go to work for the Douglass Company at Renick. He recalled working on the grade after his retirement as follows:

The trees have been cleared away and two engineers are doing some final survey work before grade excavation begins. Photo taken in Greenbrier County.

I was hired as a laborer at $1 per day. I obtained board and room for 50 cents a day at a boarding house run by the Albert Gardners, just west of Spring Creek. At that time pay was held back for one month, therefore I had to work two months before I received any pay whatsoever. I recall my first check was for $19.40 after board was taken out. Of that sum I sent my mother $10. With the rest I bought a suit of clothes for myself including shoes, white shirt, tie, hat, socks, the whole works in fact.

I was not long in that job until I was put in charge of the commissary, which was run as a convenience for the men. Most of them lived in shantys near the job and did their own cooking. All kinds of groceries, canned goods and side meat, now referred to as salt bacon, was carried, along with a barrel of cider.

(Mr. Clemons later worked on the rail laying crew until the track was completed to Cass and then joined the maintenance force on the Greenbrier line.)

The first construction work in Pocahontas County started on August 5 near Burnsides by the firm of Julian, Carzza, and Company. This company, made up of Italians from Baltimore, had the grading contract for the seven miles south of Stamping Creek. They offered wages of $1.25 a day for ten hours work. After a week's work this sum didn't seem sufficient to many of the laborers employed by the company and many of them quit when their demands for $1.50 per day were refused. Men with teams also objected to a cut from 30 cents per

hour to 25 cents and most of them also left the job. However, progress was reported in spite of the labor troubles.

The Ferguson Construction Company was awarded a contract for almost thirty miles of the work above Marlinton and construction was underway by the last part of August.

The beginnings of the work in the Marlinton area was described by a writer in *The Pocahontas Times* as follows:

Saturday (August 26), J.J. Strang of New York City established a camp on the banks of Knapp's Creek, near the Island in the town of Marlinton, and went to work Monday right in a man's corn-field. The corn was cut in a hurry and piled to one side, but it was green and will spoil. But that was not all! He cut down three sweet apple trees that had been long in growing. Nothing seems to stop the railroad now. Formerly a heavy frost would kill all railroad prospects.

Everyone admires Contractor Strang's outfit. Its glory consists principally in its fine teams, all marked with the "U.S." of the United States Army. There are about 40 mules and 16 horses, and they are all first-class animals. They are worth going a long way to see. The camp consists at present of about twenty tents, and looks like an encampment of troops. It is said these are army equipments recently sold at public auction. We Pocahontas people would rather see the munitions of war employed in building railroad than even in freeing Cubans.

In the hollow of the square formed by the tents is the long rack at which the horses and mules stand. The office tent is fitted up nicely. The dining room tent is about sixty feet long

Construction work on the grade for the new railroad, probably in Greenbrier County.

Pauline Wolfenbarger

and has two large tables. One the white men use and the other the darkies. Behind the big dining room we caught a glimpse of a tent which seemed to be occupied by a lady belonging to the encampment.

The outfit is one to be admired, and there are a lot of big strong men who direct things in a way that shows they mean business. . . .

. . . . The work began in the cornfield below Captain Jack Apperson's. . . . There were eleven scraper teams at work in a confined space, and a perfectly immense plow drawn by a magnificent span of horses and an equally good span of mules. . . .

The land owned by Capt. Apperson, the site of the first work in the Marlinton area, is along the river south of Stillhouse Run.

Robert Earle, who had been a foreman for J.J. Strang, recalled in 1940 that the "crew was mainly colored men recruited for the duration of the job in North Carolina and Virginia, who were held in a sort of benevolent subjection until such time as it pleased the management to let them settle with the quartermaster and return whence they came."

William Buckley told the author that he remembered the construction crews using mules, wagons, and tents that were army surplus from the Spanish-American War. A crew of Blacks worked on the grade through his father's fields at Buckeye, an Italian crew worked downstream, and a German crew to the north. His father, John, was a foreman for the Germans, most of whom could not speak English and were identified by number.

Once underway the construction work progressed at a rapid pace.

• The firm of Johnson, Briggs and Pitts was given a contract in late August to supply 300,000 ties for the new railroad.

• The contractor for the bridge across Knapps Creek, Crogan and Hanchel, began work on the piers in early September by opening up the quarry on Jericho on the Price land. The stones weighed approximately four thousand pounds each, one to a wagon.

• In early September it was estimated that 1500 men were at work.

• Work began on the tunnel north of Marlinton in the middle of September with A.H. Jacoby and Company having the contract.

• By early October work was underway as far north as the future site of Hosterman with six contractors at work between Marlinton and there.

• By the middle of October the two bridges across the

Camp of contractor J.J. Strang in Marlinton, located near Knapps Creek along present day Third Avenue. Contractor Strang began working in the Marlinton area in August 1899.
PCHS/NRP

Construction work on the grade for the Greenbrier Railway in Marlinton, 1899.   PCHS/NRP

Greenbrier were under construction.

• The job of moving the Temporary Court House building in Marlinton from the right-of-way began in late October and was completed the next month.

• For grading work the Chesapeake and Ohio was paying at this time 17 cents per cubic yard in earth, 28 cents per cubic yard in loose rock, and 56 cents per cubic yard in solid rock. Tunnel excavation was costing $2.25 per cubic yard.

• An advertisement for men to work on building the new railway line offered pick and shovel men $1.40 per day, cart drivers $1.40 per day, steel drivers $1.50 per day with cabins free and blankets furnished if needed. Transportation to the work site was free and board was available at $4 per month.

• In the middle of December it was reported that the first two miles of track had been laid. However, in January track laying was stopped for the winter due to freezing and thawing and the threat of landslides.

• One of the more difficult sections for the grading work was near Renick where three-fourths of a mile of limestone cliff had be to blasted to a depth of sixty feet.

• The northern abutment for the Knapps Creek bridge was completed towards the end of January 1900. Work on the bridge was delayed in February when a sudden rise in the creek, probably on the 12th, took out the cofferdam being used to construct the center pier as well as a derrick and a pump.

• Work on the two tunnels was not affected by the weather and was being done twenty-four hours a day during the winter months.

• By the first of May the Droop Tunnel was completed and twelve miles of track had been laid. One-half mile of track was being laid per day. The going price for ties was 30 cents for first class and 25 cents for second class, delivered to the right-of-way.

• Mark O. Hankins succeeded his brother, William, as engineer on the Greenbrier Railway in June.

• Eighteen miles of track were in place by the end of May and twenty-nine miles by the first of July. The temporary bridge across Knapps Creek was also completed early in July.

• In early July the engineers for the West Virginia Pulp and Paper Company began to lay off the ground at the mouth of Leatherbark Creek for the large sawmill the company planned to build there.

Quarry on Jericho Flat that supplied the stone for the Knapps Creek bridge.

PCHS/NRP

Black construction workers at one of the camps of contractor John L. Pitts, above Marlinton. Photograph taken March 7, 1900.   PCHS/NRP

One of the camps of contractor John L. Pitts, above Marlinton. Photograph was taken March 7, 1900.   PCHS/NRP

Beginning of work on the northern abutment of the Knapps Creek bridge in the fall of 1899.   PCHS/NRP

Construction camp below
Marlinton at the Kee Eddy,
1900.   PCHS/NRP

Construction work on the
grade for the new railroad
above Marlinton, 1900.
                    PCHS/NRP

Nearly completed grade for the
new railroad near Marlinton,
March 7, 1900.   PCHS/NRP

• In the middle of July it was announced that the Greenbrier Railway was ready to haul freight in carload lots to Falling Spring (Renick) and other points.

• By August work on the grade was being done near Durbin.

• By the middle of September trains were running to near the mouth of Locust Creek and the farmers of the Little Levels were having fertilizer delivered in carload lots. At about the same time John A. Argabrite claimed the honor of christening the new railroad by shipping the first carloads, two cars of stock, which were loaded at Falling Spring. The station at this location was completed in September, also. Regular train service was not to begin, however, until the track was completed to Marlinton, at the request of the engineers, so the track could be put in the best possible shape before the line was encumbered with regular traffic.

• Towards the end of September the rails were within sixteen miles of Marlinton and being laid at the rate of a mile per day. The people in Marlinton were getting anxious for the iron horse to arrive:

> The few cool nights have implanted in the marrow of our bones an aching longing to have a large house filled with black diamonds, and we are led to believe that the iron steed will accomplish this for us without the fabulous outlay heretofore incident to the use of coal. This is but one of the small advantages Marlinton will derive from a railroad; however, small favors gladly received and larger ones solicited.

• The track was in use to Smith's Mill above the mouth of Stamping Creek by the middle of October.

• In October Chesapeake and Ohio Vice-president Decatur Axtell wrote H.G. Davis that "Grading is practically done and bridges are ready on our Greenbrier Branch up to within about a mile of the forks of the river."

Finally for the people of Marlinton the big day dawned with the official "first train" on October 26, 1900. The day was reported by *The Pocahontas Times* as follows:

Construction train and camp cars for construction crew at Spring Creek. Note the temporary bridge over the creek. The locomotive is Chesapeake and Ohio Class F 4-6-0 No. 158.

Pauline Wolfenbarger

While no special committee had been appointed to consult with the weather prophets in the selection of a day for the rally no more happy selection could have been made. Conveyances of all kinds commenced to arrive at an early hour and by noon an immense crowd had assembled, horses filling all the livery stables, alleys and side streets of the town. The ox had been roasting from an early hour and when the time had come when the Injin ate the wood chuck there were many mouths ready to devour him. The special train bringing the band from Rocky Point arrived about one o'clock. This attracted many people to the railroad and some of the smaller youngsters had their first train ride. A parade was formed and the speaker of the day, Sen. N.C. McNeil was escorted to the speakers stand from which an appropriate address of welcome, happy descriptions of the past and prophecies for the future was made by the jovial Senator. At the close of the speech Ye Knights of the tournament formed in gallant array marched to the course. The competitors for the saddle and honor of crowning a Queen of Love and Beauty were Messers Clark, McLaughlin, Dr. Marshall, Galford, King and Smith.

W.D. Clark won the first prize. Will Clark owing to an infringement of the rules in carrying his lance was given second prize.

The football game was won by Marlinton by a score of 2-0 in one of the most stubbornly contested battles ever waged on the local gridiron. The addresses delivered at the coronation ball were most suitable for the occasion, "bright the lamps shown (sic) o'er fair women and brave men." Miss Daisy Mann was crowned queen. The dancing continued until an early hour. So closed one of the most eventful days in Marlinton history. The crowd is estimated from 1200 to 3000. Good order was mantained (sic) and all committees and participants in the exerdises (sic) are to be congratulated on the success of the occasion.

Regular passenger service on the new railway line did not begin for about a month, but freight by the carload lot was handled by the trains hauling construction material. At this time there were three locomotives handling the movement of traffic on the line; No. 158 worked from Whitcomb to Beards Siding, No. 334 to Marlinton, and No. 84 north of Marlinton. The cost of hauling freight to Marlinton from Ronceverte was $1 per ton, with a $15 minimum. "A jump from 72 cents the hundred (the amount charged by wagoneers) to $1 the ton in freight is enough to make one rejoice."

Regular passenger service on the new line began on December 17, 1900, operating as far as Marlinton. For more details see Chapter Five.

The new Greenbrier River line was given status as a separate division of the Chesapeake and Ohio Railway and H.C. Boughton was named as Superintendent. B.T. Dixon was assigned to the position of Trainmaster and Chief Train Dispatcher. The Track Supervisor's job went to J.R. Anderson. The headquarters for the division were located at Ronceverte.

In the meantime the work continued on the track above Marlinton with every effort being made to reach Cass as soon as possible to enable the West Virginia Pulp and Paper Company to ship pulp wood to the new paper mill at Covington.

• The track was laid across the temporary bridge across the Greenbrier River at Sharps Tunnel north of Marlinton on November 6.

Part of the crowd in Marlinton on October 26, 1900, for the "first train" celebration. Engine of the construction train is Chesapeake and Ohio F Class 4-6-0 No. 84.　　　　　PCHS

Special train at Marlinton on October 26, 1900, for the "first train" celebration on that day. The engine is Chesapeake and Ohio Railway Class F 4-6-0 No. 158. The train is located at about the present Eighth Street crossing.　　　　　PCHS

GRAND RALLY!

October 26th, 1900.

FIRST TRAIN IN MARLINTON!

BARBECUE, POLO, TOURNAMENT, FOOT-BALL, CORONATION, AND TOURNAMENT BALL!

General Manager, CAPTAIN A. E. SMITH
Speaker of the Day, SENATOR N. C. McNEIL
Secretary & Tresurer, B. N. RAYBURN
Marshall, COLONEL A. C. L. GATEWOOD
Address to Knights, S. B. SCOTT, Jr.
Coronation Address, W. A. BRATTON
Clowns, W. A. SLAVEN and B. B. BARTLETT
Judges of Tournament, LEVI GAY, W. W. TYREE, J. M. CUNNINGHAM.

THE COMMITTEES.

Committee on General Arrangements—E. D. King, L. M. McClintic, Walter Proctor, John Proctor, A. B. Kincaid, T. S. McNeel, B. M. Yeager, W. B. Sharp, A. Harrison, C. A. Yeager, B. F. Hamilton, J. H. Patterson, S. L. Brown, Levi Gay, H. A. Yeager, Uriah Bird, W. A. Bratton, R. B. Slaven, F. R. Hunter, H. R. Echols, Andrew Price, R. C. McCandlish, and A. C. Echards.

Committee on Barbecue—William and Walter Mann.

Committee on Music—C. D. Gillaspie and J. W. Yeager.

Committee on Decoration—F. P. Anderson, J. H. Patterson, Jr., W. A. Slaven, Ed Patterson, J. A. Sharp, Ike Buzzard and Carl Slaven.

Committee on Tournament—Dr J. M. Cunningham, J. O. Smith, W. W. Tyree, W. B. King, W. A. McLaughlin

Committee on Supplies—F. H. Kincaid and P. Golden.

Committee on Tournament Ball—Misses Anna V. Price, Daisy Mann, Bertie Mann, Elizabeth Magruder, Lillian Patterson, Grace Irvine, Zoe Irvine, Icy Cruikshanks, Emma King, Annie King, Elva Bird, Gertrude Bird, Fannie McLaughlin, Mollie Smith, Gertie Smith, Eliza Gatewood, Daisy Yeager, Goldie Yeager, Pearl Yeager and Bessie Edgar.——CHAPERONES—Mesdames Flora M. Bester, W. A. Mann, C. A. Yeager, L. M. McClintic, B. M. Yeager, Hubert Echols, J. A. Sharp, B. N. Rayburn, W. A. Bratton, R. C. McCandlish, A. C. Echard, A. B. Kincaid, B. B. Bartlett, R. B. Slaven, William Criser, F. H. Kincaid, A. Price, J. D. Pullins, Ed Patterson and J. H. Patterson, Jr.

PROGRAMME.

11 to 1 o'clock, DINNER, [Roast Ox]
1 to 2 o'clock, POLO GAME
2 to 5 o'clock, TOURNAMENT
3 to 5-30 o'clock, FOOT-BALL [Marlinton vs Frost]
7-30 to 12 p. m. CORONATION and TOURNAMENT BALL.
BALLOON ASSENSION at night by Prof. A. A. PICKERING.

Attraction of the Day!

"THE MOUNTAIN BEAUTIES," (The eight Craver Sisters,) of Hendricks, will furnish music for the occasion. This is the only Ladies Band east of the Mississippi River.

• Driftwood (Stony Bottom) was reached by the track laying crews on November 22. (Driftwood was one community where the railroad constuction was considered a mixed blessing, at least by the local newspaper correspondent, "We are glad to see the hands on the grade leave before they get all the turkeys and chickens.")

• High water on the night of November 25 flooded the town of Marlinton and caused some damage to the new railroad. The temporary bridges across Knapps Creek and the river at Sharps Tunnel were taken out and the grade above the tunnel was damaged. The work to rebuild the temporary bridge across Knapps Creek was finished on December 2.

• The girders for the Sharps Tunnel bridge arrived in early December. The placing of these large girders required the quick construction of a wye track at Marlinton. As it happened the girders came up the line wrong end foremost. To get the girders in the proper direction, the railroad laid a wye in the upper part of Marlinton even though they had no right-of-way from the Pocahontas Development Company. The girders were shipped two on two flat cars. Once the girders arrived, the bridge was ready for use by the end of the week. (The wye track in Marlinton was removed in August 1901.)

• The Western Union telegraph line was completed to Marlinton by the middle of December.

• One of the major objectives of the new railroad, the Town of Cass, was reached by the track by Christmas.

• On January 7, 1901, the major job of placing the permanent Knapps Creek bridge was started.

• A special train of three private cars brought Chesapeake and Ohio President Stevens, Vice-president Axtell, General Manager Boughton, General Freight Agent Hotchkiss, Chief Engineer Pierce, and Division Engineer Hankins up the line to Cass on January 22.

• Having reached Cass, the construction of the line on to Durbin seems to have been done at a more leisurely pace. Track laying began again after a winter break about the first of June. In early July it was reported that the grade below Durbin was nearly ready for ties and the stone work was underway on the bridge across the West Fork. However, by early December the track was reported to be within three miles of Durbin, meaning only about twelve miles had been laid in the preceding six months.

• Work again ceased for the winter but in early March 1902 the materials for the bridge across the West Fork at Durbin were in place and the railroad was reported to be waiting only until the threat of high water and ice passed before the bridge was constructed. Service to Durbin was predicted in a few weeks.

• Passenger service was extended to Durbin in May, so the line must have been completed to there in March or April.

The year 1902 closed with one of the more fascinating chapters in the history of the Greenbrier Railway, Pocahontas County's own "railroad war." The "war" involved the "narrows" part of the valley of the East Fork of the Greenbrier River just east of Durbin where only one railroad could be built at a reasonable expense between the

Greenbrier River bridge and Sharps Tunnel.   PCHS

-29-

hillside and the river. A second line would have to bridge the stream at least twice or entail considerable excavation. Just beyond the narrows is the site purchased in August 1902 by the United States Leather Company for a proposed tannery.

Although in December 1901 the Greenbrier Railway had filed with the Pocahontas County Clerk a plat showing its line through the narrows, the right-of-way had not been acquired. In fact, the track and depot in Durbin were on land still owned by John McGraw. In June of 1902 Col. McGraw and several of his associates chartered the Greenbrier, Monongahela, and Pittsburgh Railroad to build a line from Durbin to Point Marion, Pennsylvania. In September the Greenbrier, Monongahela, and Pittsburgh filed a location map at the Pocahontas County Court House for the section of its line between Durbin and Bartow and Col. McGraw deeded the necessary right-of-way.

At this point the Chesapeake and Ohio seems to have noticed that it might lose the potential tannery business and access to timber developments on the East Fork. The railroad reacted in the classic way shown in the movies and on Saturday night, October 4, 1902, moved a crew of 150 men to Durbin. Sunday morning the men went to work and by nightfall that day they had built one-half mile of track through the narrows. A train was run over the track and a car left chained to rails at the new terminus, located about where the lower switch to the tannery was located. Brown Beard recalled to the author that he was hired with his team to help lay the track and was paid $12.50 for the day's work.

Early Monday morning Chesapeake and Ohio lawyers appeared at the home of Circuit Judge Joseph M. McWhorter in Lewisburg to say "that they had been laying track all day on another's land and asking that the court grant them an injunction to keep it down, which was done."

Col. McGraw appealed to the Federal Court and got an injunction from Judge Nathan Goff to restrain the Chesapeake and Ohio from going on the land or using the railroad through the narrows.

The whole matter went to the courts. Special terms of the Circuit Court were held on November 1 and 18 in Marlinton with nothing resolved and another hearing scheduled for December 9. However, on the day before, December 8, the case was continued indefinitely by agreement of counsel with newspaper speculation that the matter would be settled out of court. This is what happened, as in July of 1903 the Greenbrier, Monongahela, and Pittsburgh deeded the right-of-way through the narrows to the Chesapeake and Ohio and passed quietly from the scene. Also in the same month John McGraw deeded the land for the track and depot site in Durbin to the Chesapeake and Ohio.

It is a pity that at this time we will probably never know the motives behind Col. McGraw and his people in chartering the Greenbrier, Monongahela, and Pittsburgh Railroad. Whether they were serious about build-ing the line or just wanted to pressure the Chesapeake and Ohio in some way is not known from the evidence available to the author. In a letter to H.G. Davis in October 1902, Col. McGraw wrote about the "embarrassment and trouble we have is in getting both rails and ties in over the C & O RR" and inquired about obtaining the ties and rail needed to make the connection with Davis' Coal and Iron Railway from that company, so he may have been serious. Also there was a news report in November 1902 that the Greenbrier, Monongahela, and Pittsburgh had started work on a grade beside the Chesapeake and Ohio.

Having won the War of the Narrows, the Chesapeake and Ohio was not in any great rush to build on up the East Fork. The letting of a contract for an extension to Bartow was reported in August 1903. The work was well underway in October and the grade was ready for ties and rails by the middle of November. Freight service to Bartow was available by April 1904 and the passenger trains began operating to that point in early June.

The final extension of the Greenbrier Railway was to Winterburn the following year, 1905. This line was built with the cooperation of the George Craig and Sons Lumber Company which had purchased timber land on the East Fork and Little River and was making plans to erect a sawmill at the mouth of the Little River. In March 1905 an agreement was reached between the two companies for Craig to construct the grade, build the bridges, and furnish the ties and for the railroad company to lay the track, including a side track at the mill. The agreement also included provisions on the shipment of lumber from the Craig mill. Good progress on the construction work on the grade from Bartow was reported during the same month. By the end of June the extension to Winterburn was reported to have been almost complete.

In November 1905 the agreement between the railroad and the lumber company was modified. The Chesapeake and Ohio agreed to pay Craig for the work done by the lumber company. In return Craig agreed to put in his own side track and give the railroad use of the lumber company's wye track.

With the completion of the line to Winterburn, the Greenbrier Railway reached its greatest length, 100.96 miles from Whitcomb.

Financing the New Railroad

By deed dated November 1, 1901, the Greenbrier Railway leased for forty years "its line, built and under construction, everything now held or hereafter acquired," to the Chesapeake and Ohio Railway as of October 23, 1901. The fiction of the Greenbrier line being owned by a separate company was totally ended in 1903 when the Greenbrier Railway was consolidated with the Chesapeake and Ohio. This action had been authorized by the West Virginia Legislature in February 1901 and was carried out by the stockholders of both companies at a meeting on October 20, 1903. The effective date of the merger was October 31, 1903.

The author has not located sufficient information to be certain of the exact total cost of building the railroad up the Greenbrier River; one problem is that figures vary depending upon the accounting system used. However, at the date of the consolidation of the Greenbrier Railway with the Chesapeake and Ohio, October 31, 1903, $2,013,144.10 had been spent on the actual construction of the line. This money had been expended in the following manner:

Engineering	82,812.79
Land	46,845.35
Grading (etc.)	857,275.44
Tunnels	35,298.06
Bridges, trestles, and culverts	291,230.07
Ties	120,675.49
Rails	276,008.98
Other track material	66,437.88
Track laying and surfacing	116,859.71
Ballast	44,814.84
Stations	18,036.57
Water stations	12,792.87
Fuel stations	452.08
Telegraph and telephone lines	7,494.40
Miscellaneous structures	27,691.05
Crossings and signs	5,776.98
Right-of-way fences	2,589.94
Other items	51.60

In addition, $51,987 in general expenses had been charged to the Greenbrier Railway as of this date. The largest amount, $46,741.07, was interest charged by the Chesapeake and Ohio on the money the parent company had advanced to the Greenbrier Railway. As of October 31, 1903, the cash advanced by the Chesapeake and Ohio for the building of the Greenbrier line amounted to $2,018,390.32 (the construction and general expenses minus the interest.)

Beyond the above amount the only figures the author has found are in the 1904, 1905, and 1906 Chesapeake and Ohio annual reports under the heading, "Extension of Greenbrier Railway." The total amount for the three years is $32,424.06.

In order for the Greenbrier Railway to pay its debt to the parent company, Greenbrier Railway bonds were issued. On October 6, 1900, the stockholders of the Greenbrier Railway authorized their Board of Directors to issue up to $3,000,000 in 4% bonds, to be due on November 1, 1940. On the 23rd of the same month the Chesapeake and Ohio stockholders gave approval for their railroad to guarantee the bonds. In February 1901, $2,000,000 in First Mortgage 4% Gold Bonds of the Greenbrier Railway were issued, with the Colonial Trust Company in New York City as Trustee. As the bonds were sold at a discount, $1,830,000 in cash was actually received to reimburse the Chesapeake and Ohio for the money expended on the Greenbrier line. (The additional $1,000,000 in bonds was never issued.)

By the due date of November 1, 1940, $1,396,000 of the principal had been paid on the bonds. Payment on the balance of $604,000 was extended to March 1, 1992, at 3½% interest. After its application in 1975 to abandon

the Greenbrier line, the Chesapeake and Ohio acquired the remaining bonds in 1977 and presented them to the trustee (now the Chase Manhattan Bank [National Association]). The deed of trust was released on March 28, 1979, and the Greenbrier line was free of debt—some three months after it was abandoned!

Accidents During The Construction Work

In any construction project of this magnitude accidents were inevitable and, tragically, so almost certainly were fatalities. The first fatal accident of which the author has found record occurred in early August 1899. A Greenbrier County man, name not given in the news account, was hit on the head by a fist-sized rock thrown from a blast about a quarter of a mile away. He was killed instantly in the accident that happened on the grade near Frankford.

William C. Mann was killed on November 23, 1899, while hauling rock from near his home on Indian Draft to the construction site for the bridge over the river north of Marlinton. His team ran away near the lower end of the steep Bridger Road, upsetting the load, and he was crushed by the large stone in the wagon. The stone was never recovered and is still at the site of the accident.

Another fatal accident caused by blasting occurred on December 8, 1899, at one of the camps of contractor John L. Pitts, about four miles north of Marlinton. Willis Carr, 19, was fatally injured when hit on the head by rock blown from a stump-blasting attempt. He died early the next morning. The accident occurred near the young man's home.

Two men were killed in a blasting accident on June 21, 1900, on the grade near Cass. Harvey Shanklin, 23, was killed instantly, and a Greek laborer, about 35, died early the next day from injuries. They were loading a hole with black powder when Shanklin attempted to move a rock in the hole with a crowbar, causing a spark which set off the powder. Shanklin was thrown sixty-five feet into the air and landed in the river. A third man was slightly injured. The men were employed by the firm of Bowers and Company.

An accidental explosion on February 26, 1900, near Caldwell, fortunately did not cause any deaths. It was caused by using a crowbar to unchoke a hole that already had two kegs of powder poured in it. Several men were blown into the air and several others covered with dirt but the worst that happened was one man losing three fingers and another suffering a broken leg.

In February 1900 Pocahontas County had a smallpox scare after one of the men at Camp 3 of Contractor John L. Pitts, five miles above Marlinton, came down with the disease. The patient was Arthur Rowzie, 23, who had returned to camp from a visit to his home in Rockbridge County, Virginia, in early February. On the eighth he complained of being ill but it was not until the 13th that the camp doctor, who had never before seen a case of smallpox, decided it was the dreaded disease. Upon being informed on the 14th, the Pocahontas County Board of Health established a quarantine around the camp, including the use of armed guards. Access to and from Camp 2, about a mile north of Marlinton, was also controlled as there had been contact between the two camps. About seventy-five men were quarantined in Camp 3. Bath County, Virginia, established a strict quarantine against people coming into that county from Pocahontas County.

The guards used their weapons at least twice. On the night of the 14th they fired at some men who crept out of Camp 2. These men got away but were returned from Bath County the next day. On another night a tall stump was mistaken for a man and received a load of buckshot.

The patient was isolated and waited upon by an immune Black man. Mr. Rowzie survived the disease and no new cases developed. The quarantine was lifted in early March.

For the men in the camp, "It was a very trying time. If a man got a headache, he was in a perfect agony of suspense thinking that the disease had taken hold of him. One of the foremen burned up the only deck of cards in camp, and there was more Bible reading done than at any camp on the river, it is safe to say."

There were two deaths associated with the construction work in 1901. Don Meadows, 18, was run over by the passenger train at Spring Creek on June 19. He was part of the force putting in the permanent bridge over Spring Creek and had been sent up the track as a flagman. As train No. 142 picked up speed after slowing for the construction work, the young man was seen lying across the track in a curve but the train could not be stopped before hitting him. Why he was on the track could not be determined unless he had sat down and fallen asleep or had suddenly become ill.

A week later, on June 26, an Italian laborer, Vincengo Angilette, was run over and killed at Clawson. The unfortunate man was part of a force obtaining ballast material at that point. While waiting for some flat cars to be located on the siding so they could be loaded, about twenty of the laborers climbed on a car that had been left on the main track. In shifting cars around, the train sent several from the siding onto the main track under their own momentum. Although controlled by a brakeman, these cars gave the car the Italians were on a heavy jolt. Mr. Angilette fell off the end of the car and was run over, killing him instantly.

Two members of the same crew were drowned in the river in March. On the 10th three of the Italians went across the river from their camp to buy eggs. On their return the boat upset in the high water. Only one of the three could swim and was able to reach the shore. Efforts by Jasper Friel to rescue the other two were unsuccessful. One of the bodies was found on the 12th just below the site of the tragedy but the other body was not found until

April 21, below Seebert.

A construction force laborer, William Dabney, was injured near Durbin in early March of 1902. He was riding on the pilot of the engine of the construction train and, seeing a rock on the track, Mr. Dabney jumped off to move it. But the engine, though slowing, was going faster than he had thought and he was thrown under the wheels. He suffered head injuries and a leg had to be amputated.

The Coal and Iron Railway

Although Henry G. Davis had failed to move on the extension of his railroad south into the Greenbrier Valley in spite of all the efforts made by John T. McGraw in the middle 1890s to entice him to do so, he remained interested in the project. After the West Virginia Pulp and Paper Company chose a site on the Chesapeake and Ohio for their new paper mill instead of on the West Virginia Central, Senator Davis was probably waiting for the Chesapeake and Ohio officials to make their final plans concerning an extension into the Upper Greenbrier Valley.

Davis had kept in touch with Chesapeake and Ohio officials on the possibilities of a connection between his railroad and theirs. In December 1898 he inquired of Chesapeake and Ohio President Ingalls if they should take up the question of a connection, but must not have received any immediate encouragement from him.

However, once the Chesapeake and Ohio made their final determination to construct the Greenbrier Railway, a serious correspondence began concerning a junction of the two railroads near the Forks of the Greenbrier and a traffic agreement. Davis reported to Col. McGraw in early June 1899 that "Mr. Ingalls wrote me that it was finally determined to build up the Greenbrier and he makes some suggestions as to our building this end, and the place of meeting."

Survey work out of Elkins was reported in early July.

Davis and Chesapeake and Ohio Vice-president Axtell exchanged a number of letters in the summer and early fall of 1899 concerning a junction in the Forks area. In the middle of October Davis wrote to Axtell, "we are making an estimate of the cost of extending our road southward." In the same letter he asked information on what the Chesapeake and Ohio was paying for construction work on the Greenbrier Railway.

In November Davis wrote to President Ingalls that if satisfactory arrangements could be agreed upon the interchange of traffic then "we will commence at an early day building from Elkins to the Forks to meet you."

With each passing week Davis seemed more committed to this project. Instead of building the extension in the name of the West Virginia Central and Pittsburgh, it was decided to organize a new company for this purpose. This, of course, was an almost standard procedure. So on December 14, 1899, the charter was issued for the Coal and Iron Railway which was incorporated to build a railroad from Elkins to Greenbrier County. The incorporators were H.G. Davis and S.B. Elkins, of Elkins, T.B. Davis, of Keyser, R.C. Kerens, of St. Louis, Missouri, and C.M. Hendley, of Washington, D.C. (This was the second time the Coal and Iron name was used by Davis and his associates. In April 1884 a Coal and Iron Railway was incorporated to build a railroad from Hampshire County into the coal fields in Tucker and Grant Counties. This first Coal and Iron was not built.)

In April of 1900 the Chesapeake and Ohio must have suggested that the junction point between the two railroads be changed to the head of the West Fork of the Greenbrier rather than Durbin. Davis rejected this, pointing out that all previous communications and the traffic agreement had given the Forks as the junction. He also noted that meeting at the head of the Greenbrier River would give the Chesapeake and Ohio the easy section to build and leave the Coal and Iron with only the difficult portion of the line to Elkins.

The first work let to contract on the new railroad was the two tunnels on the line. These contracts were let and the contractors at work by the early part of February 1900. By May work was underway on the grading. Perhaps reflecting more difficult construction conditions, the Coal and Iron was paying slightly more than the Chesapeake and Ohio for grading work. For earth excavation the cost was 20 cents per cubic yard, loose rock, 35 cents per cubic yard, and for solid rock, 68 cents per cubic yard. Clearing and grubbing was $30 per acre.

In September 1900 it was reported that 1500 men were at work on the Coal and Iron.

Although shorter by half than the Chesapeake and Ohio line to Durbin, 47 miles compared to 95, the Coal and Iron was a more difficult construction job. Instead of being a "water level" route, it was a mountain crossing line. The Coal and Iron had to climb one mountain to get from the Tygarts Valley River to the Shavers Fork and then cross another to get to the Glady Fork. Once on the Glady Fork the line climbed to the divide between that stream and the West Fork of the Greenbrier. Then it was an easy grade on to Durbin. Two tunnels were needed, one for each mountain crossing and both longer than the two on the Greenbrier line.

It took almost three and a half years to complete the Coal and Iron to Durbin, a fact caused, at least in part, by the difficulty of the construction work. It was well into 1901 before the tunnels were completed. Even as late as June 1903, problems with numerous slips at different points along the line as well as the sinking of fills were being encountered. The summit cut between the Glady Fork and the West Fork of the Greenbrier was a particular problem until cut wide enough.

Also, there was not the motivation for the rapid completion of this line as the Chesapeake and Ohio had to get the Greenbrier line finished to Cass. A final reason for the length of time it took to complete the Coal and Iron may have been the sale by Senators Davis and Elkins of their railroad properties to a syndicate led by

George J. Gould in January of 1902.

By the end of 1902 trains were running from Elkins to Bemis. Finally, on July 27, 1903, the last rail was laid and Elkins and points north were connected with the Chesapeake and Ohio Railway at Durbin.

At least one tragic accident marred the construction of the line. On December 27, 1900, six Austrian laborers were killed by an explosion of dynamite. The men were part of a group of thirteen who were sitting around a fire having lunch, the same fire they were using to thaw out dynamite. They had some sixty sticks of the explosive around the fire. The dynamite exploded, killing three instantly with three others dying soon afterwards. The others were all injured. The tragedy happened on the grade one and a quarter miles above Durbin.

In 1905 the Coal and Iron and the West Virginia Central and Pittsburgh became part of the expanding Western Maryland Railway, also owned by the Gould interests. The official transfer was accomplished by deed dated November 1, 1905.

C&O ROUTE	**CHESAPEAKE AND OHIO RAILWAY**	
	In Effect June 1, 1901 (Central time.)	
WEST		EAST
No 141 Daily ex Sunday	Stations.	No 142 Daily ex. Sunday
P. M.		A. M.
1.45	Cass	11.45
1.56	Forrest	11.35
2.12	Clover Lick	11.20
2.35	Harper	10.56
3.00	Marlinton	10.35
3.12	Buckeye	10.23
3.20	Dan	10.15
3.30	Seebert	10.05
3 52	Beards	9.44
4.10	Droop Mountain	9.25
4.32	Ronick	9.05
4.41	Spring Creek	8.55
5.05	Anthony	8.35
5.15	Keister	8.25
5.38	Little Sulphur	8.00
5.45	Whitcomb	7.55
5.55	Ronceverte	7.45

Sawmill of the West Virginia Pulp and Paper Company at Cass, a producer of business on the Greenbrier line for fifty-eight years. This photo is of the original mill which burned in 1922. Note the cars of logs for the mill and the loaded cars of pulp and wood ready to go to the paper mill at Covington, Virginia.　Westvaco Corporation

View of the lumber docks at Cass. Note the empty cars used to haul pulp from Cass to the paper mill at Covington, Virginia.　Westvaco Corporation

CHAPTER III
Busy Years

1901-1910

THAT THE MARKETS OF THE COUNTRY WERE READY for the resources of the Upper Greenbrier Valley was evident by the almost instantaneous industrial activity along the new railroad. The line had hardly been open a year when it was reported that "The amount of freight being handled by the Greenbrier Railway far [out] reaches the most sanguine expectations and is a cause of wonderment."

As already mentioned, freight, both inbound and outbound, was being hauled by September of 1900. The first industrial shipper may well have been the Greenbrier River Lumber Company. This company was working on its sawmill, located north of Marlinton across the river from the mouth of Stony Creek, by September 1900 and the mill was on its way to completion by the middle of October.

However, the West Virginia Pulp and Paper Company would not have been far behind if it were not the first industry to use the new railroad. The company had begun operations at the Covington mill in March of 1900 and spent the rest of the year struggling to get enough suitable wood to keep it operating. Included was attempting a log drive down the Greenbrier River in the summer time, not the best season of the year for such an activity. The company anxiously awaited the completion of the Greenbrier Railway so a steady supply of pulp wood would be available.

In October the pulp and paper company located a log camp on Beaver Creek to cut a tract of pulp wood and by the end of 1900 had a tram road connected with the Greenbrier Railway at the mouth of the creek. By the latter part of February 1901 this operation had shipped over four hundred car loads of pulp to Covington and was loading cars at the rate of 100,000 feet daily. The main company facility at Cass began shipping the first Cheat Mountain pulp wood on January 28, 1901, when two cars, Nos. 13237 and 15736, were turned over to the Chesapeake and Ohio. A regular pulp train was in operation by March. The company spent the remainder of the year getting the large Cass band sawmill ready and it began sawing in January of 1902. This mill was a steady supplier of loads to the trains on the Greenbrier line for the next fifty-eight years.

Other sawmills went into operation before or soon after the Cass mill. A circular mill began operating across the river from August in late 1899 and maybe Messrs. August and Young, the operators of this mill, had the first load of lumber for the new railroad. Other circular mills were the ones of the M.P. Bock Lumber Company at Boyer, which began operating about 1901, the Buena Vista Hardwood Company at Stony Bottom, which started in 1901 or 1902, the Hosterman Lumber Company at Hosterman, which began sawing in 1902, and Hoover Brothers, located across the East Fork from Frank, which started up in late 1902. A number of other very small mills must have started up at this time, as a list of the sawmills on the Greenbrier Division prepared by the railroad in late 1902 named forty-four, with a total daily capacity of 387,000 feet. In size the mills ranged from the Cass mill with a capacity of 60,000 feet per day to C.C. Wanless's mill at 3,000 feet per day.

The Henderson Lumber Company at Anthony was in operation by 1903 and the Grove City Lumber Company started its mill near the Droop Mountain tunnel about the same year. Harter Brothers Lumber Company set up their mill at Harter also in 1903.

In early 1905 the big band mill of the Campbell Lumber Company at Campbelltown began running and before the year was out band mills had been started up at Warntown, near Mill Point, by the Warn Lumber Company; at Winterburn by George Craig and Sons; and probably the Thornwood mill by E.V. Dunlevie. In 1906 the band mill at Watoga was constructed by the J.R. Droney Lumber Company as were the circular mills of the DeRan Lumber Company at Clover Lick and the Stony Bottom Lumber Comany at Stony Bottom. Donaldson Lumber Company at Woodman (band mill) and the Kendall and Deeter Lumber Company at Deeter (circular mill) probably also began operating their mills in 1906.

Before the end of the first decade of the Greenbrier Division's history additional band mills were in operation. The Deer Creek Lumber Company mill at Deer Creek was running by 1910 and the Maryland Lumber Company mill at Denmar started that year or the next. John Raine and Company located a small band mill on Stamping Creek in 1907 and several additional circular mills were in operation at different locations. Among the oper-

Original Cass depot and mill yard.   PCHS

ators of circular mills that were in business by 1910 were those of Hoover and Yeager at Houchins, Brown, Depp and Swanson at Sixty, and W.W. Dempsey at Big Run.

The mills on the West Fork of the Greenbrier River served by the Western Maryland Railroad also provided some traffic to the Greenbrier Division. In operation by 1905 were the band mills of the Wildell Lumber Company at Wildell, F.S. Wise at Gertrude, Pocahontas Lumber Company at Burner, Hoover-Dimeling Lumber Company at May, and P.L. and W.F. Brown at Olive, as well as several circular mills.

Besides the Cass complex, the most important individual sources of business for the new railroad were the tanneries that were established at Frank and Marlinton. The tanning industry was attracted to the Upper Greenbrier Valley by the availability of vast quantities of the hemlock bark and chestnut oak bark that were used in the tanning process of the day. Work on the Marlinton

tannery of the U.S. Leather Company began in 1903 and the tannery was in operation in early 1905. The Pocahontas Tanning Company built the Frank tannery in 1904. These two plants provided business in the form of incoming loads of tanning bark, hides, and other necessities for tanning as well as outbound loads of finished leather.

The Empire Wood Company located a kindling wood plant at Watoga in 1908. The idea was to take the wood waste from sawmills, dry it, cut it into kindling-size pieces, and bundle it for shipment to New York City. The idea was not too successful and the plant operated for only a few years. A stave mill was constructed at Clover Lick by the National Cooperage Company in 1901 but it also was not a long-lived industry. More successful was the factory at Renick operated by the Horrocks Desk Company which opened in 1904 and operated for about twenty years.

Cars of lumber ready for shipment at Cass.

Westvaco Corporation

Another natural resource of the Greenbrier Valley, limestone, was crushed for railroad ballast and other uses by the Renick Stone Company at its quarry near Renick. The quarry opened in 1907, under the name Greenbrier and James River Stone Company, but the name was changed the following year.

The long-established agricultural industry of the Valley was quick to begin using the new railroad. As already related, farmers were receiving supplies by rail as early as September of 1900 and the first shipments of stock left Renick that same month. Stock pens were located at several points along the line and stock was shipped by rail until well after World War II. In 1910 it was reported that stock shipments from the Greenbrier Valley averaged 1200 car loads of sheep and cattle each season.

The everyday material needs of the expanding population of the Upper Greenbrier Valley were also filled by rail. Today we forget that at the turn of the century, almost everything came by way of railroad cars, once a community was connected to the national rail network. From car loads of coal, food, store goods, farm supplies, household furnishings, etc., to mail and the individual items ordered from the catalogs, it all came in by train. The first automobiles and the fuel to power them came by rail. The coming of the railroad also provided the Valley with Western Union telegraph service, which was the only quick way of communicating in the early 1900s.

The growth of business on the Greenbrier division can be seen by the statistics giving the amount of freight originating on the line. For the fiscal year ending June 30, 1903, some 191,677 tons of freight were picked up by the Greenbrier Division freight trains with freight revenue that year of $220,360.68. The figures grew to 245,591 tons and $278,312.33 in revenue in 1903-1904; 293,225 tons and $299,855.95 in 1904-1905; and 378,926 tons and $407,530.77 in the fiscal year ending June 30, 1906. As can be seen from these figures, freight tonnage and revenue almost doubled in four years as the development of the resources of the Upper Greenbrier Valley took place.

In each of these four years, Cass, not surprisingly, was the biggest single source of freight, growing from 107,826 tons in 1902-1903 to 196,687 tons in 1905-1906. In 1902-1903 the next busiest stations were Marlinton (17,377 tons), Renick (8,086 tons), Boyer (7,517 tons), Anthony (6,912 tons), Clover Lick (6,353 tons), Seebert (5,393 tons), Hosterman (4,384 tons), North Caldwell (3,416 tons), and Beard (2,936 tons). In 1905-1906 the stations after Cass with the greatest tonnages were Marlinton (42,940 tons), Durbin (19,604 tons), Boyer (15,419 tons), Winterburn (11,937 tons), Renick (11,736 tons), Seebert (11,276 tons), Anthony (8,818 tons), Hosterman (8,237 tons), and North Caldwell (6,334 tons).

As would be expected, freight train operation on the Greenbrier Division showed a great deal of variation over the years and depended upon the amount of business available. The most definitive source of information on train operations is, of course, schedules, but not too many have been located for the early years of the Greenbrier line. Of course, schedules do not tell the entire story, particularly for freight service, as many freight trains were run "extra" as business dictated and never appeared on a schedule.

In June of 1901 *The Pocahontas Times* reported to its readers, "Two local freights are on the road each making one trip a day from Ronceverte to Cass, passing the passenger at Marlinton." These trains would have been one each way and numbered 145 and 146. No. 145 made the trip from Cass to Ronceverte and No. 146 the Ronceverte to Cass run.*

The schedule for June 4, 1905, gives two scheduled freight trains, in addition to the four passenger trains:

WEST 145		EAST 146
	Bartow	
5:00 a.m.	Durbin	5:10 p.m.
6:40	Cass	3:40
9:00	Marlinton	12:10
10:50	Seebert	10:50
12:40	Renick	8:12
3:00 p.m.	Whitcomb	6:10 a.m.

Service is daily except Sunday.

This schedule may not give the complete story as *The Pocahontas Times* reported the month before concerning freight service as follows: "In order to handle the increased business, an extra freight was put on Monday (May 8). One freight runs from Durbin to Ronceverte daily. Another plys (sic) between Durbin and Marlinton and the third between Ronceverte and Marlinton."

---

*Note: On Chesapeake and Ohio schedules all train movements were considered either east bound or west bound. On the Greenbrier line the direction of travel was west for trains going down river and east for trains going up river, no doubt based on the direction of travel along the main line in relation to Ronceverte, the headquarters for the Division. The author will use east and west in giving schedules, but for the convenience of the reader, will use north and south or up river and down river in the text.

This procedure of operating freight trains over only a portion of the Greenbrier line was a standard one until the Depression. The exchange point for the trains serving only a portion of the line varied over the years depending upon traffic. At different times Cass, Clover Lick, and Marlinton were the exchange points. In the schedule for June 2, 1912, Cass is the dividing line:

WEST 149	147	145	
2:30 p.m.			Winterburn
3:00			Bartow
3:30 p.m.	7:00 a.m.		Durbin
	8:30	6:00 a.m.	Cass
	8:50 a.m.	6:30	Sitlington
		8:02	Marlinton
		10:17	Seebert
		12:45	Renick
		3:30 p.m.	Whitcomb

EAST 146	148	
	12:30 p.m.	Winterburn
	12:00	Bartow
	11:15	Durbin
3:25 p.m.	9:30	Cass
3:10	9:00 a.m.	Sitlington
1:15		Marlinton
11:50		Seebert
9:25		Renick
6:50 a.m.		Whitcomb

These trains ran daily except Sunday. Under this schedule, trains 147, 148, and 149 made up a day's work for one crew, starting at Durbin at 7 a.m., going to Sitlington as No. 147, back to Winterburn as No. 148, and finally back to Durbin as No. 149. The reason for running No. 147 to Sitlington is not known to the author unless it was to handle the traffic at the mill at Deer Creek. Trains 145 and 146 required separate crews and engines, of course.

Motive power for the freights in these early years on the Greenbrier were Chesapeake and Ohio Class F 4-6-0 and Class G 2-8-0 locomotives. Photos exist showing both types in use on the Greenbrier in the first years of the line. We can, however, assume that the G class engines soon became the most common power since the F class engines were generally used on passenger trains.

In this first decade of the Greenbrier Division there were several changes in superintendent. As of March 1, 1902, Mr. Boughton was transferred to the Kentucky Division and H. Pierce, Division Engineer for the Kentucky Division, became Greenbrier Division Superintendent. On April 1, 1905, Mr. Pierce was appointed Engineer of Construction and the Greenbrier line came under the Superintendent of the Huntington Division, E.W. Grice. John W. Haynes was appointed as Assistant Superintendent to be in charge of the Greenbrier Division. Mr. Haynes was appointed as Greenbrier Division Superintendent on July 1, 1906, following a splitting of the Huntington Division into the Clifton Forge and Huntington Divisions.

Part of the freight hauled in the early years on the Greenbrier line was the bark used in the tanning process at the tanneries at Marlinton and Frank. This photograph, taken in early 1904, shows piles of bark at the Marlinton tannery.
PCHS/NRP

The tannery at Frank, a customer on the Greenbrier line for 80 years, from its construction in 1904 until train service was ended to Frank in early 1984. The tannery was built by the Pocahontas Tanning Company and is now operated by the Howes Leather Company.
PCHS

The Sitlington depot was destroyed by fire in October 1908. The fire was discovered early on the morning of the 29th but efforts to put out the fire were unsuccessful. Arson was the suspected cause but the author has not found if any arrests were ever made. The building was soon replaced.

One perhaps unexpected result of the construction of the Greenbrier Railway was the change, at least temporarily, of the politics of Pocahontas County from Democrat to Republican. In March of 1900 N.C. McNeil wrote to S.B. Elkins, "The construction of a railroad in this country is going to give the county to us in a very short time." Mr. McNeil's remark was prophetic as in 1904 Pocahontas County voted Republican for president and in the 1908 election the county supported the full GOP ticket.

1911-1920

By the middle part of the second decade of the Greenbrier Division's history, a number of the original lumber companies had finished cutting their timber and closed their mills. However, a number of new mills opened to keep traffic at a high level.

The mill at August closed in 1909; DeRan Lumber Company shut down at Clover Lick in 1911; Harter Brothers ceased operating in either 1911 or 1912; and the Hosterman operation around 1912. The Warn Lumber Company closed out its mill near Mill Point in late 1913; the Campbell Lumber Company mill cut its last log in February of 1914; and John Raine and Company on Stamping Creek finished the same year. Also finishing about the middle part of the decade were the Donaldson Lumber Company at Woodman, the Grove City Lumber Company at Droop Mountain Tunnel, and the Kendall and Deeter Lumber Company at Deeter.

A closed saw mill sometimes gave the railroad a last spurt of business, however. In April 1916 it took forty cars to move the Campbell mill from Campbelltown to a new location near Rainelle.

On the Western Maryland almost all of the mills were closed by the middle teens. F.S. Wise at Gertrude closed about 1910; P.L. and W.F. Brown finished about 1913; the mill at May, started by the Hoover-Dimeling Lumber Company, was closed by Gilfillan, Neil and Company in April 1914; the Pocahontas Lumber Company shut down its mill at Burner about 1915; and the Wildell Lumber Company finished in 1915 or 1916.

To compensate for these mill closings, big band mills operated by the Spice Run Lumber Company at Spice Run and the F.S. Wise Lumber Company at Clover Lick began operating in 1913. After finishing at Mill Point the Warns moved to a new location, Raywood, and started their band mill there in 1915. The American Column and Lumber Company opened a small mill at Buckeye in late 1914. By 1915 the lumber operation at Boyer, now the North Fork Lumber Company, had replaced a smaller mill at Boyer with a large band mill near the mouth of Brush Run. On the Western Maryland the Mountain Lick Lumber Company purchased the mill at Olive and extended its life to 1919 or 1920.

In late 1914 the Kendall Lumber Company began to harvest the timber on land on Marlin and Thorny Creek Mountains owned by the Thorny Creek Lumber Company. The Chesapeake and Ohio gained twice from this operation since the Thorny Creek Lumber Company also owned the mill at Thornwood and decided to use it to produce the lumber rather than build a new mill at the timber. Thus the railroad first got to haul cars of logs from the lumber railroad on Thorny Creek to Thornwood and then cars of lumber from the mill. Kendall also had a spur line up a small stream about a mile south of Harter.

In 1915 the Spice Run Lumber Company began the construction of its logging railroad from the Chesapeake and Ohio at Mill Run, across Droop Mountain, to Hills Creek. In this case the lumber company train ran over the Chesapeake and Ohio tracks from Mill Run to Spice Run instead of the railroad company hauling the log cars. However, the lumber company would have been required to pay for the privilege of running over the railroad's tracks.

Other lumber companies also had logging lines joining the Greenbrier Division. The West Virginia Pulp and Paper Company had lines up Trout Run, built by 1916, up Allegheny Run, completed in 1916, and up Deever Run, built in the late teens. George Craig and Sons Lumber Company built a railroad from Houchins into timber on Burner Mountain in 1915. A.D. Neill, who purchased the Clover Lick mill from F.S. Wise, had a logging railroad switching from the Chesapeake and Ohio just south of the Greenbrier River bridge near Harter; built about 1920. As far as the author knows, the pulp and paper company ran its own trains over the Chesapeake and Ohio; in the other two cases the arrangement for getting the cars of logs to the mills is not known.

In addition to these logging railroad lines, a great many sidings were put in over the years to load logs for various lumber companies, as well as tan bark and pulp wood. The Greenbrier River Lumber Company, for example, depended upon the Chesapeake and Ohio to bring in most of the logs for its mill at Marlinton.

The Cass operation of the West Virginia Pulp and Paper Company was expanding towards its peak years of the early 1920s and provided a tremendous amount of business for the Greenbrier line trains. By 1910 shipments of lumber, pulp wood, and slabs often exceeded 1000 carloads per month. In May of 1910 a total of 1149 cars left Cass, an average of slightly over 44 cars per day. To utilize the waste bark, a tanning extract plant was erected by the pulp and paper company between Cass and Deer Creek. Ground was broken for this plant in late 1913 and it began operating in early 1915. This plant produced hemlock and spruce bark extracts, and a limited quantity of chestnut wood extract. During World War I, a considerable quantity of osage orange dyewood extract was produced in both liquid and powdered form to be used in the dyeing of khaki cloth, in place of fustic dyewood extract.

Smaller sawmills, with an operational life of only a few years, also added to the car loadings on the line. A.V. Miller located a mill at Deever Run about 1909, moved to Pine Flats about 1911, and moved again in 1916 to Nida. Paul Golden put in a mill and created a new train stop, Golden, in 1917. In the late teens the Vulcan Last Company established a plant at Spice Run, across the river from the sawmill, which operated for a few years.

As it had done with earlier operations, the Chesapeake and Ohio helped some of these companies by leasing them rail to be used in building their logging railroads. Both Spice Run and F.S. Wise leased four miles of rail and the necessary accessories and Warn leased enough rail for twenty miles of track for its Raywood operation. These leases and later ones all followed the same pattern and called for a yearly rental for use of the rail equal to 6 percent of its value. The value was figured at $20 or $25 per long ton for 50 to 75 pound rail in early years. Showing the effect of wartime inflation, the value had grown to $40 per long ton by the early 1920s. Angle bars were leased at $1 or $1.50 per pair. Other companies leasing rail were the Marlin Lumber Company and the Spring Creek Lumber Company.

In at least one case, the railroad also supplied a bridge to a lumber company. A two span truss bridge that had been over the Calf Pasture River in Virginia was furnished to the Deer Creek Lumber Company. After the lumber operation was completed, the bridge was donated by the railroad to the County Court. The author has not determined what the Court did with this gift.

In addition to the normal traffic involving lumber, other wood products, coal, agricultural products, store goods, etc., the Greenbrier Division trains occasionally hauled loads of a more unusual nature. On March 19, 1912, sixteen head of elk were unloaded at Marlinton for the Allegheny Sportsman Association for its game preserve at Minnehaha Springs. The elk came from a preserve in Iowa. The following year fifty elk came from Yellowstone National Park. Twenty-five arrived on January 28 and the other twenty-five on February 3.

Modern conveniences and contraptions were to arrive eventually on the Greenbrier. Section Foreman Thomas E. Clemons at Spring Creek received the first motor car on the division in January of 1913. As an experiment, his section was doubled in length to twelve miles to see if the use of motor cars could reduce the number of track maintenance sections. The experiment proved to be a success and the following year the number of sections of the Greenbrier Division was reduced from eighteen to ten, all with motor cars. Ironically, with the reduction, Mr. Clemons lost his job on the Greenbrier due to a lack of seniority and went to Paint Creek.

In the last part of 1913 the office of the train dispatcher for the Greenbrier Division was moved from Ronceverte to Marlinton. A warehouse building was moved to beside the Marlinton depot from its original location across the track and in early November Train Dispatcher A.B. McCrary was in his new office. The track supervisor also moved his office into this building. However, the train dispatcher's office didn't remain in Marlinton for too many years and was returned to Ronceverte in February 1916. The building continued to serve as the office for the track supervisor until the last supervisor retired in 1972. It also housed the Western Union telegraph office for a number of years.

The West Virginia Public Service Commission was organized in 1913 to regulate utilites in the state, including railroads. The first case to come before the commission that involved the Greenbrier Division was interesting, if not earth shattering. The Marlinton and Academy Telephone Company and F.W. Ruckman, of Mill Point, filed a complaint in July 1913 against the Chesapeake and Ohio and the Ronceverte and Elkins Telephone Company charging that the railroad allowed the Ronceverte and Elkins Company to place a phone in the Seebert Station but had refused the Marlinton and Academy Company permission to do the same on several occasions. The railroad pointed out that it had a contract with the Ronceverte and Elkins company giving it the exclusive privilege to install a phone in the depot. The Public Service Commission, observing the inconvenience to the subscribers of the Marlinton and Academy Company in their use of the railroad due to this lack of a phone, the fact that the Marlinton and Academy Company had more subscribers in the area than the other company, and the growing acceptance of the telephone as a business necessity, recommended that the railroad permit the complaining company to install a phone at Seebert. Over the objections of the Ronceverte and Elkins Company, the Chesapeake and Ohio agreed to do so.

A similar complaint was filed in January 1914 by the Marlinton and Clover Lick Telephone Company concerning installing one of its phones in the Clover Lick depot. The case was quickly settled and the phone installed in March.

The creation of the new mill town of Raywood brought about the establishment of a new agency station on the Greenbrier line. A depot building was constructed by the Warn Lumber Corporation in late 1915. Although many stops were created by the various saw mills that were put into operation over the years, Raywood was the only agency station established after the early 1900s.

During World War I an engine was kept at Cass to do the yard work there. After working the Cass yard, this crew would make a trip to Durbin and back.

The amount of freight loaded on the Greenbrier Division during the second decade of the line's history remained high. During the fiscal year ending June 30, 1913, 490,573 tons of freight originated at the various stations along the line. Freight revenue that year was $596,261.65. The figures dropped to 476,032 tons and $525,364.92 for

Extract plant operated by the West Virginia Pulp and Paper Company at Deer Creek, below Cass. This plant used waste bark to produce various extracts used in tanning and was in operation from 1915 to 1928.　　Westvaco Corporation

Watoga was one of the many sawmill towns that appeared along the Greenbrier Division in the early 1900s. The sawmill is in the right side of the photograph. The facility in the center of the picture was a kindling wood plant. The sawmill was in operation from 1906 to about 1920.　　PCHS

One of the many sawmills in the Greenbrier Division was the one operated by the Spice Run Lumber Company at Spice Run in Pocahontas County, just north of the Greenbrier County line. This mill operated from 1913 to about 1926. Thomas W. Dixon, Jr.

Loading poles at Bartow, June 1927.   U.S. Forest Service

Sawmill and town of the Harter Brothers Lumber Company at Harter, north of Marlinton. This mill operated from 1903 to about 1911 and was typical of the many small sawmills that were once located along the Greenbrier Division.   PCHS

Horrocks Desk Company factory at Renick, which operated from about 1904 to about 1925.
PCHS

the next year. Although there was a slight increase in freight tonnage in 1914-1915 to 477,344, revenue had another decrease to $470,043.41. However, during the fiscal year ending June 30, 1916 the figures for both freight tonnage and revenue increased to 561,578 tons and $572,019.96.

Cass, as before, was the biggest single source of freight on the Greenbrier Division during these years, loading 177,266, 202,437, 221,857, and 199,430 tons each year respectively. In 1912-1913 the stations after Cass originating the most freight were Winterburn (87,618 tons), Marlinton (51,279 tons), Seebert (32,539 tons), Denmar (28,236 tons), Durbin (18,213 tons), Boyer (11,123 tons), Beard (8,813 tons), Woodman (8,684 tons), and Renick (7,510 tons). Following Cass in 1915-1916 were Thorny Creek (71,057 tons), Winterburn (64,931

tons), Denmar (26,554 tons), Clover Lick (22,539 tons), Raywood (20,730 tons), Marlinton (19,978 tons), Spice Run (19,810 tons), Beard (18,515 tons), Durbin (17,344 tons), Hosterman (12,153 tons), and Seebert (10,787 tons). In just the comparison of these two years, the changes in the lumber industry along the Greenbrier Division can be observed. Woodman is gone from the second list and Marlinton and Seebert have dropped down due to mill closings while Spice Run, Raywood, and Thorny Creek appear. (Thorny Creek was the source of logs for the mill at Thornwood and not a mill site. Likewise, the tonnage at Hosterman was most likely logs headed for the Cass mill.) The absence of Boyer as one of the top freight producers in 1915-1916 (only 5,354 tons that year) was probably only a temporary situation, as that mill had another eleven years to operate.

F-10 Class 4-6-0 No. 189 and freight train. The crew is, left to right, _____ Turner, _____, Lem Walker, Forrest Clinebell, J.E. Hall, and Jetter Smitson.
PCHS

1921-1929

By 1920 the end of the big lumber boom in the Upper Greenbrier Valley in the not too distant future was obvious to anyone who cared to observe the signs. The third decade of the history of the Greenbrier line saw the virtual completion of the first cutting of the vast timber resource of the valley that had been the main stimulus for the building of the railroad.

The American Column and Lumber Company at Buckeye finished in May 1917; George Craig and Sons at Winterburn and the Maryland Lumber Company at Denmar both shut down in 1918; the Thornwood mill, now operated by the Thorny Creek Lumber Company, closed in April 1920; the Watoga Lumber Company (originally J.R. Droney Lumber Company) also sawed its last log in 1920; and the mill at Deer Creek, now Range Lumber Company, was finished by 1922.

The last two band mills to cut virgin timber in the valley both began operation in 1921. They were the mills of the Marlin Lumber Company at Stillwell and the Spring Creek Lumber Company at Spring Creek.

In addition to the decline in freight business on the Greenbrier line due to the closing of most of the saw mills and the withering away of the towns associated with them, it was during the 1920s that the motor truck began to make its presence felt in the hauling of freight.

However, in spite of the slow decline in local freight (and passenger) business that set in during the 1920s, these years were no doubt the busiest period in the Greenbrier line's history. The reason for this was the increased use of the line as a through route with cars interchanged with the Western Maryland at Durbin. In late 1923, Chesapeake and Ohio President W.J. Harahan announced that an agreement had been reached with the Western Maryland Railroad for the interchange of traffic at Durbin. The news release announcing the agreement stated that the result will be "A more direct and expeditious through freight route between Eastern and Western cities. . . ." The news release continues:

> For years the Chesapeake and Ohio has been operating a through freight route known as the "Blue Ridge Dispatch," which has always been popular and will be continued. The Durbin route, Mr. Harahan said, is an additional facility for the benefit of shippers made feasible by the direct connection afforded with the Western Maryland. Through trains will operate between Ronceverte, and Elkins, W.Va., and over the Western Maryland, without change of locomotive or crew.
>
> With the opening of the Durbin route, the Chesapeake and Ohio will establish a Commercial Agency in Philadelphia.
>
> On account of increased freight traffic originating in that territory, the Chesapeake and Ohio Railway has just established in a Commercial Agency at Pittsburgh, Pa., ..."

The plan for not changing locomotives or crews never did materialize, but the "manifest" trains with cars for interchange were operating over the Greenbrier line by January of 1924.

In preparation for this service a large amount of heavier rail was laid on the Greenbrier line in 1923 and 1924.

The through freight business did prove to be very suc-

cessful and a second manifest train began operating in October of 1924. The increased interchange business at Durbin required the construction of an additional side track there in 1925 to handle the cars moving between the two railroads. The new track was laid on the west side of the existing Western Maryland track beginning on the west leg of the wye track and extending 2595 feet to the upper part of the Western Maryland yard. This track was used by the Chesapeake and Ohio to deliver cars to the Western Maryland. If this track could not hold all such cars, then the additional cars were placed on the siding on the east side of the Western Maryland main line. Chesapeake and Ohio engines were permitted to operate on the Western Maryland track to a point 100 feet north of the uppermost switch in the Western Maryland yard. To deliver cars to the Chesapeake and Ohio, the Western Maryland used the portion of the Chesapeake and Ohio passing track that was east of the depot platform. Western Maryland engines could operate on the Chesapeake and Ohio track to a point 100 feet east of the switch of the passing track.

G-5 Class 2-8-0 No. 704 at Renick in August 1928.

Wendell A. Scott

The schedule for April 3, 1927, listed the following freight trains:

WEST

147	145	93	
TTS	TTS	Daily	
7:50 a.m.			Winterburn
8:20		3:00 p.m.	Durbin
10:10		3:55	Cass
12:50		4:33	Clover Lick
2:00 p.m.	7:00 a.m.	5:45	Marlinton
	8:30	6:14	Seebert
	12:15	7:15	Renick
	2:10 p.m.	8:20 p.m.	Whitcomb

EAST

96	152	150	148	146
Daily	Daily	TTS	MWF	MWF
		7:45 a.m.		
8:00 a.m.	5:00 p.m.	7:00 a.m.	2:00 p.m.	
5:30	3:55		10:30	
4:58	3:27		9:25	
3:55	2:45		7:00 a.m.	2:00 p.m.
3:23	1:47			1:30
2:02	12:15			9:30
12:45 a.m.	10:45 a.m.			7:20 a.m.

By this schedule, trains 146, 147, 148, 149, and 150 provided the local service on a three day a week basis with Marlinton as the interchange point. A turn-table had been installed at Marlinton in late 1920 and that station had probably served as the division point for the local freight trains since then. Trains 93, 96, and 152 were the manifest trains.

The Chesapeake and Ohio promoted trains 93 and 96 as the "Durbin Route." In 1926 No. 96 originated at Cincinnati, leaving at 2 a.m. each day and arriving at Durbin at 8 a.m. the next day. From Durbin the traffic moved over the Western Maryland to Shippensburg, Pennsylvania. From there the cars went by the Reading Railroad, the Central Railroad of New Jersey, the New York, New Haven and Hartford Railroad, and other connecting lines to their various destinations in the eastern and northeastern states.

Cars for No. 93 came to Durbin by the reverse of the above route. Another section of No. 93 came from the east with traffic from Norfolk, Richmond, Washington, and other points. At Hinton the sections were made into a single No. 93 which operated as far as Chicago. No. 93 left Durbin at 3 p.m. daily. The combined No. 93 left Hinton at 5:15 a.m., the next day with a 10:30 p.m. arrival at Cincinnati. The train arrived at Chicago at 8 p.m. the second day out of Durbin. Sections of No. 93 also went to Louisville, Kentucky, Toledo, Ohio, and Elkhorn City, Tennessee.

A schedule does not tell the full story of the amount of traffic on a line of railroad, however, as many trains are run "extra." *The Pocahontas Times* in February 1926 reported that six manifest trains were being operated up the river (eastbound) and commented "With the four passenger trains each day, the local freight trains and the west bound freight and the six east bound manifest trains each day, the Greenbrier Division is a busy piece of rail-

Renick Stone Company quarry north of Renick, 1928. The quarry operated from 1907 into the 1940s.
Wendell A. Scott

road track." The same article reported that continuous telegraph service at Marlinton and Durbin began on February 12 with three operators on eight hour shifts. Cass and Renick were reported to each have two shifts of operators.

As the interchange station between the two railroads, Durbin was particularly busy. At the peak of the through freight business there were eight employees at the Durbin depot—agent, three operator/clerks, cashier, passing report clerk, billing clerk, and freight hostler. (The freight hostler was responsible for moving the less-than-carload freight from the cars of one railroad to the other.) In addition there were three engine watchmen and a mechanic to take care of the locomotives that waited at Durbin between runs. By agreement with the Western Maryland, the Chesapeake and Ohio depot was used by both companies with the Chesapeake and Ohio responsible for staffing. Expenses of maintaining and operating the station were divided with the Chesapeake and Ohio paying 60 percent and the Western Maryland 40 percent. This percentage was later changed to 70 percent and 30 percent.

The pump house for the water tank at Durbin also contained the batteries that supplied the power for the telegraph system. The Greenbrier Division telegraph system consisted of three lines. One connected the agents with the division dispatcher at Ronceverte, the

Tipple at the Renick Stone Company quarry, 1928.
Wendell A. Scott

second made connection with main line points such as Clifton Forge, Richmond, Huntington, and Cincinnati, and the third line was for the Western Union company.

The trains on the Greenbrier were not big by modern day standards; four double header freight trains going up the river with about two hundred loaded cars total on February 6, 1926, was considered worthy of being noted in the paper. A down river manifest train with one hundred and forty-two cars on September 13, 1929, was called the longest train ever to operate on the Greenbrier.

During most of the 1920s the freight trains were pulled by the G Class 2-8-0 locomotives. The greatest number of cars one of these engines could pull northbound on the Greenbrier line, which was the up grade direction, was about thirty. Therefore, it was often necessary to use two engines on the trains from Ronceverte to Durbin.

Mr. J.E. Hall, Jr., was a fireman on the manifest trains during the late 1920s. He recalled that the trains averaged about fifty cars, so two engines were usually needed. On the up river trip water would be taken three times; at Renick, Marlinton, and Clover Lick or Cass. Clover Lick was preferred by the crews because at Cass the train had to be left below the road crossing while the engines took water and it was hard to start the train on the stiff grade at Cass. Coal was taken at Marlinton on the journey to Durbin. On the return trip to Ronceverte water was taken only at Marlinton and it was not necessary to take coal.

In looking for a way to haul larger trains on the Greenbrier with more cars per engine, the Chesapeake and Ohio had to turn to the H Class 2-6-6-2 Mallet locomotives as the curvature on the line prevented the use of two cylinder locomotives larger than the G class. To prepare the line for these heavier engines, (over 200 tons versus about 90 tons for the 2-8-0s), the railroad budgeted $253,006 out of an overall 1929 improvement budget of $18 to $19 million for the purpose of strengthening a number of the bridges on the Greenbrier line. The biggest jobs were the replacement of the bridges across Knapps Creek at Marlinton, the West Fork of the Greenbrier River at Durbin, and one span of the bridge over the Greenbrier River at Watoga (the other span had been replaced after a train wreck in 1925). The through truss bridges over Knapps Creek and the Greenbrier at Watoga were replaced with heavier bridges of the same type, while the through truss bridge at Durbin was replaced with a plate girder bridge. The other large bridges replaced were those over Spring Creek, Locust Creek, Stamping Creek, Steven Hole Run, Beaver Creek, and Clover Creek. Work was begun on the bridge project in March 1929 and all the bridge work was completed by February 1930. Additional heavier rail was also installed in the late 1920s and the early part of the 1930s. The Mallets were put into service on the Greenbrier line on September 20, 1929, and remained the usual freight engine on the line until the last few months of steam engine operations.

An unusual freight shipment is reported in June 1924

View of Clover Lick about 1903. Note the siding going to the stave mill operated by the National Cooperage Company and the short siding in the foreground. The freight train consists mainly of cars of pulp wood, no doubt en route from Cass to Covington, Virginia.
PCHS

View of Clover Lick, about 1910. Note the changes from the previous photograph. The siding on the east side of the main track no longer serves the now closed stave mill, but goes behind the depot. From this siding, a spur goes off across the trestle to the mill of the DeRan Lumber Company, located a short distance up Glade Run.
PCHS

Frank S. LaBar, of the LaBar Rhododendron Nurseries, Straudsburg, Pennsylvania, has completed his annual digging and shipping in Pocahontas county this year. The output was 75 cars, mostly rhododendron, though there was also a big shipment of laurel. Mr. LaBar has been coming to the Greenbrier Valley for the past fifteen years, and he says he has in sight supplies of plants for twenty more years. The season's payroll amounted to $14,000 and it was largely distributed where it did the most good—to farmers and their boys. It is of interest to note that the laurel was shipped to a cemetery on Long Island, which is beautified at the expense of J. Pierpoint Morgan.

In late March of 1926 a train load of forty-seven tank cars filled with olive oil came over the line.

In the latter part of 1924 the status of the Greenbrier line was changed from that of a division to a sub-division, becoming part of the Clifton Forge Division.

In addition to the major track and bridge work carried out in the 1920s, other physical improvements were made on the Greenbrier line. The installation of a turntable at Marlinton in late 1920 has already been mentioned. In early 1923 the Marlinton water tank, located between Eighth and Ninth Streets, was replaced by a new tank located adjacent to the turntable at the upper end of the Marlinton yard. The wooden water tanks at Anthony and Renick were replaced by 50,000 gallon steel tanks in early 1925 and the 50,000 gallon wooden tank at Clover Lick was replaced with a steel tank of the same size in 1927. A new wooden water tank was built at Durbin in late 1928 and the tank hooked into the town water system to save pumping. The Western Maryland put in a water tank at the upper end of its yard in Durbin, adjacent to the highway crossing, in late 1924.

In June 1923 the Chesapeake and Ohio let a contract for a new freight and passenger station at Cass to replace the badly crowded one at that busy (in 1923) location. The new depot was completed in September.

In April 1927 the telegraph system on the Greenbrier line was supplemented by the installation of a telephone system connected with the train dispatcher's office. Telephone units were installed at thirteen locations along the line and the necessary wires strung on the trackside poles.

As the golden 20s were coming to an end so was the lumber boom in the Upper Greenbrier Valley. The Buena Vista Hardwood Company at Stony Bottom closed in the middle part of the decade. The Spice Run Lumber Company finished about 1926. The big mill of the North Fork Lumber Company cut its last log in September 1927. At Raywood, the Forest Lumber Company, successor to the Warn Lumber Corporation, went into bankruptcy and cut its last log in February 1928. The band mill at Clover Lick, now owned by the Raine Lumber Company, closed in 1929. The Horrocks Desk Company at Renick closed about 1925 and the extract plant near Cass shut down in 1928.

With the closing of the sawmills the associated communities also withered away, some almost immediately, others in a slower fashion over the years. So the railroad

George W. Stevens, President of the Chesapeake and Ohio Railway, 1900-1920.   COHS

not only lost the outbound shipments of lumber but the incoming loads needed to supply an industry and town as well as people to ride the passenger trains. Steadily improving roads and increasing numbers of cars and trucks were also beginning to make an impression on the amount of business coming to the Chesapeake and Ohio. These facts were made evident in the 1920s when the railroad began making requests to the West Virginia Public Service Commission to cut back on passenger service and to close stations. (The cutbacks in passenger service are covered in Chapter Five.)

The first depots to have been closed must have been the ones at Hosterman and Winterburn although the exact dates have not been located. The mill at Hosterman was shut down about 1912, if not before, and the last activity there of any size was the West Virginia Pulp and Paper Company logging line up Allegheny Run built in 1916. The author has found a reference to an agent at Hosterman in 1918 and the paper company seems to have finished its logging along the Greenbrier line by the end of 1919, so the Hosterman depot probably closed around 1920.

The closing of the Winterburn mill in 1918 and the Thornwood mill in 1920 would have left the agent at the Winterburn depot with very little to do. Passenger service to Winterburn ended in July of 1923. When the Winterburn depot building was removed in 1926 it was noted in railroad records that it had not been in service for several years.

In July 1928 permission was requested from the Public Service Commission to close the agency stations at

Anthony, Bartow, Beard, and Sitlington. The railroad cited a large decline in revenue at each depot. At Anthony the Chesapeake and Ohio claimed that revenue had declined by almost half in six years, from $9,176.99 in 1921-22 to $4,638.26 in 1927-28. At Beard the decline had been even more dramatic over the same period, going from $90,128.91 to $7,922.36. This sharp decrease was no doubt caused by the closing of the Spice Run Lumber Company's mill, which did its business through the Beard station.

In the application to close the Bartow station the railroad pointed out that the Durbin depot was only two and a half miles away by paved road and was open from 5 a.m. to 9 p.m. with an agent, three clerks, a station helper, and two operators. At Sitlington it was claimed that the total revenue for 1927 was only $2,219.89.

The Public Service Commission granted permission to change all four stations to non-agency status as of August 31, 1928. However, it did require that a suitable shelter be maintained for the use of passengers and for the protection of the less-than-carload freight shipped to the stations.

As the closing of the sawmill at Raywood in 1928 would have reduced the business at the station to almost nothing, the Chesapeake and Ohio made the request to change that depot to non-agency status the next year. The Public Service Commission granted permission to do so in June 1929 but required the railroad to provide suitable facilities to shelter passengers and freight.

Mr. Wendell Scott spent time as a boy with his grandparents across the river from Renick. He recalled to the author the "action" across the river on the Greenbrier line in the late 1920s and early '30s:

The local went up around dinner time—I remember well, a little consolidation—600 class with a crowned stack, working the "yard" just above Renick. Two pictures of the "Renick Stone Company," no, three—will be along in a week or so—it was a source of revenue. The local would set off the necessary number of hopper cars on a blind siding, where they would be gravity run through the loading hoppers to be later picked up. The up "manifest," often double-headed, would go up following the morning "up passenger," unless it was held up too long at Ronceverte for #16, the local running behind #4. The westbound freights were mostly pulp wood loads, the empties eastbound. I remember the slack running out—violently, at times, as double-headers jockeyed for position at the water tower. A local man, one "Lant Sharp," ran the pumping station— tended the boiler, cleaned the firebox (dumped the ashes into the river) and, when necessary, shoveled down coal from the rear to the gate on the engines. I remember hearing the trains stop for water, after dark, when I was a child, and hearing the muffled voices of the crew, and the "clang" of the tank lid when they slammed it shut.

A G-1, No. 666 as I recall—2-8-0, worked the local freight on the division as late as 1928 or so. This engine had a flanged stack. Like the G-5s and A-10, they were all saturated steamers and had a soft exhaust, even when working hard. When drifting down to the water tank east of Renick, the back-pressure would draw in the exhaust smoke leaving a sort of a stair-case effect drifting behind.

G Class 2-8-0 locomotive at the original Marlinton water tank. This tank was located between Eighth and Ninth Streets.   PCHS/NRP

Train arriving in Marlinton with a load of elk for the game preserve of the Allegheny Sportsman Association at Minnehaha Springs, March 19, 1912.

PCHS

F-10 Class 4-6-0 No. 189 with freight train at Seebert.

PCHS

Track crew with one of the first motor cars used on the Greenbrier Division, 1913.   PCHS

Track crew near Sitlington, about 1908.   PCHS

Track crew at Stony Bottom, 1904.   PCHS

CHAPTER IV
Depression and the Final Years

Depression and World War II

AS WOULD BE EXPECTED, THE GREAT DEPRESSION HAD a tremendous effect on the amount of traffic on the Greenbrier line. Much of the remaining locally originated freight disappeared and the trains of through freight were taken off the schedule.

Only three large sawmills on the line were still operating as the 1930s opened and two were soon shut down. The Marlin Lumber Company's mill at Stillwell sawed its last logs in July of 1932 and the Spring Creek Lumber Company closed its mill in late 1934. Only the mill of the West Virginia Pulp and Paper Company at Cass continued to run through the Depression years, but with a reduced output.

The Marlinton tannery closed in the summer of 1930 and remained idle for ten years. The tannery at Frank did remain in operation during the '30s.

The Depression also greatly reduced the amount of through traffic over the Greenbrier.

All of this was reflected in the reduced number of freight trains operating in the 1930s. The schedule for July 24, 1932, had only one freight train in each direction:

WEST 147		EAST 150	146
8:05 a.m.	Winterburn	8:00 a.m.	
8:35	Durbin	7:30 a.m.	2:30 p.m.
9:40	Cass		1:30
10:10	Clover Lick		12:30
11:20	Marlinton		11:20
11:50	Seebert		10:45
1:05	Renick		9:35
2:15 p.m.	Whitcomb		8:10 a.m.

Service was daily except Sunday.

In July of 1933 the Chesapeake and Ohio applied to the Interstate Commerce Commission to abandon the track between Bartow and Winterburn. Approval was forthcoming and operations were discontinued on the 2.72 miles of track from a point 1000 feet east of the Bartow station to the end of track at Winterburn on October 5, 1933. In 1939 an additional 742½ feet of the main track at Bartow was taken out of service.

In June 1935 the railroad requested permission from the Public Service Commission to be relieved of keeping the stations at Beard and Sitlington for passengers and less-than-carload freight, to eliminate the need for caretakers. Permission was granted in August to eliminate the passenger facilities. The Chesapeake and Ohio came back to the commission in October to again request permission to end the less-than-carload service and the caretakers at these points. Persistence paid off for the railroad, as the request was granted in January.

In April of 1939 a similar request was made for Anthony and permission was granted in May.

The Depression years did see a few industries begin operating on the Greenbrier line to counterbalance to some extent the more numerous closings. In 1934 the Ruth-Bell Lumber Company started up a saw mill on land leased from the Western Maryland Railway at Durbin. In 1935 the Williams and Pifer Lumber Company put a mill on Chesapeake and Ohio property at Marlinton. At Spring Creek the S.J. Neathawk Lumber Company located a circular mill on the site of the band mill and started up in 1936.

The schedule for the Greenbrier line for March 21, 1937, was similar to the schedule for July 1932 with one freight train in each direction, operating daily except Sunday. Bartow was now the end of the line rather than Winterburn.

WEST 147		EAST 150	146
7:40 a.m.	Bartow	7:40 a.m.	
7:50	Durbin	7:30 a.m.	2:45 p.m.
8:30	Cass		1:30
9:55	Clover Lick		12:30
11:20	Marlinton		11:20
11:45	Seebert		10:45
12:40	Renick		9:35
1:50 p.m.	Whitcomb		8:20 a.m.

In January 1938 two train loads of palm nuts, about one hundred cars total, went over the line. The shipment was for the Palm-Olive soap factory at Cincinnati and had come from South America to Baltimore, Maryland.

A potential source of car loads for the Greenbrier line was the plan of the Greenbrier Ore Company in the late 1930s to develop the iron ore deposits on Browns Mountain. The development of the local ore had been a long time dream of many people and the existence of the ore in Pocahontas and Greenbrier Counties had been used in the 1890s to help attract the railroad builders, as related in an earlier chapter. It was hoped that the demand for iron and steel due to the war in Europe would finally make working this local ore profitable.

The Greenbrier Ore Company got as far as actually mining some ore and began hauling it to the railroad at Marlinton on August 20, 1940. The following year it was reported that the ore was being crushed and shipped to rolling mills at Ashland, Kentucky, but by the end of 1941 the company was the defendant in various cases in the circuit court. Although it was reported in June 1942 that the ore piled at Marlinton had been purchased by another group and shipments were to begin soon, it is doubtful the Chesapeake and Ohio got many car loads from this venture. The Greenbrier Ore Company was adjudged to be bankrupt in November 1942. Probably about the only thing the railroad got out of the affair was a big pile of low grade iron ore on its yard at Marlinton.

Much more important as a source of business for the railroad was the sale of the Marlinton tannery to the International Shoe Company by the United States Leather Company in November 1940. The new owners began almost immediately the process of re-activating the plant. The boilers were fired up on January 8, 1941, and the first car of hides came in on the 10th. By the next month three hundred hides were being put to soak daily and the outbound loads of leather began the latter part of May. By the spring of 1942 the daily output was up to eight hundred hides which meant a car load of finished leather every two days. The value of the tannery to the railroad as a customer was even more important for inbound shipments as it took three car loads of hides, chemicals, and other supplies to make one car of leather.

Just prior to United States involvement in World War II, freight service on the Greenbrier line was being provided by trains three days a week. The schedule for April 27, 1941, was:

| WEST | | EAST | |
147		150	146
TTS		TTS	MWF
7:40 a.m.	Bartow	7:40 a.m.	
7:50	Durbin	7:30 a.m.	2:45 p.m.
8:30	Cass		1:30
9:30	Clover Lick		12:30
10:41	Marlinton		11:20
11:00	Seebert		11:00
12:40	Renick		9:35
1:50 p.m.	Whitcomb		8:20 a.m.

The war years brought a final burst of heavy usage to the Greenbrier line both in the form of increased local business as well as through traffic. Wartime restrictions reversed the loss of business, both freight and passenger, to the truck and automobile. For example, the freight business at the Marlinton station had an increase of $22,314.21 for March 1942 over March 1941.

On Tuesday, March 31, 1942, local freight service returned to a daily basis except Sunday, with a train each way.

Also in the summer of 1942 trains of strictly through traffic returned to the line. In order to avoid congestion in its Potomac Freight Yard at Washington, D.C., the Chesapeake and Ohio began sending trains of coal by way of the Greenbrier line and the Western Maryland to Baltimore. When this increased traffic was announced in July it was expected that two hundred cars of coal in three manifest trains would be run over the line daily.

H-4 Class 2-6-6-2 No. 1359 leaving Marlinton en route to Ronceverte with a freight train.　　　PCHS

As this increased traffic was about to begin the local papers and railroad officials worried about the carelessness of motorists grown used to fewer trains on the Greenbrier line. *The Pocahontas Times* commented, "In this connection it should be noted these trains running extra increase the hazards at crossings. Then too the crews are from the main line and do not understand the careless habits of our people. A recent check up on 25 cars at the Main Street crossing in Marlinton showed only three drivers who looked either way." In *The Marlinton Journal* the agent at Marlinton, John G. Beard, expressed his concern that the people have become familiar with the schedules of the few trains that have been running and thus become careless at crossings. He emphasized, "But now, for safety's sake, everyone should remember that 'all the time is train time.' "

J.E. Hall, Jr., returned to the Greenbrier line as a fireman on the coal trains. He related to the author that three trains were run up the line every day with an average of seventy-five cars powered by two H Class 2-6-6-2 engines. The trains originated at Hinton. From Hinton to Ronceverte one engine was forward and the other was in the rear of the train due to heat conditions in the tunnels on the main line. At Ronceverte, where coal and

water were taken, the rear engine was moved forward. Coal and water were taken again at Marlinton. On the return trip the engines usually ran light as the empty coal cars were routed a different way back to the coal fields. On the return trip water was taken at Marlinton.

At the height of wartime traffic in 1943 the following stations were in use on the Greenbrier Division:

• North Caldwell—agent.
• Anthony—this station was open on an irregular basis with an operator on the second shift, 3 to 11 p.m., depending on trafic.
• Spring Creek—agent.
• Renick—agent, operator, and station helper with the station open for two shifts.
• Seebert—agent.
• Marlinton—agent and two operators with station open for two shifts. The freight station had clerk, cashier, and laborer.
• Clover Lick—agent with an operator on duty on the second shift depending on traffic.
• Cass—agent, operator, and clerk with station open two shifts as needed.
• Durbin—agent, two operators, clerk, and laborer with station open two shifts.

H-4 Class 2-6-6-2 No. 1347 photographed at Ronceverte in the early 1940s. This locomotive was used on Greenbrier Branch freight trains and pulled the last freights on the line powered by a Mallet type steam engine on February 11 and 12, 1953.
Wendell A. Scott

Meet between the Greenbrier passenger train and a freight train, June 26, 1945. The freight engine is H-4 Class 2-6-6-2 No. 1414.
Charles A. Brown

Under the direction of Track Supervisor James Madison there were seven maintenance sections—North Caldwell, 16 miles, Renick, 16 miles, Seebert, 16 miles, Marlinton, 12 miles, Clawson, 13 miles, Cass, 13 miles, and Durbin, 11.7 miles. Each section had a foreman and a crew of six to eight men.

Southbound freight train at Renick powered by K-1 Class 2-8-2 No. 1112. K Class engines were used on the Greenbrier Branch for a time in the middle 1940s.
Wendell A. Scott

The Final Years

At the end of the war the coal shipments ceased and with restrictions dropped on the use of cars and trucks, the decline in business on the Greenbrier Subdivision resumed.

In 1948 freight service was still on a daily except Sunday basis on the following schedule (September 26, 1948):

WEST		EAST	
147		150	146
7:30 a.m.	Bartow	7:30 a.m.	
7:50	Durbin	7:15 a.m.	2:45 p.m.
9:05	Cass		1:00
9:30	Clover Lick		12:35
10:30	Marlinton		11:30
10:58	Seebert		10:58
12:40	Renick		9:15
1:50 p.m.	Whitcomb		8:00 a.m.

By the time of the schedule of March 31, 1951, freight service had been reduced again to three days a week with a train to Durbin on Monday, Wednesday, and Friday as No. 146 and to Bartow and back to Ronceverte on Tuesday, Thursday, and Saturday as trains 150 and 147. The schedule for trains 147 and 150 was the same as in 1948. Train 146 had a 7:30 a.m. departure from Whitcomb, 8:45 from Renick, 9:45 from Seebert, 10:30 from Marlinton, 12 from Clover Lick, 1 p.m. from Cass, and a 2:45 arrival at Durbin.

Since the H Class Mallets had been introduced on the Greenbrier line in 1929 they had been the usual motive power for freight trains. In 1945 the Chesapeake and Ohio began using K Class 2-8-2 engines on the Greenbrier freights. After about two years the H Class locomotives returned, possibly because the K Class engines were too hard on the track in the sharp curves on the Greenbrier.

In the final years of steam power on the line, H Class engines 1347 and 1414 were the most commonly used with No. 1328 occasionally making the run. As diesels began to bump modern steam power from main line service, these engines began to appear on the branch lines to replace older motive power. On February 11, 1953, No. 1347 was the last Mallet to leave Ronceverte on a Greenbrier line freight train. The next freight train out of Ronceverte on February 13, was pulled by a K-4 Class 2-8-4 No. 2788.

Mr. Wendell A. Scott remembered the K-4s in use on the Greenbrier in a letter to the author, "Used to pulling 160 loaded hoppers west of Hinton, it was something to see one of them handling twenty or so cars on the Greenbrier. No fuss, no struggle—they moseyed out with an exhaust as gentle as a compound."

K-4 Class 2-8-4 No. 2760 at Renick, pulling freight train No. 146 to Durbin. K-4 Class locomotives were used on the last steam powered Greenbrier Branch freight trains in 1953 and 1954.

Wendell A. Scott

day, June 25, 1954, and returned to Ronceverte on Saturday, June 26, pulled by K-4 Class No. 2781. On Monday, June 28, 1954, the freight train went to Durbin behind diesel No. 5812.

The last steam engine pulling a Greenbrier passenger train had run earlier that year on Saturday, Monday, and Tuesday, January 16, 18, and 19. The locomotive was No. 1058, a G-9 Class 2-8-0.

The last steam locomotive used on the Greenbrier Subdivision in regular service was No. 992, a G-7s Class 2-8-0, which powered a work train on December 19, 20, and 21, 1955.

Steam power reappeared occasionally during the remaining twenty-three years of the Greenbrier line's life, generally in connection with the Cass Scenic Railroad.

On December 9, 1964, Meadow River Lumber Company Shay No. 7 came up the line en route to a new home on the Cass Scenic Railroad. A second Meadow River engine, Heisler No. 6, made the trip to Cass over the Greenbrier Subdivision on December 14, 1966.

The Cass to Durbin section of the line has been used a great many times by Cass Scenic Railroad steam engines, either taking trains to an off line destination such as the Forest Festival in Elkins or the Strawberry Festival in Buckhannon or hauling rail fan trips along the Greenbrier River. Regularly scheduled trips to Durbin were begun by the Cass Scenic Railroad on July 7, 1984, operating on Saturdays, Sundays, and Tuesdays.

Steam power returned to the Greenbrier line in grand style in the summer and fall of 1971 in the form of former Reading Railroad 4-8-4 locomotive No. 2102 pulling a series of nine Ronceverte to Durbin excursion trains. No. 2102 was the largest two cylinder steam locomotive to operate on the Greenbrier.

The first freight train on the Greenbrier line powered by a diesel locomotive ran on July 1, 1953. The locomotive involved was No. 5882. This was during the annual coal miners' vacation time and the railroad had a temporary surplus of diesels. After five trips with diesels on the head end, the K-4 Class steam engines were again assigned to the Greenbrier local freight. Diesels, however, continued to appear as power on the Greenbrier trains over the next year. Finally, the last steam-powered freight train on the Greenbrier line ran to Durbin on Fri-

Agent/Operator at Renick, August 20, 1958.

Wendell A. Scott

The last steam engine to run on the section of track below Cass was Cass Scenic Railroad Heisler No. 6 which powered a special train to Pioneer Days in Marlinton in July 1978. The trip to Marlinton was made on July 6 with trips for the public operated from the Marlinton depot on July 7 and 8. The return to Cass was made on the 8th.

Other special trains, not involving steam locomotives, were run over the Greenbrier line in its final years. In August of 1963 the West Virginia Centennial Train came to Marlinton. The eight car train arrived in time for a 1 p.m. opening on the 19th and departed on the afternoon of the 20th. On May 13 and 14, 1967, an excursion train from Huntington to Elkins and return passed over the Greenbrier Subdivision. The following May a special train of sleeping and private cars was in Cass on the 25th and 26th for the dedication of the Cass Scenic Railroad line to Bald Knob. In the summer and fall of 1973 and 1974 and the fall of 1975 a number of excursion trains were run from Ronceverte to Cass. More detail on the special passenger trains is given in Chapter Five.

Station closings began again in 1952. The Chesapeake and Ohio filed a request with the Public Service Commission that year to close the Clover Lick station, citing expenses exceeding revenue. The commission approved change from agency to non-agency status, effective November 1.

The Spring Creek station was the next to go. The Greenbrier Lumber Company (originally S.J. Neathawk Lumber Company) closed its mill at Spring Creek in 1954, switching the revenue situation at the depot from profit to loss. The railroad made its request to close the station in May 1955 and the necessary permission was granted by the Public Service Commission on July 1.

The freight depot at Marlinton was closed in the middle 1950s.

In November 1956 the railroad received Public Service Commission permission to discontinue for freight purposes and eliminate from all tariffs the following Greenbrier line non-agency stations: Whitcomb, Camp Allegheny, Hopper, Loopemount, Keister, Golden, Horrick, Rorer, Droop Mountain, Spice Run, Locust, Burnsides, Kennison, Violet, Stillwell, Clawson, Harter, Big Run, Raywood, Wanless, Boyer, Whiting, and Frank.

By 1953 the number of maintenance sections had been cut to five: North Caldwell, 20 miles, Renick, 20 miles, Marlinton, 19 miles, Clover Lick, 20 miles, and Durbin, 18.8 miles.

The freight schedule for October 28, 1956, was:

WEST		EAST	
147		150	146
TTS		TTS	MWF
7:30 a.m.	Bartow	7:30 a.m.	
7:50	Durbin	7:15 a.m.	3:30 p.m.
8:40	Cass		2:10
9:05	Clover Lick		1:15
10:18	Marlinton		12:30
10:43	Seebert		11:50
11:50	Renick		11:00
1:20 p.m.	Whitcomb		9:40 a.m.

Former Reading Railroad 4-8-4 locomotive No. 2102. In the summer and fall of 1971 this engine powered a series of excursion trains from Ronceverte to Durbin. This photo was taken at the Marlinton water tank.

Marshall Booker

Meadow River Lumber Company Shay No. 7, newly lettered for the Cass Scenic Railroad, pauses at Marlinton on December 9, 1964, while heading for its new home. John P. Killoran

Meadow River Lumber Company Heisler No. 6, enroute to a new home on the Cass Scenic Railroad, passing the Marlinton water tank on December 14, 1966. John P. Killoran

Marlinton, December 29, 1977.   WPM

Dismantling the freight depot at Marlinton, November 1976.
WPM

The continued existence of the Greenbrier line received a severe blow at the end of June 1960 when the Cass sawmill was closed by the Mower Lumber company after over fifty-eight years of operation. The Cass mill had been sold to Mower by the West Virginia Pulp and Paper Company in 1942.

The middle part of the 1960s saw the closing of all but two of the remaining agency stations as the Chesapeake and Ohio was able to easily document expenses exceeding revenue. The first to close was Seebert. The Public Service Commission granted permission to close this

depot by an order dated June 12, 1963. On November 16, 1965, permission was granted to change Cass to non-agency status.

Closure of the Renick station was not long after Cass with permission granted by the Public Service Commission on January 25, 1966. The following year North Caldwell was closed after authority was received on April 25, 1967. These closures left Marlinton and Durbin as the only agency stations on the line.

In June of 1972 the Western Maryland requested permission from the Public Service Commission to change its operation at Durbin to non-agency status for carload traffic only. This was approved by the PSC on November 1, 1972.

In February 1968 the Chesapeake and Ohio closed out its engine facilities at Ronceverte and the Greenbrier local freight train began operating out of Hinton.

Then in the spring of 1970 the International Shoe Company closed the Marlinton tannery. This event, without much doubt, assured that the Greenbrier line would not survive for many more years.

By 1970 the number of maintenance sections had been reduced to three—Durbin, Marlinton, and North Caldwell. On February 1, 1972, Track Supervisor James E. Madison retired and the position was not filled. Soon after, the Greenbrier Branch sections were eliminated and maintenance crews brought in off the main line as needed. To provide for track inspection after the elimination of on branch maintenance forces, the railroad began sending a road/rail vehicle over the line prior to trains.

In May of 1975 the telephone and telegraph system on the Greenbrier line was taken out of service.

However, the years following World War II saw a few new users of rail service established along the Greenbrier Subdivision. Track crews put in side tracks at MP 3 near North Caldwell to serve the asphalt plant of the Interstate Amiesite Company in the summer of 1948; at MP 95 near Durbin for the mill of the J.B. Belcher Lumber Company in September 1962; at Bartow in July and August 1963 for the sawmill of Green Bank Mills, Inc. (now operated by the Interstate Lumber Company); and at Stillwell for the R.S. Burruss Lumber Company's sawmill in April of 1964 (now the Kramer Lumber Company). The Westvaco Corporation located wood yards at Marlinton in April 1966 on existing track and on the Western Maryland at Durbin.

Beginning in 1947 there were several attempts made to mine coal in the Briery Knob section of Pocahontas and Greenbrier Counties. This coal was trucked to Seebert for loading on rail cars. These attempts were not too successful and the reason may have been the quality of the coal. At least it wouldn't burn very well in caboose stoves according to Harry Dolan, who was a trainman on the Greenbrier for many years.

The Greenbrier Branch played a role in the construction of the 140 foot and 300 foot telescopes at the National Radio Astronomy Observatory at Green

Clover Lick, January 5, 1978.   WPM

Marlinton, December 21, 1978.   WPM

Bank. Major components for both structures came by rail in the 1959-1964 period. Bartow was the unloading point for the final haul to Green Bank by truck. The largest pieces were for the 140 foot scope and were the 162 ton polar axis that arrived in September 1959; a second polar axis of 215 tons delivered in December 1963 (the first axis was not used due to design problems); the 138 ton yoke hub shipped in late March 1964; and the spherical journal which weighs 150 tons and arrived in April 1964. The 17½ foot diameter of this last piece was dictated by the bridge and tunnel clearances between its place of manufacture in Pennsylvania and Bartow. The journal went through the Droop Mountain Tunnel with only three inches to spare.

In addition to the material for the Observatory, another special shipment in 1959 was the beams for the new highway bridge being constructed across the Greenbrier River in Marlinton. Each beam is 100 feet long and weighs 12½ tons. The length of the beams required extra caution in the Droop Tunnel.

In addition to traffic originating or terminating on the line, a considerable amount of traffic was still being routed over the Greenbrier on its way to off-line destinations. In 1973 the Chesapeake and Ohio reported 733 carloads originating or terminating at Durbin and Bartow, 511 at Marlinton and Cass (almost all Marlinton, of course), and 1142 cars as through traffic. The effect of the closing of the Marlinton tannery is shown by the reduction of Marlinton and Cass carloads from 1196 in 1967 to the 511 in 1973.*

The biggest part of the originated traffic would have been wood chips from Burrus and Interstate Lumber Companies and pulp wood from the Marlinton Westvaco yard, all going to the Westvaco plant at Covington. Most of the rest of the outbound shipments would have been lumber from the two sawmills and some leather from the Howes tannery at Frank. Cars of hides to the Frank tannery would have been the largest single part of the inbound loads. Coal shipments to Cass and other points would have made up the next largest segment of the inbound traffic. Even though the total number of cars for 1973 seems large, divided by trains six days a week, it comes out to less than eight cars per train.

In February 1974 the Public Service Commission gave the railroad permission to eliminate Anthony, Beard, and Clover Lick from its freight tariffs.

In the spring of 1974 the Chesapeake and Ohio reduced the frequency of train service on the Greenbrier line from three trains per week to one. This train usually operated from Hinton to Durbin on Wednesday and back to Hinton on Thursday. This reduction in service had an almost immediate and unfortunate effect on the traffic load at Marlinton. The Westvaco pulp yard closed in March 1975, the company claiming that it was not economically feasible to operate the yard with train service only one day per week. Burrus Lumber Company also switched its wood chip business over to trucks due to the lack of capacity on its siding to hold sufficient cars for a week's production of chips. These actions resulted in traffic to and from Marlinton dropping to 269 cars in 1974 and 140 cars in 1975.

In 1976 traffic on the Greenbrier Branch consisted of 955 cars as follows: Marlinton, outbound—31, inbound—15; Cass, outbound—2, inbound—113; Durbin, outbound—36, inbound—211; Bartow, outbound—372; through traffic, coal—160, other—151.

On March 18, 1975, the Chesapeake and Ohio Railway filed an application with the Interstate Commerce Commission for authority to abandon 92.04 miles of its Greenbrier Branch from a point just north of North Caldwell to near Durbin. In a related proceeding, filed on February 4, 1976, authority was requested for the lease of the 2.84 miles of line from Durbin to Bartow by the Western Maryland Railway so operations could con-

*Note: The traffic figures in this and following paragraphs come from data supplied by the Chesapeake and Ohio during the abandonment proceedings and does not include traffic to or from North Caldwell as that point was not part of the line up for closure.

tinue on that section of line. The Chesapeake and Ohio application gave the reasons for the request to abandon as declining traffic, cost of operating the line exceeding the revenue generated, and the cost of rehabilitation that would be needed on the line in a few years if it continued in service.

A hearing on the proposed abandonment was conducted by the Interstate Commerce Commission on August 15-17, 1977, at the Pocahontas County Court House in Marlinton. Administrative Law Judge Walter J. Alprin presided. Representing the Chesapeake and Ohio were attorneys Rene J. Gunning and Peter Schudtz.

Presenting the railroad's case for the abandonment were E.R. Lichty, General Manager Operations Planning; William L. Bailey, Jr., Assistant Regional Sales Manager; I.J. Warren, Director of Real Estate and Industrial Development; Ben J. Johnson, Director of Quality Control; Oscar Becker, Cost Analyst; and Ted Grizafi, Assistant Engineer for Coal Properties.

Among the items coming out of the testimony by the railroad's witnesses were:

• no recent requests had been received by the railroad for data on industrial sites in the Greenbrier area but also no effort had been made by the railroad to promote the area.

• rehabilitation work estimated to cost $2,532,609 would be needed on the line soon if it were to remain in service. Also, $388,802 would be the average cost per year to maintain the line after rehabilitation. (Actually spent on maintenance in 1975 and 1976 were $10,821 and $24,452.)

• income to the Chesapeake and Ohio from Greenbrier Branch operations in 1976 was given as:

Marlinton/Cass traffic	$ 31,806
Durbin/Bartow traffic	219,508
Through traffic	119,015
	$370,329

Adding in the income to the other two railroads making up the Chessie System, the Baltimore and Ohio and the Western Maryland, total Chessie System income from Greenbrier line traffic in 1976 was $438,804.

If the abandonment took place it was estimated that income of $359,261 would come to the Chessie after a rerouting of the traffic that would remain.

• It was claimed that operating the Greenbrier Branch in 1976 cost the Chesapeake and Ohio the following:

Direct branch line cost	$348,565
Off-branch costs of Marlinton/Cass traffic	11,441
Durbin/Bartow traffic	125,813
Through traffic	87,572
	$573,391

Adding Baltimore and Ohio and Western Maryland costs brought the Chessie System total to $630,917.

Thus it was claimed that the Chesapeake and Ohio lost $203,062 in 1976 on the Greenbrier line operations and the Chessie System as a whole $192,113.

Last loaded car to be shipped from Marlinton, a car of lumber from Burrus Lumber Company on Trailer Train bulkhead flatcar No. 80522. It was picked up at the mill at Stillwell on December 20, 1978, and taken on to Hinton on the 21st. WPM

Last loaded car to be delivered to Marlinton, a load of coal in Chesapeake and Ohio hopper No. 49467. It arrived on December 14, 1978.   WPM

The estimated cost to the Chessie System to handle the traffic that would be re-routed from the Greenbrier was given as $225,842 for a profit of $103,419 if the Greenbrier Branch was abandoned.

• Based on the above figures, it was estimated that in order for the Greenbrier line to break even at least 600 additional cars would have to originate or terminate on the line. If rehabilitation costs and the estimated annual maintenance cost after rehabilitation were figured in, then the additional cars needed would increase to 1,978 for one day per week service or 2,158 for three day per week service.

Appearing in opposition to the abandonment at the hearing were Clifford Worth, General Traffic Manager for the Westvaco Corporation; Everett Tibbs, Superintendent of the R.S. Burrus Lumber Company sawmill at Marlinton; William L. Hurst, Sales Manager for the Burrus Company; Edward G. Frazee, Vice-president of Interstate Lumber Company; Harry Widney, Vice-president of Howes Leather Company; Noel W. Barnhart, President of Energy Enterprises; Herbert Bryan, representing Alla-Ohio Valley Coal Fuel, Inc.; Arnold Elkins, a coal operator; Donald Fogus, Executive Director of West Virginia Forests, Inc.; J. Steven Hunter, representing the Pocahontas County Commission and the Pocahontas County Development Authority; and Scott McNeil and B.F. Harrall, both speaking as private citizens.

Mr. Worth discussed several reasons his company opposed the abandonment of the Greenbrier line. He said that the line figured in Westvaco's plans for providing the Covington and Luke paper mills with coal and pulpwood. Included in the plans were the possibilities of loading coal mined in Nicholas County at Seebert and re-opening the Marlinton woodyard if adequate rail service was available.

Mr. Tibbs and Mr. Hurst both reviewed the need for rail service for the products of the Marlinton mill and expressed concern about a possible loss of business due to the higher cost of truck shipment of lumber. Mr. Tibbs described the existing service by the railroad as "very bad" with delays in getting lumber cars of up to four or five weeks. He also discussed the change from rail to truck for shipping woodchips due to the cutback to one train per week. (Mr. Bailey, in response to a question during this testimoney for the railroad, admitted that the Chesapeake and Ohio had made no effort to retain this business.)

The problem of getting lumber cars was also discussed by Mr. Frazee.

Mr. Widney expressed concern about the future of rail service for the tannery at Frank (as we shall see, his concern was well founded).

Mr. Barnhart, Mr. Bryan, and Mr. Elkins all discussed potential coal developments in eastern Nicholas County and the loading of this coal at Seebert. (In his testimony for the railroad, Mr. Grizafi had suggested that this coal, if it was mined, could be loaded as easily at Richwood as Seebert.)

Others testifying at the hearing were John Killoran, Executive Director of the West Virginia Railroad Maintenance Authority; Robert Mathis, a planner with the West Virginia Department of Natural Resources; and John Ratliff, representing the United Transportation Union. The first two discussed plans for the future use of the Greenbrier Branch right-of-way, if approval of the abandonment was received, and Mr. Ratliff requested job protection for any employees involved.

Judge Alprin's initial decision was issued by the Interstate Commerce Commission on January 12, 1978. Probably to no one's surprise, he ruled "that the present and ably to no one's surprise, he ruled "that the present and

Last train from Hinton to Durbin, December 27, 1978, at Seebert. WPM

Last train from Hinton to Durbin, December 27, 1978, at Renick. WPM

future public convenience and necessity permits the abandonment" of the Greenbrier line as requested by the Chesapeake and Ohio and the lease of the Durbin to Bartow section to the Western Maryland.

Two exceptions were filed to the initial decision. The first was filed by the Chesapeake and Ohio itself and was in objection to the labor protection conditions contained in the decision. The second exception was filed by the Interstate Lumber Company and claimed that the decision was not based on the evidence as presented at the hearing.

Train crew, December 27 and 28, 1978. Left to right, J.L. Ryan, brakeman, W.C. Cole, brakeman, L.R. Ratliff, conductor, and W.W. Bulmer, engineer.   WPM

Last train on the Greenbrier Branch, December 28, 1978, at Anthony.   WPM

Early on the morning of December 28, 1978, the last train on the Greenbrier Branch prepares to depart from Durbin.
                                                        WPM

By an order issued on August 16, 1978, the Interstate Commerce Commission, accepted, with modification, the initial decision of Judge Alprin as its decision. The modification involved the labor protection conditions and was based on a decision made by the Commission since Judge Alprin had made his ruling in the Greenbrier case. Interstate's claim that the decision was not based on the evidence was rejected. The decision was effective thirty days from the date of issue.

On September 27, 1978, the Chesapeake and Ohio issued a notice that it would abandon the Greenbrier Branch on or about December 29, 1978, and concurrently lease to the Western Maryland Railway the Durbin to Bartow track. The Interstate Commerce Commission issued its final certificate of abandonment on October 25, 1978.

The last loaded cars to be delivered to Marlinton were a box car for the Southern States Cooperative store and a hopper of coal. The box car, Louisville and Nashville Railroad No. 109169 was brought in by the train the week of November 12-18. The hopper, Chesapeake and Ohio Railway No. 49467, arrived on December 14. The last loaded car out of Marlinton was a load of lumber from Burrus Lumber Company. Loaded on Trailer Train bulkhead flat car No. 80522, it went out on the train on December 21. (It was picked up at the mill on the 20th.)

On Wednesday and Thursday, December 27 and 28, 1978, the last freight trains made their way to Durbin and back to Hinton. Pulling the last two trains was engine No. 2311 with caboose No. 3306. The crew consisted of L.R. Ratliff, Conductor, W.W. Bulmer, Engineer, and J.L. Ryan and W.C. Cole, Brakemen.

The consist on December 27 was:

To Howes Leather Company
   YS 1023—empty boxcar
   ATSF 48665—empty boxcar
   ATSF 9573—boxcar of hides
   ATSF 42093—boxcar of hides
To Interstate Lumber Company
   C&O 84491—empty chip car
   C&O 84847—empty chip car
   C&O 84616—empty chip car

First step in removing the track—lifting the rails and ties from the ballast. Photograph taken in Marlinton, August 5, 1979.
WPM

Pulling the spikes from the ties at Horrock, August 30, 1979.
WPM

To Western Maryland Railway
WM 63838—empty hopper car
CP 381109—boxcar of potash, en route to Biglerville, Pennsylvania
C&O 26062—boxcar of miscellaneous company material, en route to Hagerstown, Maryland.
IC 400475—boxcar of wood products, en route to Trenton, New Jersey

The last freight train to operate the entire length of the Greenbrier line made its passage down the river with almost no notice on December 28, 1978. Only one person (the author) watched its departure from Durbin and a small crowd gathered at the Marlinton depot. The train went through Ronceverte unnoticed. In addition to the crew, riding the last trip were E.G. Woodson, Trainmaster from Clifton Forge, Virginia, and Paul McLaughlin. The consist that day was:

Loaded cars
CI 1849—hopper car of coal en route to Chattanooga, Tennessee
B&O 470117—boxcar of railroad company material
C&O 84831—wood chip car to Covington
C&O 158256—wood chip car to Covington
C&O 84085—wood chip car to Covington
C&O 84861—wood chip car to Covington
Empty cars
CBQ 24520
BN 195642
CBQ 22334
NP 31476
ATSF 16635

At the end of business the next day, December 29, 1978, the last two agency stations, Durbin and Marlin-

ton, closed their doors for the last time. The agents were Ray Looney at Durbin and Paul Bowden at Marlinton.

To complete the history of the Greenbrier Branch following the abandonment, we need to go back to 1976, the year the West Virginia Railroad Maintenance Authority was created. Immediately after its organization, the Railroad Authority undertook a study of the Greenbrier as one of its first tasks. Based on this study, the authority decided that the amount of traffic on the portion of the line that the railroad was seeking to abandon was too small for the length of the line for the State of West Virginia to oppose the abandonment application. Therefore, during the abandonment procedure, the Railroad Authority and the Chessie System discussed the possible uses of the right-of-way if the Interstate Commerce Commission approved the request to abandon the Greenbrier line. As a result of these discussions a plan for the future of the line was worked out.

For its part the Chessie System made the following offer to the state:

1. Donate the entire 92.04 miles of right-of-way to the state, with the exception of two parcels in Marlinton.

2. Donate all improvements, except rails and ties, on the 92.04 miles to the state, including the depot at Marlinton.

3. Donate to the state all land and improvements at Durbin, including the depot, not needed by the Western Maryland Railway to maintain the freight service between Durbin and Bartow.

4. Sell to the state the track between Mile Post 78 and Durbin for the estimated net salvage value of $598,730.

The state of West Virginia agreed to the above proposal by the railroad and laid out to the public its plan for the Greenbrier line as follows:

1. The track between Cass and Durbin will be purchased to maintain a rail access to the Cass Scenic Railroad and for possible freight service to Cass.

2. The line below Cass will be placed in a "rail-bank" and its physical integrity retained so if the need ever develops, rail service can be re-instated.

3. The line below Cass will be leased to the Department of Natural Resources for recreational use.

4. The depot at Marlinton will be donated to the town.

Following the abandonment of the Greenbrier line in 1978, a number of the parts of the plan took place more or less as expected.

The Chessie System moved quickly to have the track taken up from the Greenbrier line. In December of 1978 the track material between North Caldwell and Mile Post 78 was sold to Midwest Steel, of Charleston. Midwest, in turn, contracted with the firm of Skelly and Wallans, of Toronto, Canada, to do the actual removal work.

Skelly and Wallans began the work of taking up the rails and ties in July 1979. The first thing that was done was to lift the rails and ties from the ballast by using a track tamping machine. This was followed by crews with spike pullers and bolt machines. The rails and ties were picked up and hauled by truck to stockpiles located at North Caldwell, Renick, and Marlinton.

The track removal work was completed by the late spring of 1980. However, the economic turndown of the early 1980s caused the bottom to drop out of the market for used rail and the large piles of rails only slowly disappeared. At the end of 1984 some of the rail still remains at several places along the line.

The ties were sold to Railroad Cross Tie Sales Company, Inc., of Georgia, and were disposed of more rapidly.

At least part of the Greenbrier line survives in the State of Ohio. As part of the rehabilitation of a former Conrail line between Cambridge and Pleasant City, the State of Ohio purchased eight miles of rail that came from the Greenbrier. This rail was welded into longer lengths by the Chessie System rail welding facility and laid by contractor in 1983.

Once the track removal work was nearing completion, the actual transfer of the property from the railroad to the state was made by deed dated June 20, 1980. A bill of sale with the same date transferred the track from Mile Post 78 to Durbin.

In Marlinton, a non-profit organization, Marlinton Railroad Depot, Inc., was incorporated in September 1979 to be responsible for the depot and adjacent office building on behalf of the town. This organization received two Historic Preservation Grants-in-Aid, totalling $21,250, from the West Virginia Department of Culture and History for the exterior restoration work on the depot.

The major exterior restoration work was done by a contractor, Zimmerman Construction Company, and begun in the spring of 1981. The work involved needed carpentry work, a new roof of simulated slate to look like

Spring Creek, August 30, 1979.　　　　　WPM

Loosening the track bolts at Beard, September 6, 1979.　WPM

the original, painting, and restoring the front side of the depot to its original look by putting back the second freight door. The paint scheme chosen was yellow with red and white trim as used by the Chesapeake and Ohio from about 1910 through the 1920s.

Work on restoring the interior and beautifying the grounds was done by residents from the Anthony Correctional Center and numerous volunteers from the community. Funds for this work came from donations from community organizations and businesses. The Marlinton Woman's Club made the depot one of its major community improvement projects for several years.

Marlinton, October 22, 1979.   WPM

Loading rail from the Greenbrier Branch into a gondola car
for shipment, at North Caldwell, December 15, 1979.   WPM

Knapps Creek Bridge, October 26, 1979.   WPM

The Chessie System donated four cars for display on track left in front of the depot by courtesy of Midwest Steel. The cars are a caboose, box car, flat car, and a track workers' camp car.

The depot building was opened to the public in the summer of 1983 and at this writing contains a craft shop and tourist information center as well as displays on the history of the Greenbrier Division.

The Durbin depot, while remaining state property, has also undergone renovation for community use. It was leased by the state to the Pocahontas County Senior Citizens for use as a senior citizen center for upper Pocahontas County. The bulk of the funds to restore the exterior of the building and renovate the interior was a $50,000 grant from the Governor's Community Partnership Grant Program made in November 1982. The restoration and renovation work was contracted to the Worlidge Construction Company and began in the spring of 1983. The paint scheme selected for the Durbin depot was the same as that used on the Marlinton depot. The center was put into use in the fall of 1983.

Unfortunately, the other plans for the future of the Greenbrier line have not come to realization as hoped.

The right of way from North Caldwell to Cass was leased to the Department of Natural Resources for use as a recreational trail and has been designated as the Greenbrier Trail. However, a lack of funding has limited the maintenance and development of the trail to a bare minimum as of this writing.

The use of the Cass to Durbin portion of the Greenbrier line proved to be minimal. No demand for using Cass as a destination or loading point for freight ever developed and even the coal for the Cass Railroad locomotives came by truck rather than rail. The only use of the line was an occasional shipment for the Cass Railroad and a few rail fan excursions each year, although the Cass Railroad finally began running regular tourist trains to Durbin in the summer of 1984.

But most unfortunate was the decline of the traffic on the Western Maryland line to Durbin and the remaining small part of the Greenbrier line from Durbin to Bartow. Prior to the abandonment of the Greenbrier Subdivision it was hoped that one positive result might be increased business on the Western Maryland Durbin line, thus

North approach to the Droop Tunnel, December 20, 1979.
WPM

Piles of rail joints at Renick, December 20, 1979. WPM

Piles of spikes at Renick, December 20, 1979. WPM

securing its future. At the time of the Greenbrier abandonment proceedings, the only traffic of significance over the Western Maryland line to Durbin was interchange traffic from the Chesapeake and Ohio and cars from the Westvaco pulp yard at Durbin. With the abandonment of the Greenbrier line, the interchange cars would be gone, but it was believed diversion of the traffic from Frank and Bartow as well as the pulp wood loads would provide the traffic needed to ensure rail service to the Durbin area.

However, this increase in traffic on the Western Maryland line did not take place; instead the number of cars on the trains to and from Durbin decreased following the closing of the Greenbrier Branch. Interstate Lumber Company decided not to ship chips and sawdust to the Westvaco plant at Luke, Maryland, and so this business did not go to the Western Maryland. Also the pulp yard at Durbin reduced the number of shipments by rail, claiming that reductions in service and increased rates made truck service more feasible. This left the Howes Leather Company tannery as the only customer of any significance on the line. Traffic to Howes consisted of inbound loads of hides and an occasional car of chemicals and an occasional outbound car of leather.

In June of 1983 the Chesapeake and Ohio Railway, the Western Maryland Railway, and the Baltimore and Ohio Railroad made application to the Interstate Commerce Commission to abandon the Western Maryland line from Greenbrier Junction to Durbin and the Chesapeake and Ohio line from Durbin to Bartow. (The Baltimore and Ohio was involved because it was in the process of taking over all Western Maryland operations.) The reasons given in the application for the request to abandon the lines were that the operation of them had been unprofitable, the track and tunnel near Glady needed rehabilitation, and the assets dedicated to these lines could be better utilized.

Due to a problem with the way the company handled the public notification of the application to abandon the line to Durbin, the ICC required that the application be resubmitted. This was done and the new application was dated September 28, 1983.

In the abandonment application the Chessie System detailed the traffic on the line for 1981, 1982, and the first three months of 1983 as follows:

	1981	1982	1983
Howes Leather	234	189	30
Westvaco	74	71	25
Interstate Lumber	1	1	0
Other	12	2	0
	321	263	55

The number of trains run were 44 in 1981, 40 in 1982, and 11 in the first three months of 1983.

For these periods the railroad claimed revenue of $167,054, $138,268, and $35,994 from operation of the line to Durbin, compared to avoidable costs for the same periods of $202,124, $181,362, and $46,901. To rehabilitate the line the application gave figures of $475,339 to purchase and install needed ties, $110,981 for surfacing work, and $565,000 for work on the Glady Tunnel. Following the rehabilitation work, an estimate of $183,956 was made for the needed annual maintenance cost.

Protests to the abandonment were received from the Howes Leather Company, Interstate Lumber Company, Railway Labor Executives Association, United Transportation Union, West Virginia Department of Natural Resources, and West Virginia Public Service Commission.

The major issues raised by the protestants were continuation of service to the customers on the line, maintaining a rail access for the Cass Scenic Railroad, labor protection for the effective employees, and whether the Chessie System had an implied contract with the State of West Virginia to continue the line to Durbin following the purchase of the Cass to Durbin track by the state in 1980.

The Monongahela National Forest submitted a comment on the abandonment supporting continued rail service by some agency. If this was not possible and the abandonment took place, the Forest Service urged that the right-of-way be transferred to public ownership.

None of the protests moved the Interstate Commerce Commission to schedule a hearing in this case. Due to improper filing by several protestants, only the protests by the labor organizations and the Public Service Commission were considered by the ICC. The implied contract

Stillwell, January 15, 1980.　　　　　　　WPM

Ties stockpiled at Marlinton, May 5, 1980.　　　WPM

Stockpiling ties at Marlinton, January 15, 1980.　　WPM

argument was dismissed by the Commission as not a proper issue to be considered in an abandonment proceeding. As for the protests by labor organizations, the ICC stated that it felt the standard labor protection conditions that were included in all recent abandonment decisions would be sufficient. The Commission ruled that the discontinuance of the rail service would not result in a serious adverse impact on Pocahontas and Randolph Counties nor on the environment.

By a decision dated December 6, 1983, the Commission gave its approval to the abandonment request. Based on this authority, the Chessie System discontinued service on the line to Durbin as of 12:01 a.m. on February 15, 1984.

Actual train service to Durbin had ended somewhat before that date. The final train ran on September 25, 1983. That day engines 6536, 6459, 5978, and 6546 ran light from Elkins to Durbin and hauled back a number of cars that had been in storage in the Durbin yard.

During the time the abandonment was under consideration by the Interstate Commerce Commission, the Chessie System made two offers to the State of West Virginia in an attempt to mitigate two of the problems cited by those opposed to the elimination of the line. These problems were the loss of rail service to the Howes Leather Company tannery at Frank and the loss of a rail connection for the Cass Scenic Railroad.

One of the offers from the Chessie was to sell the Western Maryland line from Greenbrier Junction to Durbin to the state for $300,000, which was approximately half of the estimated scrap value of the track material on the line.

The other offer was to donate to the state sufficient track material from the Durbin line for the rebuilding of the former rail link between Old Spruce and Spruce on Cheat Mountain. This would connect the Cass Railroad with the Elkins to Webster Springs line of the Western Maryland.

Under both offers the state was to be responsible for providing service to the tannery from either Greenbrier Junction or Spruce.

Unfortunately the state agency involved, the Department of Natural Resources, sat on these proposals and made no official response to the Chessie System's offers. Finally, under pressure from local people and with the urging of State Senator Jae Spears and other legislators, the Department of Natural Resources agreed in March 1984 to the offer of track material for the Spruce-Old Spruce connection. The 1984 Legislature appropriated $100,000 in the 1984-85 state budget to be used on this project. In October the Chessie System made the donation of the track material on the Durbin to Bartow portion of the Greenbrier line. The Cass Scenic Railroad track crew began the work of taking up this track the same month.

As this is written in late 1984 the following items need to be resolved before the Greenbrier Branch slips completely into the footnotes of history:

Rail stockpiled at Marlinton, May 5, 1980.　　WPM

Marlinton, February 2, 1980.　　WPM

• arrangements have to be completed for the removal of the Durbin to Bartow track and its relaying from Old Spruce to Spruce. Included is an agreement with the Mower Lumber Company on the exact location of the connecting line.

• the Department of Natural Resources and the Chessie System need to work out a permanent arrangement for the use by the Cass Scenic Railroad of the track between the West Fork bridge and the Durbin depot as well as the wye track. The solution will probably be the purchase of this track by the state.

• rail service for the tannery. The Department of Natural Resources does not plan to attempt such service even after Old Spruce-Spruce line is built due to the difficulties of handling modern freight equipment on the Cass Railroad, especially in the winter. To provide the tannery with rail service of a sort, discussions have been held between Chessie and Howes Leather Company concerning the unloading of freight cars at Cheat Bridge for trucking on to the tannery.

• disposition of the Western Maryland line to Durbin. It will, without doubt, be removed by Chessie in 1985. The right-of-way will probably be purchased by the U.S. Forest Service.

REGULAR PASSENGER SERVICE ON THE GREENBRIER began on December 17, 1900. The first train consisted of engine No. 98 (C. and O. A Class, 4-4-0 wheel arrangement), a coach, and a combination passenger coach/ baggage car. The train arrived at Marlinton slightly behind time, having been delayed at Beaver Creek where a siding was being installed. The initial schedule for the Chesapeake and Ohio Railway's newest division was as follows with trains to run daily except on Sunday:

WEST		EAST
1:00 p.m.	Marlinton	12:00 noon
1:20	Buckeye	11:40
1:30	Beaver Creek	11:30
1:45	Seybert	11:15
2:15	Beard's	10:45
2:40	Droop Mountain	10:20
3:15	Renick	9:45
3:25	Spring Creek	9:35
4:00	Anthony	9:00
4:15	Keister	8:45
4:50	Little Sulphur	8:10
5:00	Whitcomb Junction	8:00
5:15 p.m.	Ronceverte	7:45 a.m.

Arriving on the first train was the Marlinton Agent, S.I. Fleshman, who set up a temporary office in the post office. The fare was 4 cents per mile with a ticket from Marlinton to Ronceverte costing $2.35.

As the newly laid track settled in and was better ballasted, the schedule for the passenger train began to show improvement. A new schedule went into effect on February 1, 1901, with an hour improvement in time. The train left Ronceverte at 7:45 a.m. with arrival in Marlinton at 11 a.m. The return trip from Marlinton began at 2:45 p.m., arriving at Ronceverte at 5:55 p.m.

Mail service by train was to begin on February 20, 1901, but none arrived on that day. On the 21st a small sack of twelve letters and one newspaper came by train and it took several days for the mail to get onto a regular basis. Particularly pleased were the readers of daily papers that came by mail who observed that "Richmond, Baltimore, Charleston seem about as near neighbors as Huntersville used to be. To read a Friday's paper on Saturday is more relishing than to wait until Monday or Tuesday for Friday's news."

February also saw the departure from Marlinton of the first couple to begin their honeymoon by train in the per-

sons of Asa W. McNeil and Uema Etta Beverage. They were married on the 25th.

After a number of delays, passenger service was extended to Cass with a new schedule on June 1, 1901. The stations above Marlinton listed in this schedule were Harper (probably Clawson), Clover Lick, Forrest (Sitlington), and Cass. The stations below Marlinton were the same as in the original schedule, except that Beaver Creek was now called Dan. Again there was an improvement in train speed with the eastbound train, No. 142, leaving Ronceverte at 7:45 a.m., arriving at Marlinton at 10:35, and Cass at 11:45. The return trip, as train No. 141, began at 1:45 p.m., back to Marlinton at 3:00, and arrived at Ronceverte at 5:55. The service was still only six days a week.

Railway Post Office service on the Greenbrier train probably began with the extension of the passenger

A-6 Class 4-4-0 No. 53 at the Marlinton depot.   PCHS/NRP

Bartow depot and a 4-4-0 (A Class) passenger engine.   PCHS

Waiting for the train at Renick.   PCHS/NRP

train's run to Cass; at least the first reference the author has found to a Greenbrier RPO route is listed as the Cass and Ronceverte RPO, beginning in 1901.

In addition to the extended service up the river, the Greenbrier passenger train had new equipment assigned to it in early June. The consist was now made up of a combination mail and baggage car and two coaches. Motive power remained one of the Class A 4-4-0 steam locomotives. Engines of this type generally handled the Greenbrier line passenger trains until the end of regular steam powered passenger service on the line in 1930.

Marlinton was the terminating point for an excursion on August 11, 1901, with 542 passengers descending upon the town. They arrived in ten cars behind engine No. 158. After eating at the various local restaurants and hotels, the crowd spent the afternoon looking the town over before departing at 6 p.m. Although the town had been a little apprehensive before the crowd arrived due to concern about a possible disorderly element, the good behavior of the excursionists and the fact they left several hundred dollars behind left the townspeople with the willingness "to see as many excursions as the railway company cares to give us."

Although this would not always be the case, by the end of 1901 the passenger trains had achieved a degree of regularity "that the Pocahontas County people set their time by it and from Marlinton to Droop the Cooks (sic) commence to get dinner when they hear the passenger whistle."

Passenger service was extended to Durbin in May of 1902. Although a few trips may have been made earlier in the month, the official day of regular service beginning to Durbin was May 26. A schedule for that date has not been located but the schedule that went into effect on February 1, 1903, is as follows:

WEST 141		EAST 142
1:00	Durbin	12:01
1:40	Cass	11:20
2:43	Marlinton	10:15
5:15 p.m.	Ronceverte	7:45 a.m.

The trains operated daily except Sunday. With this change in the terminus to Durbin the Railway Post Office became the Durbin and Ronceverte RPO.

Coinciding with the completion of the Coal and Iron Railroad to Durbin in July 1903 was the doubling of the passenger service on the Greenbrier Division with the addition of a train in each direction. The new schedule, which took effect on Sunday, August 2, also added Sunday service, and provided a morning train from Durbin and an evening train from Ronceverte. As No. 141, the train left Durbin at 6:50 a.m., arrived at Marlinton at 8:33, and at Ronceverte at 11 a.m. The return trip, as No. 144, left Ronceverte at 4 p.m., arrived at Marlinton at 6:29, and Durbin at 8:10 p.m. (The original No. 141 became No. 143.) This new service was of special benefit to those people living north of Marlinton and Ronceverte, allowing them to go to either town to transact business and return home the same day. Also, a connection in Ronceverte with a westbound train on the main line made it possible for Pocahontas and Greenbrier County people to reach Charleston within a day.

Coal and Iron passenger service from Elkins to Durbin began on August 1, 1903, with one train each way. The train left Elkins at 8 a.m. and arrived at Durbin at 11:45. The return trip left Durbin at 3 pm, with a 6:45 arrival at Elkins.

On October 7, 1903, Train 141 consisted of fourteen cars, filled with people going to a show of some type at Ronceverte. A special excursion train from Elkins to Ronceverte also ran that day.

Travelers on the Greenbrier Division got a present from the Chesapeake and Ohio at the beginning of 1904 with a fare reduction. The 4 cents per mile rate was reduced to 3.2 cents per mile.

Bartow received passenger service starting on June 6, 1904, with the extension of the run of Trains 142 and 143 to that point. With this extension in service the Railway Post Office route name was changed to the Travellers Repose and Ronceverte RPO. (The post office for the area remained at Travellers Repose until February 1906 when it was moved to Bartow and the name changed.)

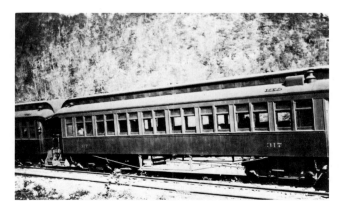

Coach No. 317 at Spice Run on October 20, 1914. This car was built by the Pullman Company in July 1887.   COHS

Parlor car No. 474 at Spice Run on October 20, 1914. This car was built by Barney and Smith in August 1889. Parlor car service was operated on Train 142 and 143 from 1910 until 1918.   COHS

The schedule going into effect on the Greenbrier line on June 19, 1904, was:

WEST

141	143	
	2:35 p.m.	Bartow
6:50 a.m.	2:44	Durbin
7:31	3:24	Cass
8:38	4:28	Marlinton
10:01	5:46	Renick
11:00 a.m.	6:45 p.m.	Ronceverte

EAST

142	144	
12:40 p.m.		Bartow
12:30	8:15 p.m.	Durbin
11:49	7:36	Cass
10:47	6:32	Marlinton
9:29	5:13	Renick
8:30 a.m.	4:10 p.m.	Ronceverte

The Coal and Iron was now running two trains each way between Elkins and Durbin. Trains arrived at Durbin at 10 a.m. and 2:35 p.m. The return trips left Durbin at 12:40 p.m. and 3:15 p.m.

The final extension of passenger service was made on November 18, 1905, when the first passenger train went to Winterburn. Winterburn, which had a wye track where the trains could be turned, became the terminus for all Greenbrier Division passenger trains and this gave Bartow additional service as well. The schedule for July 6, 1906, gave the arrival time for No. 142 at Winterburn as 12:50 p.m. and its departure as No. 143 at 2:40 p.m., while No. 144 arrived at 8 p.m. and laid over for the night, leaving at 6:45 a.m. as No. 141.

With the new terminal point for Greenbrier Division passenger trains came another name change for the Railway Post Office, to Winterburn and Ronceverte RPO.

The Coal and Iron Railroad was now part of the Western Maryland Railway and its passenger service to Durbin by the schedule of November 19, 1905, was:

WEST

8:00 a.m.	12:35 p.m.	Elkins
8:51	1:24	Fishing Hawk
9:07	1:46	Glady
9:48	2:19	Burner
10:00 a.m.	2:35 p.m.	Durbin

EAST

2:35 p.m.	7:00 p.m.	Elkins
1:49	6:08	Fishing Hawk
1:30	5:52	Glady
12:57	5:17	Burner
12:40 p.m.	5:00 p.m.	Durbin

In late November of 1905 Sunday passenger service on the Greenbrier Division (Trains 141 and 144) was discontinued but for how long is not known at this writing.

During these early days of the Greenbrier Division's history the passenger trains had no problem finding places to stop. The already existing communities, together with the new sawmill towns, gave rise to the saying that a train had to back up after leaving a station in order to have a distance to whistle for the next station. The schedule for June 4, 1905, lists the following stations and flagstops: Whitcomb (station), North Caldwell (s), Bowes (flagstop), Keister (f), Anthony (s), Spring Creek (s), Renick (s), Horrock (f), Rorer (f), Droop Mountain (f), Spice Run (f), Beards (s), Burnside (f), Seebert (s), Dan (f), Buckeye (s), Munday Lick (f), Marlinton (s), August (f), Clawson (f), Harter (f), Clover Lick (s), Stony Bottom (f), Sitlington (s), Cass (s), Wanless (f), Hosterman (s), Boyer (f), Whiting (f), Durbin (s), and Bartow (s).

As the years went by the opening of new sawmills would create additional stops for the passenger trains. Winterburn has already been mentioned and among the

Train time at Marlinton—early 1900s.

PCHS

Waiting for the train at Clawson. The identity of the woman is not known.   PCHS

others would be Tottens, Hopper, Loopemount, Brink, Woodman, Deeter, Golden, Locust, Denmar, Kennison, Watoga, Stillwell, Sixty, Thorny Creek, Big Run, Raywood, Deer Creek, Cup Run, Pine Flats, Nida, Frank, and Houchins.

With this development in the lumber industry along the Greenbrier Division, ridership on the passenger trains increased rapidly during the early years. During the fiscal year ending June 30, 1903, some 33,611 passengers boarded the trains on the line providing $36,672.66 to the Chesapeake and Ohio. Marlinton was the busiest depot with 7,154 passengers, followed by Seebert, 4,210, Cass, 4,033, Renick, 3,090, Durbin, 2,949, Clover Lick, 1,544, Hosterman, 1,418, Forrest (Sitlington), 1,291, Anthony, 1,237, and Buckeye, 1,015. Only seven people got on the trains at Burnsides, paying $3.50 for the privilege.

During the next fiscal year the number of passengers more than doubled to 71,269, with revenues of $52,966.06. For the next fiscal year ending June 30, 1905, total passengers were 92,451 and revenue $69,747.99. Marlinton remained the busiest station during both years.

The next fiscal year (1905-06) saw the completion of the Greenbrier line to its greatest length and 107,755 passengers boarding trains 141, 142, 143 and 144. Passenger revenue for the year was $85,725.02. Dur-

bin edged out Marlinton as the busiest depot, 19,218 passengers to 19,110. The next busiest stations were Cass, 13,190, Seebert, 9,977, Renick, 6,896, Bartow, 4,651, Winterburn, 4,515, Anthony, 3,469, North Caldwell, 2,812, Clover Lick, 2,775, Hosterman, 2,650, and Buckeye, 2,363. Bowes had the least number of passengers with 164.

Unfortunately, as we know, the process would begin to reverse itself as the sawmills began to shut down and towns disappear, but this part of our story will come later.

At various times there were reports that the Greenbrier line was being considered as part of a through route for passenger service. In late 1903 consideration was given to routing the Chesapeake and Ohio's premier train, the Fast Flying Virginian, to New York City by way of Durbin and Hagerstown, Maryland, but it was soon discovered that sharp curves between Durbin and Elkins would not accommodate the Pullman cars. In the summer of 1905 thought was given by the Baltimore and Ohio Railroad to instituting a through Pullman service between Pittsburgh and Hot Springs, Virginia, by way of Clarksburg, Grafton, Elkins, Durbin, and Ronceverte, to be operated at night, but the service was never started. In late 1909 there was a proposal by the Western Maryland Railway for a through car service between Ronceverte and Cumberland, Maryland. The idea was to attach a parlor car to train No. 142 and send it on to Cumberland on the connecting Western Maryland train at Durbin, to arrive in Cumberland at 7 p.m. The returning car would leave Cumberland at 7 a.m. to make connection with train No. 143 at Durbin. However, the plan, like the others, was never activated.

In February 1907 the passengers on the Greenbrier Division and elsewhere in West Virginia got a present from the State Legislature in the form of a law mandating a coach fare of 2 cents per mile. The law set a 5 cents minimum and required the fare to be the nearest multiple of 5 to the result of multiplying the distance by 2 cents. Naturally the Chesapeake and Ohio Railway and the other railroads operating in West Virginia challenged the new law in the courts. The case went all the way to the United States Supreme Court and was not settled until 1913, in favor of the law. During the years the law was under litigation in the courts the Chesapeake and Ohio had been charging its pre-law fares but had to issue passengers with coupons for the value of their tickets above the 2 cent rate. Those people who had had the foresight to keep the coupons received a nice monetary windfall in 1913. The Coupon Commissioners were in Marlinton on September 8 "and had a very busy day, receiving and receipting for hundreds of packages of coupons. These packages would aggregate many thousands of dollars." The railroad did not lose out entirely as its "trains were crowded with people coming with their coupons and those of their neighbors." The return of the 2 cent rate in July was welcomed with the comment that now "the ordinary passenger will not have to sell a cow every time that he takes a trip to buy a mileage book."

In late 1907 and early 1908 the Chesapeake and Ohio went through a period of cutting back service wherever possible. Among the casualties were the Greenbrier Division's trains 141 and 144, discontinued on February 2, 1908. In this day of the automobile and paved roads it is difficult to realize the effect of the discontinuance of these trains on the area they served, particularly to those living north of Marlinton. People living north of there had adjusted their business and social lives to the trains and the ability to go to Marlinton, their county seat and shopping center, attend to their business, and return home the same day. The same was no doubt true for people in Greenbrier County for access to Ronceverte and their county seat at Lewisburg. Public outcry immediately followed this action by the railroad, and petitions, signed by "thousands," were directed to the company. "Notwithstanding the demeanor of absolute monarchy assumed by certain official puppets, railroads are yet in a legal sense, at least, public carriers. The matter has been looked up, and it is found that a railroad cannot discontinue train service if it can be shown that public necessity requires its continuance." It was believed by local citizens that the necessity of trains 141 and 144 to the public could easily be shown, in court if necessary. The public pressure must have had its effects as Nos. 141 and 144 resumed operating on June 28, 1908.

Passenger service on the Greenbrier reached its height of luxury on June 7, 1910 when a parlor car was added to trains 142 and 143. "We are coming out of the woods fast. Superintendent Haynes has put a nice, new parlor car on trains 142 and 143. On its initial trip Tuesday, it was well filled and we are sure it will be profitable. For a half cent a mile additional fare, a clean, comfortable seat is secured in an easy riding car."

First a combination baggage/parlor car was used, but as the service did prove to be popular, a full parlor car was substituted by June 1912. Mrs. Alice Moore told the author of her fond memories of the black porter on the car, Uncle Henry. When she would be en route to visit her uncle in Charleston as a child, he would make sure she got on the proper train at Ronceverte. This service continued until World War I caused cutbacks in 1918 and was not restored after the war. The Greenbrier line was one of the few Chesapeake and Ohio branch lines in West Virginia to rate first class service.

The schedule on the Greenbrier for June 2, 1912, was:

WEST 141	143	
6:00 a.m.	2:20 p.m.	Winterburn
6:20	2:45	Durbin
7:00	3:25	Cass
8:02	4:30	Marlinton
9:25	5:50	Renick
10:40 a.m.	7:00 p.m.	Ronceverte

EAST 142	144	
12:55 p.m.	8:10 p.m.	Winterburn
12:30	7:45	Durbin
11:50	7:05	Cass
10:45	6:00	Marlinton
9:25	4:39	Renick
8:15 a.m.	3:30 p.m.	Ronceverte

Nos. 141 and 144 operated daily and Nos. 142 and 143 ran daily except Sunday. The other station stops on this schedule were Bartow, Boyer, Hosterman, Sitlington, Clover Lick, Buckeye, Watoga, Seebert, Denmar, Beards, Spring Creek, Anthony, and North Caldwell. The flagstops were Houchins (141/144 only), Frank, Wanless, Pine Flats, Deer Creek, Stony Bottom, Big Run, Harter, Clawson, August, Violet, Burnsides, Locust, Spice Run, Droop Mountain, Rorer, Horrock, Woodman, Keister, Brink (141/144 only), Bowes, Hopper (141/143 only), and Whitcomb.

Western Maryland trains arrived at Durbin at 10:20 a.m. and 2:30 p.m. They left Durbin for Elkins at 12:30 p.m. and 4 p.m. Service on the Western Maryland was daily except Sunday.

In March of 1913 there was a news report of the Western Maryland reducing its passenger service to Durbin to one train each way. The remaining train arrived at Durbin at 2:20 p.m. and departed for Elkins at 2:50 p.m. However, in November a schedule for two trains each way is given as follows:

WEST 51	53	
8:00 a.m.	12:20 p.m.	Elkins
10:10 a.m.	2:30 p.m.	Durbin

EAST 52	54	
12:45 p.m.	5:00 p.m.	Elkins
10:30 a.m.	2:50 p.m.	Durbin

However, in a 1914 Chesapeake and Ohio schedule, there is only one Western Maryland train to Durbin given, arriving at 2:30 p.m. and leaving at 2:50 p.m., daily except Sunday. No other reference has been found that lists more than one Western Maryland train to Durbin after the November 1913 schedule.

The number of passengers boarding the Greenbrier Division trains continued to grow during the second decade of the line's history. During the fiscal year ending June 30, 1913, total passengers were 151,478 and revenue from these passengers of $90,191.32. For the next year the total number of passengers was 183,933 with revenue of $87,838.88. This drop in revenue while the number of riders increased was no doubt due to the upholding of the 2 cents a mile law by the courts, as discussed earlier.

The total number of passengers dropped a little during the year ending June 30, 1915, to 178,561, but jumped during the next year to 192,833. This is the last year for which the author has figures but this is probably near the largest number of passengers boarding the trains on the Greenbrier line. There may have been a slight increase during the World War I years, but soon after that the decline in passengers, as discussed shortly, began. Revenue from passengers for the years ending June 30, 1915 and 1916 was $78,818.78 and $79,226.41 respectively.

In all four of these years the busiest depots for passengers were Marlinton, Durbin, Cass, Seebert, and Renick, in that order. The top ten for 1912-13 were Marlinton, 26,267, Durbin, 21,986, Cass, 15,075, Seebert, 13,898, Renick, 8,556, Thornwood, 6,036, Clover Lick, 4,842, Denmar, 4,379, Winterburn, 4,106, and Beard, 3,690. In 1915-16 the list was Marlinton, 35,056, Durbin, 25,019, Cass, 21,748, Seebert, 10,351, Renick, 9,077, Winterburn, 8,186, Clover Lick, 7,381, Spice Run, 6,575, Buckeye, 6,279, and Denmar, 5,429.

In 1917 the United States entered World War I and one of the effects on the Greenbrier line was that trains 141 and 144 were discontinued for about four months. Citing a shortage and increased cost of the labor and materials needed to maintain these trains as well as the extraordinary demand being made upon its track and equipment in moving troops and materials needed in the war effort, the Chesapeake and Ohio applied to the Public Service Commission for permission to discontinue these trains. In an order dated June 15, 1917, the PSC granted the necessary permission and the trains were taken off on July 1. As in 1908, efforts were quickly underway to have these trains restored with protests and petitions. In addition to the reasons given the previous time, it was pointed out that trains 141 and 144 served as a "school bus" for a number of students attending Edray District High School at Marlinton and enabled them to live at home rather than having to board in town in order to go to school. Taking all the protests into account and knowing that the Federal government planned to have the massive movements of men to training camps completed by the middle of October, the PSC ordered in September that the trains be put back in service as soon as practicable after October 15. In the same order the railroad was allowed to increase fares on the Greenbrier Division from 2 cents to 2½ cents per mile in response to the claim by the Chesapeake and Ohio that passenger service on the line was being operated at a loss. The trains were placed back in operation on October 28, 1917.

Both sets of trains received new equipment in the form of coaches painted in Chesapeake and Ohio Railway yellow in 1919; 142 and 143 in May and 141 and 144 in June.

Following the end of World War I the growing use of the automobile and improved roads, together with the closing of most of the sawmills in the Greenbrier Valley, began to have their effect on the number of passengers riding the Greenbrier Division. In October of 1920 the railroad applied to the Public Service Commission for permission to discontinue trains 141 and 144 between Durbin and Winterburn. In June 1921 the PSC ruled

that the trains could be discontinued between Bartow and Winterburn, effective on June 19. As there were no turning facilities at Bartow, No. 144 would go in reverse to Durbin for the night and then return to Bartow in reverse in the morning in order to begin its trip back to Ronceverte as No. 141.

However, the railroad may not have exercised the authority to discontinue trains 141 and 144 between Bartow and Winterburn. The public timetable for the fall of 1922 shows service to Winterburn by these two trains and when the Chesapeake and Ohio returned to the Public Service Commission in April of 1923 with another request to reduce passenger service on the Greenbrier Division, it was for permission to discontinue all four trains to Winterburn.

The 1923 petition to the Public Service Commission was for authority to discontinue trains 141 and 144 between Durbin and Winterburn and trains 142 and 143 between Bartow and Winterburn. This request was approved by the PSC with an effective date of July 8, 1923. As mentioned before, Bartow had no turning facilities, so after the end of service to Winterburn, train 142 would turn at Durbin and then back on to Bartow to complete its run. With this change in service the Railway Post Office was renamed the Bartow and Ronceverte RPO.

The 1922 schedule mentioned above was dated September 15 and was as follows:

WEST

141	143	
6:40 a.m.	2:25 p.m.	Winterburn
7:00	2:45	Durbin
7:42	3:25	Cass
8:55	4:35	Marlinton
10:27	6:07	Renick
11:45 a.m.	7:25 p.m.	Ronceverte

EAST

142	144	
1:25 p.m.	9:05 p.m.	Winterburn
1:05	8:45	Durbin
12:22	8:02	Cass
11:12	6:55	Marlinton
9:46	5:26	Renick
8:32 a.m.	4:12 p.m.	Ronceverte

Nos. 141 and 144 operated daily and Nos. 142 and 143 daily except Sunday. A Western Maryland train was scheduled to arrive in Durbin at 2:35 p.m. and depart at 3 p.m., daily except Sunday.

The Greenbrier line schedule for February 10, 1928, lists the passenger trains as follows:

WEST

141	143	
	1:20 p.m.	Bartow
6:15 a.m.	2:20	Durbin
6:55	3:00	Cass
8:02	4:08	Marlinton
9:30	5:34	Renick
10:45 a.m.	6:45 p.m.	Ronceverte

EAST		
142	144	
1:20 p.m.		Bartow
1:05	7:40 p.m.	Durbin
12:15	6:55	Cass
11:02	5:45	Marlinton
9:30	4:20	Renick
8:07 a.m.	3:05 p.m.	Ronceverte

As usual, trains 141 and 144 ran daily and trains 142 and 143 ran daily except Sunday. The other station stops on the schedule were Clover Lick, Seebert, Beard, Anthony, and North Caldwell. Connecting service on the Western Maryland was a train arriving at Durbin at 2:10 p.m. and departing for Elkins at 2:35 p.m., daily except Sunday.

Although freight traffic on the Greenbrier line was heavy during the 1920s, as described in a previous chapter, passenger traffic began the decline, both locally and nationally, that would eventually lead to the extinction of passenger service on the Greenbrier as well as make the passenger train in general an endangered species. The major threat, of course, was the growing use of automobiles on roads that began to be greatly improved after World War I. Then in the 1930s air transport began to seriously compete for the traveller. The author has not located any ridership figures for the trains on the Greenbrier line, but on the Chesapeake and Ohio Railway as a whole the total passengers in 1920 were 8,767,811, dropping to 5,811,872 in 1925, and only 3,418,376 in 1929. The bulk of this decline was in local traffic.

As one way of cutting the cost of passenger service, the Chesapeake and Ohio began to investigate the possible use of self-propelled gas/electric cars on branch lines and for local trains on the main lines. In April 1926 such equipment was tried out on several trips on the Greenbrier.

In late 1928 the railroad announced that it was ordering six gas/electric cars from the J.G. Brill Company at a cost of $300,000. As built, these cars were identical with their exteriors painted standard Chesapeake and Ohio Pullman green, while the interiors of the passenger sections were dark brown on the sides with cream colored ceiling. They were divided into four compartments—engine and control, Railway Post Office, baggage and a forty seat passenger section. To satisfy the laws of Virginia, the passenger section was divided into twenty-seven seats for whites and thirteen for blacks. In 1949 five of the six cars were modified by having the gas engines replaced by diesel engines and the passenger section reduced in size to either twenty-four or sixteen seats. Numbered 9050 through 9055, these were the "doodle-bugs" fondly, or perhaps not so fondly, remembered by former passengers on the Greeenbrier and other lines of the Chesapeake and Ohio.

On June 20, 1929, the steam powered equipment on trains 142 and 143 was replaced by one of these motor cars pulling a combination coach/baggage car. Which one of the Brill cars this was is not known to the author, but in the final years of passenger service on the Green-brier, Nos. 9054 and 9055 were most commonly used.

The Great Depression was only about six months old when the Chesapeake and Ohio applied to the Public Service Commission in early April 1930 to receive permission to discontinue trains 141 and 144. The railroad cited increasing losses in operating these trains and reduced need for them due to improved local roads. Railroad officials claimed a loss of approximately $14,500 in 1929 on these trains and estimated that the loss for 1930 would be $25,000 based on the first few months of the year.

This application was not a surprise to the people in the Greenbrier Valley but concerns were raised in several areas. As in 1908 and 1917 when the same trains were taken off, objections were based on the convenience of these trains to the people living north of Marlinton and other shopping points, as the trains enabled them to come to town on business and return the same day. Also these trains provided the express service and the only Sunday service.

At a meeting on April 21 Assistant Superintendent E.D. Glenn met in Marlinton with local leaders to review the railroad's position. He could offer nothing to help those living north of town, but indicated that changes in express service on the main line would enable express to be put on trains 142 and 143 with an actual improvement in service. He said also that trains 142 and 143 would operate seven days a week to provide Sunday trains.

On June 30, 1930, the Public Service Commission approved the railroad's petition to eliminate Nos. 141 and 144. The Chesapeake and Ohio posted notices that the trains would be discontinued on July 21 and that Nos. 142 and 143 would begin operating seven days a week.

The schedule for the remaining passenger service on the Greenbrier line, dated July 15, 1930, was as follows:

WEST		EAST
143		142
12:30 p.m.	Bartow	12:30 p.m.
1:55	Durbin	12:15
2:30	Cass	11:30
3:30	Marlinton	10:20
4:42	Renick	8:54
5:50 p.m.	Ronceverte	7:50 a.m.

Service was daily. The other station stops were Clover Lick and Seebert. Flagstops listed on the schedule were Hosterman, Sitlington (station stop for No. 142), Clawson, Buckeye, Denmar, Beard, Spring Creek (station stop for No. 142), Anthony, Keister, Loopemount, North Caldwell (station stop for No. 142), and Whitcomb. The Western Maryland train arrived in Durbin at 1:45 p.m. and departed at 2 p.m., daily except Sunday.

In July of 1932 the Chesapeake and Ohio made an application to the Public Service Commission for a further cutback in passenger service on the Greenbrier by proposing the elimination of trains 142 and 143 and substituting a daily mixed freight and passenger train which would also handle mail and express. Opposition to this request from local citizens was vigorous. Hearings were held in Charleston on July 29 and in Marlinton on September 16. In response to the protests, the railroad agreed to withdraw its application for mixed train service in return for permission to discontinue the passenger trains on Sunday. On September 24 the PSC issued the necessary order for the elimination of Sunday runs by trains 142 and 143.

The schedules for December 12, 1937, and April 28, 1940, were the same, as follows:

WEST 143		EAST 142
12:40 p.m.	Bartow	12:40 p.m.
1:55	Durbin	12:31
2:30	Cass	11:44
3:30	Marlinton	10:41
4:42	Renick	9:15
5:50 p.m.	Ronceverte	8:05 a.m.

Service was daily except Sunday. On the Western Maryland a train arrived at Durbin from Elkins at 1:45 p.m. and began its return trip at 2 p.m.

In 1940 the Greenbrier Subdivision was included in an experiment by the Chesapeake and Ohio to attempt to increase the use of branch line passenger trains in West Virginia by lowering fares. The Public Service Commission approved a rate of one and a half cents per mile, one way, with an additional reduction for round trips. The new fare went into effect on February 10 and continued until September 30. On the Greenbrier the railroad advertised one way fares of 60 cents from Marlinton to Durbin, a saving of 39 cents, and 90 cents from Marlinton to Ronceverte, a saving of 58 cents. Round trip fares for the same trips were 90 cents and $1.35 respectively, half of the previous fare in each case.

The author has found no reference to the results or continuance of these experimental fares. The involvement of the United States in the Second World War the following year brought increased business to all trains without the need for special fares, of course.

The next cutback in service came in 1942 when Bartow lost the passenger train. The Public Service Commission issued an order on July 13, 1942, allowing the Chesapeake and Ohio to discontinue the train to Bartow but required the railroad to provide motor vehicle transportation between Durbin and Bartow. In a period of a little over a month only eight people were so transported, using a Durbin taxi, so the PSC allowed total elimination of service to Bartow in an order dated October 13, 1942. The Railway Post Office on trains 142 and 143 was renamed for the last time and became the Durbin and Ronceverte RPO.

The connecting service on the Western Maryland made a change of a more substantial nature in 1942. In September the railroad applied to the Public Service Commission to discontinue its trains 53 and 54 between Elkins and Durbin. In an order dated October 27 the

PSC denied this request due to the people living between Bowden and Durbin having no other form of transportation and the very poor roads. In late November the Western Maryland returned to the PSC with a request to substitute mixed freight and passenger service for the passenger train. Approval was given for this change in an order dated December 7, 1942.

During World War II, of course, with restrictions on the use of private vehicles, business was good for trains 142 and 143 on their runs up and down the Greenbrier River as it was for all passenger trains. But following the war it was only a matter of time before the small train on the Greenbrier would fall to the tax supported onslaught of the automobile, bus, and airplane.

Following the war there wasn't much change in the schedule of trains 142 and 143. The schedules for September 26, 1948, and April 27, 1952, were the same, as follows:

WEST 143		EAST 142
1:40 p.m.	Durbin	1:15 p.m.
2:10	Cass	12:23
3:03	Marlinton	11:23
4:10	Renick	10:08
5:00 p.m.	Whitcomb	9:10 a.m.

The schedule for October 28, 1956, was the same for No. 143, but the times for No. 142 were one hour and five minutes earlier.

In March of 1954 the Western Maryland Railway applied to the the Public Service Commission for permission to change its service to Durbin from a daytime schedule to a night schedule. At this time the railroad was in the process of switching to diesel locomotives and it wanted the change in schedule in order to dieselize its Elkins-Cumberland and Elkins-Durbin passenger services with the purchase of only two diesel locomotives. Under the proposed schedule the passenger service to Cumberland would operate during the day. After arriving back in Elkins from Cumberland at 6:20 p.m., the train would then depart for Durbin as No. 153 at 6:30 p.m., arriving in Durbin at 8:55 p.m. The return trip, as No. 154, would leave Durbin at 9:25 p.m. and arrive at Elkins at 11:55 p.m. The train to Durbin would remain mixed freight and passenger. The railroad claimed to be losing $90,000 a year on the Cumberland-Durbin service and stated to the PSC that the only alternative to this schedule change would be to seek total abandonment. By an order dated April 26, 1954, the PSC approved the change as of May 3.

This change in the Western Maryland schedule no doubt eliminated most, if not all, of the passengers who may have transferred from the train of one railroad in the Greenbrier Valley to the train of the other. It probably also eliminated most of the remaining passengers on trains 153 and 154. The final Western Maryland day schedule was:

Young men going off to war—special troop train in Marlinton on April 29, 1942. The locomotive is F-15 Class 4-6-2 No. 450.   PCHS

Unloading the mail from the RPO section of Motor Car No. 9055 at Marlinton on June 26, 1945. The 9055 and its coach were en route to Durbin when the photograph was taken and thus are Train No. 142.

Charles A. Brown

2356

Train time at Marlinton—June 26, 1945.

Charles A. Brown

| WEST | | EAST |
153		154
11:05 a.m.	Elkins	4:30 p.m.
1:30 p.m.	Durbin	2:00 p.m.

In 1956 a prediction of an increased number of passengers on the little train that ran along the Greenbrier River was made by a writer in Greenbrier County:

> The route along the river is justly considered one of the most scenic in the nation—though a nation has not discovered it yet, and our own people are too accustomed on the one hand and too unaccustomed on the other to recognize it. It has been obscured by the motor age and highways miss it.
>
> The day is probably not far off when people of the nation will discover the scenic enchantment that a trip up the Greenbrier Division affords. . . . . There will be a renaissance of travel on the Greenbrier Division.

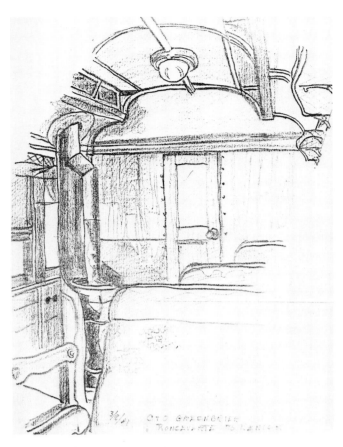

Interior of a Greenbrier coach. Drawn by Wendell A. Scott, March 8, 1941.

Although an attempt was made in the early 1970s to capitalize on the scenic beauty of the Greenbrier line, as will be related shortly, the 1950s were not the time for this automobile oriented society to discover the charm of. the ride on the train that ran to Durbin and back.

The fate of trains 142 and 143 was sealed in March of 1957 when the Post Office Department discontinued using the trains to carry the mail. The last day for mail service by train was March 8. The next month the Chesapeake and Ohio filed a request with the Public Service Commission to discontinue Nos. 142 and 143. Hearings were held on June 17 and July 8. The railroad testified that in the fifteen months from January 1, 1956, through March 1957, No. 142 had had a daily average of only 1.9 passengers per mile (averaging only slightly over eight passengers per day) and No. 143 had averaged only 1.5 passengers per mile daily (an average of not quite seven passengers per day). The railroad stated that revenue from the trains in 1956 was $21,645.06 from the mail contract but only $5,739 from passengers and express. To continue the service it was estimated that operating costs would be over $39,000 annually with revenue of less that $6,000.

Ironically, as rail passenger service in the Greenbrier Valley was nearing its end, the idea of through passenger service over the Chesapeake and Ohio and the Western

Maryland Railways reappeared. In January 1957 the Western Maryland filed with the Public Service Commission a request for permission to discontinue its trains 9 and 10 between Cumberland, Maryland, and Elkins. The PSC held a hearing on this request in February. However, following the hearings on the Chesapeake and Ohio's request to discontinue No. 142 and 143, the PSC held a number of meetings with the two railroads and their operating unions to explore the possibility of providing service between Ronceverte and Cumberland by a diesel rail car. The proposal was for three round trips per week, Ronceverte to Cumberland and return. However, numerous objections were raised to this idea and no way was found to reduce the cost to a reasonable level. The negotiations on this proposal were terminated near the end of November.

Not surprisingly, following the failure of the through service proposal and high cost/low use evidence presented by the railroads, the PSC approved the requests of both companies to abandon their passenger trains on or about January 6, 1958, by orders dated December 24, 1957. Among those who had objected to the discontinuance of the Chesapeake and Ohio trains were farmers who shipped milk to Ronceverte but arrangements were made for the tri-weekly freight train to handle these shipments.

The final runs of trains 142 and 143 were made on Wednesday, January 8, 1958. The crew on this day consisted of I.F. Clinebell, Conductor, C.M. Lynch, Engineer, J.H. Sims, Express Messenger, and J.M. Humphreys, Baggageman.

The final passenger schedule on the Greenbrier line was:

WEST 143		EAST 142
1:40 p.m.	Durbin	12:34 p.m.
f 1:53	Hosterman	f 12:01
2:10	Cass	11:42
2:30	Clover Lick	f 11:19
f 2:48	Clawson	f 10:57
3:03	Marlinton	10:42
3:27	Seebert	10:22
f 3:42	Beard	f 10:07
4:10	Renick	9:39
f 4:16	Spring Creek	9:32
f 4:32	Anthony	f 9:16
f 4:56	North Caldwell	8:50
5:00	Whitcomb	f 8:46
5:15 p.m.	Ronceverte	8:41 a.m.

Not shown on the schedule were flagstops at Camp Allegheny, Hooper, Loopemount, Keister, Woodman, Golden, Horrock, Rorer, Droop Mountain, Spice Run, Locust, Den Mar (sic), Burnsides, Kennison, Watoga, Violet, Buckeye, Stillwell, Thorny Creek, Harter, Big Run, Stony Bottom, Sitlington, Raywood, Wanless, Boyer, and Whiting.

Passenger service on the Western Maryland Railway from Elkins to Durbin continued for over a year longer. In early March 1958 the railroad applied to the Public

A-16 Class 4-4-2 No. 291 pulling the Greenbrier Branch passenger train while the usual motor car is in the shop. Photograph taken at Renick about 1947.   Wendell A. Scott

Train 143 approaching Renick as it makes its way from Durbin to Ronceverte, 1944.   Wendell A. Scott

Service Commission for permission to discontinue the passenger component of mixed trains 153 and 154. In its application the railroad claimed that No. 153 carried only 1.37 passengers per day in 1957 and No. 154 carried only 0.28 passengers per day that year. Revenue averaged $31 per month for No. 153 and $7.50 per month for No. 154. The Western Maryland also pointed out that since the Chesapeake and Ohio was now only running its freight train to Durbin on Monday, Wednesday, and Friday, it was having to run a train on Tuesday, Thursday, and Saturday for passengers only. The railroad claimed a $41,000 loss to run those three extra days.

In July the PSC issued an order requiring the Western Maryland to continue the service on Monday, Wednesday, and Friday. Being determined to eliminate all passenger service (the Durbin trains were the last passenger service on the Western Maryland), the railroad got the West Virginia Supreme Court to order a new PSC hearing. The result was a PSC order on March 31, 1959, authorizing total discontinuance of the passenger service. On Friday, April 10, 1959, Western Maryland trains 153 and 154 made their last runs as mixed trains and ended railroad passenger service in the Upper Greenbrier Valley.

The final schedule for these trains was:

WEST 153		EAST 154
6:30 p.m.	Elkins	11:55 p.m.
6:38	Canfield	11:44
6:47	Lumber	11:33
6:52	Meadows	11:28
6:55	Faulkner	11:25
6:59	Bowden	11:21
7:07	Weese	11:13
7:14	Flint	11:06
7:18	Walker	11:02
7:24	Bemis	10:56
7:34	Cheat Junction	10:46
7:43	Glady	10:37
7:53	Beulah	10:27
8:03	Wildell	10:17
8:19	May	10:01
8:47	Olive	9:33
8:55 p.m.	Durbin	9:25 p.m.

All the stations were flagstops except Elkins, Bowden, Bemis, Glady, and Durbin.

Following the ending of the last passenger service to Durbin, Mrs. P.F. Eades wrote in *The Marlinton Journal* as follows:

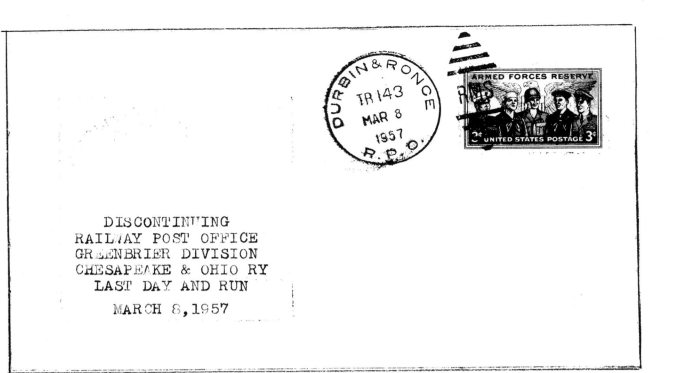

Last passenger train came into Durbin Friday, April 10. The writer has lived in Durbin for the past sixty years and saw the last log drive with its accompanying arks go down the Greenbrier River. Later saw the C&O railroad come into Durbin in 1902. Then some time later the (railroad) known (as the) Coal & Iron came into Durbin. E.D. Baker of Beverly, engineer, was in charge of this division and made his home with my parents, Mr. and Mrs. C.G. Sutton. Durbin is surely isolated now as no passenger trains, no bus line or no means of transportation unless one owns a car. It's not much better off than it was sixty years ago when we came here by covered wagon and in a carriage with a fringe around the top. The only difference is much better roads.

During the final twenty years of the life of the Greenbrier Subdivision, passenger carrying trains returned occasionally to the line, including an attempt to carry out the 1956 prediction of trains being operated for the scenic value of the line.

In May of 1967 the Greenbrier line was part of the route of an excursion which ran from Huntington to Elkins and return. Called the "West Virginia Highlands Special," the excursion was sponsored by the Collis P. Huntington Chapter of the National Railway Historical Society. The train ran to Elkins on May 13 and returned on the 14th. A Chesapeake and Ohio passenger diesel pulled the train, which was made up of four C. and O. sixty passenger coaches, a C. and O. baggage car, two Norfolk and Western gondola cars converted for passenger use, and the former Baltimore and Ohio Pullman car, "Emerald Waters," owned by the Huntington Chapter.

The following May saw what was no doubt the most impressive passenger train to ever operate over the Greenbrier line. Consisting of eleven sleeping cars, the train was sponsored by the National Railway Historical Society as part of the activities involved with the opening of the Cass Scenic Railroad from Whittaker Station to Bald Knob. Cars for the "Mountaineer Special" originated at Washington, D.C.; Louisville, Kentucky; Cincinnati, Ohio; Richmond, Virginia; Huntington, and Charleston and were brought to Hinton on May 24 as part of the Chesapeake and Ohio's "George Washington" passenger trains. Early on the morning of the 25th the cars left Hinton for Cass as a separate train, arriving in time for the dedication activities that day. The special train returned to Hinton on the afternoon of the 26th and the cars were returned to their cities of origin by the east and west bound "George Washingtons."

Recognizing the potential of the Greenbrier Subdivision as a route for a regular scenic train, a number of people in Greenbrier County began planning for a scenic railway operation from Ronceverte to Durbin in early 1970. Although initially it was hoped to make a few runs in 1970, train operations did not begin until 1971. Arrangements were made with Steam Tours, Inc., of Akron, Ohio, to operate the trains with their 4-8-4 steam locomotive, former Reading Railroad No. 2102. During the summer and fall of 1971 nine trips were operated between Ronceverte and Cass with the train going on to Durbin for turning. Engineer on No. 2102 on these runs was J.E. Hall, Jr.

The 1971 excursions proved popular and an expanded schedule of trips was set for the 1972 season. However, problems developed and the 1972 trips had to be cancelled.

To continue the trains, the operation went back to

strictly local people and the Greenbrier Scenic Railroad was organized. This organization operated excursions in the late summer and fall of 1973, the summer and fall of 1974, and the fall of 1975. These years the trains were powered by diesel locomotives.

Although the trains generally operated with a full load of passengers, rising costs and the plans by the Chesapeake and Ohio to close the Greenbrier Branch caused the 1975 season to be the last. The final run was on Saturday, October 18. The schedule for the 1975 trips was:

EAST		WEST
8:00 a.m.	Ronceverte	4:00 p.m.
9:50	Marlinton	2:45
10:55 a.m.	Cass	1:30 p.m.

Motor Car No. 9055 at Ronceverte prior to its departure up the Greenbrier Branch, about 1952. Note the changes in No. 9055 between this photograph and the photos on page 81. In 1949 the passenger section of the car was reduced in size, a diesel engine replaced the gas engine, and a new paint scheme was applied.   C&O Railway photo/COHS

Train 143 at Renick, 1950s.   Wendell A. Scott

Daily Train From Ronceverte To Durbin Makes Last Run

Chesapeake & Ohio Railroad Co. employes (sic) and a passenger are shown on the passenger station platform at Marlinton Wednesday as the passenger train which is operated daily over the Greenbrier Branch from Ronceverte to Durbin made its last run. Shown left to right, are J.H. Sims, of Ronceverte, express messenger, who has worked intermittenly on the branch since 1924; C.M. Lynch of Ronceverte, engineer, who has been in railroad service for 50 years, mostly on the Greenbrier Branch; J.M. Humphreys of Hinton, baggageman, who has been working as an extra employe (sic) for the railroad for only a short time; I.F. Clinebell of Ronceverte, conductor, who has been in the service of the Chesapeake and Ohio Railroad for over 50 years on the Greenbrier Branch, except four years on the main line; Gephart Geiger of Stony Bottom, who was a passenger train which is operated daily over the Greenbrier Branch from Ronceverte to Durbin made its last run. Shown left to right, are J.H. Sims, of Ronceverte, express manager, who has worked intermittently on the branch since 1924; C.M. Lynch of Ronceverte, engineer, who has

The railroad company was recently granted permission by the West Virginia Public Service Commission to discontinue passenger service on the Greenbrier Branch after it was shown that the company was losing a large amount of money yearly by keeping the train in operation.

From Beckley (W.Va.) Post-Herald, January 11, 1958

CHAPTER VI
Accidents

ALTHOUGH GREAT STRIDES IN SAFETY HAD BEEN made in railroading in the latter part of the nineteenth century, with the use of air brakes and automatic couplers being two of the major innovations, it was still a fairly dangerous occupation as the new century opened. The Greenbrier line turned out to be safe for passengers, but, unfortunately, the same was not true for employees and those who were uninvited visitors to railroad property.

In the little over seventy-eight years of the existence of the Greenbrier Branch at least thirty-six people were killed as a result of train operations. Of these, fourteen were railroad employees and only one was a passenger. Of the rest, most were either people trying to hop a ride on a moving train or people under the influence of alcohol who wandered onto the tracks at the wrong time. Two fatal accidents involved a train and a road vehicle.

As would be expected, the causes of accidents were varied. Slides were a continuous problem for many years and caused a fair share of accidents and train delays. Other causes included broken rails, rotten ties, rolling stock failure, and on at least two occasions, animals on the track. In short, it was impossible to operate a busy, single-track railroad, that at times was not maintained as well as it should have been, without at least a few accidents. To the credit of the men who were actually responsible for the operation of the trains on the Greenbrier, none of the accidents seems to have been the result of employee negligence. Two definite cases of deliberate attempts to cause accidents have been located but fortunately neither was successful.

1900-1910

The first accident found by the author involving a fatality due to regular train operations on the Greenbrier line occurred in late 1900, probably in November. The accident happened in Greenbrier County. A brakeman, name not given in the news account, was standing between two freight cars with a foot on each when they became uncoupled and he fell between them. Both legs were cut off and he lived but a few hours.

A brakeman lost both feet in an accident north of Sharps Tunnel on the night of December 9, 1900. Jack Lilliard was riding on a boxcar, the first of eight cars of construction material being pushed by engine No. 334. In the big curve above the tunnel the car jumped the track and went into the river. Lilliard jumped to the hillside as the car left the rails, but fell back on the track. The front truck of the next car passed over his feet.

One of the deliberate attempts to cause an accident occurred in early 1901. The track was completed to Cass but regular service had not been extended to that point. Engineer Charles I. Smith remembered the incident after his retirement as follows:

> "As an incentive to the trainmen, the chief engineer was allowing an extra day for each man who would run a train of flat cars from Marlinton to Cass and return with a load of logs. One day I thought I would try it, and had proceeded only a short way out of Marlinton when a man flagged the train near the entrance to a tunnel and told me there were rails across the track. I eased the train to a stop and sure enough five or six rails were piled across the tracks on the other side of the tunnel. If that man had not flagged us, we would have gone into the river. The people up there didn't want the railroad and this was a deliberate move to halt it."*

Train operations caused three deaths in 1901, in addition to the two deaths associated with construction work that year. On March 3, a Chesapeake and Ohio employee, Ernest G. Chattin, about 18, attempted to board the caboose of a moving freight train at Forrest (Sitlington) and fell under the wheels. His left thigh was badly crushed. He was brought to Marlinton but was injured beyond the powers of Drs. Cunningham and Marshall to save him and he died that evening. Mr. Chattin was part of the carpenter force on the railroad.

The second death caused by train operations in 1901 was that of John Burr, 46. Mr. Burr, a brakeman, fell from a car near North Caldwell on April 16 and was seriously injured. He died in the Clifton Forge Hospital the next day.

A collision between engine No. 85 and a hand car on November 23 resulted in the death of William Walker. The accident occurred in a curve above Cass. Mr. Walker was thrown from the car against the engine and received head and leg injuries. He died on the passenger train while en route from Cass to the hospital in Ronceverte.

The first wreck involving a passenger train located by the author occurred in December of 1901. The engine

*Arrit, Gay, *Historical Sketches of the Allegheny Highlands*. (Allegheny Historical Society, Covington, Virginia, 1982), page 129.

Passenger train No. 143 and a freight train stuck in the snow at Droop Mountain on February 8 and 9, 1905. Photograph taken by Mrs. Virginia Clark Sharp.

Mrs. Ruth Sharp Beebe

and mail car of train 142 were derailed on the 13th at Keister. The lower switch to the passing siding was partly open causing the engine to attempt to ride on both tracks at once. By the tone of the news report whatever had caused the switch to be improperly aligned must not have been considered a deliberate attempt to cause an accident. There were no injuries but the wreck train from Clifton Forge was required to get the train on its way again, six hours late.

The following year, 1902, was another tragic one with three deaths. A freight wreck on March 25 resulted in the death of Greenbrier Division Trainmaster B.T. Dixon and serious injuries to the fireman, Daniel Sherwood. The train, traveling downriver, hit a rock on the track four miles above North Caldwell and the engine and tender left the track and went into the river. Mr. Dixon was caught by the tender and crushed. He died early the next morning from the injuries in the Clifton Forge Hospital. The engineer jumped clear and was not hurt.

A brakeman by the name of Hayes McDowell was fatally injured when he fell between the cars of his freight train at Renick on either September 11 or 12. He lost a leg and suffered other injuries from which he died the following day.

The final railroad related death in 1902 was that of Lee Collins, about 21, on November 26 at Hosterman. He

was participating in the "sport" of jumping on and off the man stop and was thrown under the wheels when he attempted to jump off. Both legs were cut off and his death resulted.

A demolished locomotive and eight freight cars in the river were the results of a freight train hitting a tree on the tracks on June 7, 1902. The accident occurred near Beard. The engineer and fireman escaped injury but the two brakemen and the conductor suffered minor injuries.

One death marred train operations in 1903. Emory Weiford, about 20, was killed instantly on October 7 at the Marlinton depot. He attempted to board train 144 as it was leaving the station and fell under the wheels.

Late in August 1903 dynamite was found on the Greenbrier line track in Pocahontas County sufficient in quantity to wreck a train. Note was made of a similar incident on the logging railroad on Cheat Mountain about two years previously. The exact location of the dynamite was not given in the news account. Fortunately it was found by a track walker and the next train flagged before striking the dynamite.

The Greenbrier Division escaped another fatal accident until 1905 when one of the worst accidents involving a passenger train occurred. On April 25 a tree fell in passenger trains as they were leaving stations. He leapt on a coach as the train was pulling away from its Hoster-

front of the evening passenger train to Durbin (No. 144) as it approached Hosterman. The engine went into the river and the two cars, a baggage car and a coach, turned over on their sides, caught fire, and burned. Albertus A. Culp, 27, a Chesapeake and Ohio main line fireman who was riding in the cab to his home in Durbin, was killed. Uriah Bird, of Marlinton, was the most seriously injured of the passengers, suffering internal injuries. Engineer C.H. Dean and Fireman J.A. Cooper suffered cuts and bruises. The West Virginia Pulp and Paper Company operated a special train to bring the injured back to Cass. From there they were brought to the Marlinton hospital by a special train sent from Ronceverte. (The engine involved in this wreck, Class A 4-4-0 No. 42, was credited with the deaths of seven men, counting Mr. Culp, to this date.)

The engine, tender, and four cars of passenger train No. 142 were derailed on July 4, 1905, a mile above Marlinton but there were no injuries. The cause of the wreck was a rail loosened by a tree sliding onto the track.

The dangerous mixture of alcohol and railroads was the probable cause of the one death in 1906. A lumberman named Jack Brown was hit at Cass by one of the passenger trains on February 10 and died from his injuries the next day. He had been drinking and sat down close to the track. Both legs and one arm were cut off by the train.

Two deaths occurred in 1907, including the only death of a passenger in the history of the Greenbrier line. An employee of the Warn Lumber Company, Morris Johnson, 24, was killed on April 17 when he jumped from a moving passenger train at the lumber company's switch near Seebert to save the walk back from the Seebert station. He was fatally injured by hitting his head on a rock.

A hobo named Phillips was killed in a freight train wreck near Wanless on May 8. A number of the cars went into the river. This was not a good day for railroading in the Greenbrier Valley, as the wrecking train, en route to this accident, put four cars in the ditch a mile above Whitcomb. Finally, a Western Maryland Railway engine, coming to transfer passengers around the freight wreck, derailed at Burner above Durbin.

There were also two deaths in 1908, both of company employees. On June 25 Charles Marks, 35, tender of the coal tipple at Marlinton, was fatally hurt when hit by a freight car. He was at work near the tipple and stepped aside to let a switch engine pass. His attention was on the engine and, being hard of hearing, he did not notice the approach of a car that had been shifted onto the track that he was standing on. He died the same day from his injuries.

A brakeman named Powell, about 30, died of injuries received on July 24. He was riding on the steps of the tender of an engine pushing a car up to the tipple of the rock quarry near Renick. Somehow he fell off and was caught by the locomotive's driving rods, throwing him against a rock cliff. He was immediately taken to Ronceverte where a special train was being prepared to take him to the hospital but he died just as Ronceverte was reached.

The final death during the first decade of the history of the Greenbrier line was that of engineer Charles H. Dean, one of the original passenger engineers on the line. His train, No. 141, was approaching Durbin from Winterburn early on the morning of February 8, 1910, when it hit two large bulls on the track, opposite the tannery. One bull was shoved aside, but the other one, weighing 1900 pounds, derailed the engine. The tender smashed against the cab and caught Mr. Dean and Tom Gilhooley, the fireman. Mr. Dean died from his injuries on February 14 at the Hinton Hospital. Mr. Gilhooley had his left arm cut off but survived. At least one passenger car was derailed but there were no injuries among the passengers.

During the 1905-1907 time period the lives of the men operating trains on the Greenbrier Division must have become very harried from wondering where and when the next derailment was going to occur. Passengers probably also began to wonder what the odds might be that their trip would be completed within a reasonable approximation of the hour (or day) that the schedule called for. Over forty derailments and delays made it into the pages of the local papers from the middle of 1905 through 1907 and these were certainly not all that occurred.

Slides were a continuing problem as they would be for many years until the hillsides that were disturbed by the construction work finally stabilized. Blame was also placed on the railroad operating trains on the Division of a greater length than track with numerous curves could safely handle. However, the major cause of the problems during these years was the deterioration of the ties. When the Greenbrier line was constructed, ties were not treated in any way and thus their life expectancy was only a few years. By 1906 the original ties on the Greenbrier line were nearing the end of their lives at a time of increasing traffic. Judging by the newspaper accounts of the period, the Chesapeake and Ohio must have let tie replacement fall way behind the rate of tie deterioration.

By late 1906 the situation was such that the local papers were becoming very blunt in their criticism of the railroad's management and urged the populace to write Chesapeake and Ohio President George Stevens concerning the dangerous condition of the ties.

A correspondent to the *Marlinton Messenger* in early 1907 pointed out that passengers who knew the true condition of the track sat in the back of the coaches ready to jump. A writer to *The Pocahontas Times* from Harter a year earlier had a different sort of complaint. Track crews had taken rails from the track into the Harter sawmill in order to make track repairs and cut the mill off from rail service for a week.

The public outcry brought Mr. Stevens and his entourage on an inspection trip up the Greenbrier Division on January 2, 1907. Although the editors of both Marlinton papers commented on his ability to find tight spikes and sound ties, Mr. Stevens did give assurance that a major program of tie replacement was scheduled for 1907. A portion of the report of *The Pocahontas Times* on Mr. Stevens' trip went as follows:

President Stevens, General Manager Doyle, and a number of lesser lights, of the Chesapeake & Ohio Railway Company, came up the Division Wednesday on a tour of inspection. We do not know the impression they carried back as they came in their well appointed private cars, and may not have been moved to echo the sentiments of a bone racked passenger of one of our passenger trains who gravely asked the conductor why rails were not laid on some of the ties to make traveling easier. And then too they carried their rations with them, and were not harassed by the fear of missing a meal on account of the time limit of six miles an hour on a certain piece of track.

While Mr. Stevens was here he had a word with us, and gave us a seegar which made a pretty fair smoke. While too politic to admit that the road was not in first class condition, and went so far as to point out to us certain and sundry ties which would have been a credit to a trunk line. He said that work of renewing the track would go steadily forward, and that so much had not been done this season as was contemplated on account of the bad weather. A requisition has been made for sixty thousand new ties, sufficient to lay about a fourth of the entire line. He assured us that the present rail would be replaced by heavier steel, and that at least fifteen miles would be laid this year. Some of this would be put at the lower end, and a part near Marlinton. We were admonished to treat the railroad fairly and we believe we have always done so. Our airing the matter of the bad condition of the line at this time was prompted by no other motive than to get ties that will not crush and run splinters in our feet when we walk on the track on the Greenbrier Division.

Mr. Stevens is a tall, big handsome, gray haired man, a born figure with an air which distinguishes him from those of us who have debts and the devil to pay and know it. He has evidently cultivated the habit of appearing to see only the brighter and better things of life, for in walking over a short distance of track he would find and comment on the tight spikes and the sound ties though they numbered but one in five. What a horse trader he would have made.

However, the railroad must have been slow to carry out the promises of its president as the situation was not improved by the middle of the year. In June, according to *The Times*, the number of wrecks averaged one every other day from one cause or another with seven wrecks and a number of slides in one ten-day period. The paper minced no words in assigning the blame to "The niggardly policy which of late years has characterized the management of the C. and O." in allowing the track on the Greenbrier line to deteriorate. In addition to bad track conditions, blame for accidents was placed on using old, worn-out rolling stock, loaded beyond its original capacity. It was hoped that now that the good working weather was available, "the railway company will put in play their much vaunted, twentieth century ability to accomplish things and give us a road bed that will not unduly endanger the lives of the traveling public nor their faithful servants." The willingness of the railroad to sustain the financial losses due to the accidents instead of spending the money to repair the track was also a source of wonder to *The Times* as was its callous disregard for the safety of passengers and employees.

But by later in the year things did improve on the Greenbrier line as the railroad finally did go to work on a maintenance and rebuilding program. In the middle of

July it was reported that heavier rail was being laid between Cass and Durbin as well as on the lower section of the line, ties were being installed on all sections, and slag ballast was being hauled in.

President Stevens had gone over the line again on June 24 and perhaps this had spurred the responsible officials to get to work.

By October it was reported that 50,000 new ties had been laid, over twenty miles of heavier rail laid, and about 300 cars of slag ballast put down. By the next year (1908) trains were operating on the Greenbrier Division with a minimum of problems.

President Stevens made his third visit to the Greenbrier Division during the year when he and other officials came over the line on a tour of inspection on December 3.

Not all traffic tie-ups could be blamed on the lack of maintenance by the Chesapeake and Ohio, of course; Mother Nature had to take a share of the blame over the years. A case in point was a snow and sleet storm of monumental proportions that hit the Greenbrier Valley on February 8, 1905. This storm brought traffic on the Greenbrier line to a complete halt and trapped passenger train 143 for twenty-four hours in a snowdrift at Droop Mountain. The train, en route to Ronceverte, had been fighting snowdrifts for miles until finally reaching a drift that proved too much for the 4-4-0 locomotive. It could go neither forward nor backward. A thirty-five car freight train was also trapped just ahead of the passenger train. Drifts were soon above the car windows and a long, cold night was soon upon the forty passengers.

The nearest extra engine was at Cass and it took ten hours to arrive. By daylight over a hundred men were at work and the track was cleared to the Droop station, a distance of two miles. The cars were so drifted in that they could be loosened from snow only one at a time. To free the baggage car the two engines had to back off and ram it. It was supper time before the work was completed and the train arrived at Renick. It was then on to Ronceverte, only about thirty-six hours late.

Among the passengers on the snowbound train were a couple on their honeymoon, Mr. and Mrs. Charles McCoy, from Wanless. To help pass the time during the long night, a glee club was organized.

Mrs. Ruth Sharp Beebe was on the train as a child of 10 and recalled the snowbound night in 1979 as follows:

My mother, Virginia (Jennie) Clark Sharp, my sister Mary, and I had been visiting my grandmother, Annie Clark, at what was known then as Academy, now called Hillsboro. My sister and I attended the schools there until time to return home, which is Wyoming.

It was a dreary day when we boarded the little train at Seebert, I think. All went well until we reached Droop Mountain. It was snowing hard, and if I remember, there was a river just below us. As we were going round the mountain, the snow became master of the situation and we came to a grinding halt. There was much confusion, maybe the train would be pushed into the river. I think it was about 4 p.m. and darkness soon came upon us. I remember well the bride and groom, Mr. and Mrs. McCoy. To a child of ten years the idea of being marooned on a train in a snow storm, and having a group of people serenading you most of the night brings back a romantic dream not soon forgotten.

My grandmother had sent along a bounteous lunch of fried chicken, sandwiches, etc., and my aunt, Mrs. Rella Yeager, had made macaroon cookies, all of which my mother had us divide with other children on the train. The next morning the conductor took mother to the baggage car. She got her cameras out of the trunk packed to go west. Some of the men pulled her through the snow, up the side of the mountain, and she took the pictures I am enclosing.

Over the miles and through the years that incident has stayed very vividly in my memory, also the beautiful times I had that winter in West Virginia. . . . When mother complained of the weather in Wyoming we would remind her of the time she was snowbound in West Virginia.

Other wrecks could be blamed on neither the railroad or Mother Nature. On May 8, 1906, train 148, the through freight from Ronceverte, was slowing at Boyer to set off cars when suddenly an engine, running without cars or crews, came out of the darkness and struck the train. Fortunately, although both engines were badly damaged and four freight cars demolished, there were no injuries to the crew other than cuts and bruises. The lone engine had come from Durbin but how was the question of the hour. The finding of a cap and hat soon led authorities to two men, Walter Jones and Fred Halt. It turned out that they wanted to visit a friend at Hosterman and decided the quickest and cheapest way to get there was to take the engine. They got the engine watchman at Durbin drunk and took off, neglecting, however,

to consult with a timetable to see if the way was clear. They jumped off the engine when they saw the train at Boyer.

Human error was the cause of what might have been a disastrous accident on July 19, 1909. Passenger train 143 was at Marlinton ready to leave and no word had been heard from a northbound freight that had passed Seebert some time before. On the assumption that the freight had taken the siding at Buckeye, although it had no orders to do so, the passenger train was allowed to depart. On the long stretch of track below Marlinton the two trains came in sight of each other with time to stop. With over 300 people on the passenger train, had they met in a curve the death toll in the resulting wreck could have been high. The freight had been delayed north of Buckeye by a horse stuck in a bridge and had encroached on the passenger train's time in getting it loose. However, it still had the "block" and with nowhere to side track, it came on.

One of the worst slides on the Chesapeake and Ohio occurred on the Greenbrier line at Woodman (two miles north of Anthony) on April 7, 1910. The slide started some 470 feet above the track and was eighteen to forty feet deep on the rails. It took a force of one hundred men and a steam shovel over a week to clear the slide as material would come in as fast as it was removed. Passengers, mail, and express could be transferred, but freight service was totally cut off until the thousands of cubic yards of material were removed.

Wreck of Train No. 141 at Frank on February 8, 1910, caused by two bulls on the track. Engineer Charles H. Dean died of injuries received in the wreck.
PCHS

This photograph fits the description of a wreck at Milepost 59 (north of Marlinton) on September 26, 1910. The fireman suffered minor injuries while the engineer escaped without injury.
PCHS

1911-1920

Although there were no passenger fatalities or even serious injuries of passengers in the second decade of the history of the Greenbrier line there were several potentially bad accidents involving passenger trains.

On January 21, 1911, a rock rolled in front of train 141 below Stony Bottom giving engineer R.P. Boyd no time to stop. The engine, 4-4-0 No. 65, derailed and went into the river and the baggage car was derailed. Mr. Boyd received only cuts and bruises but fireman D. M. O'Leary was badly scalded and cut. None of the passengers was injured.

A slide near Spice Run derailed the engine and tender of train 144 about a week later, on January 29, 1911. The coaches remained on the track and the passengers escaped with only a good shaking up. The engineer, Windy Marcus, and fireman were slightly injured.

Engineer J.M. Sampson, the regular engineer on Nos. 142 and 143, had bad luck on two Fridays in a row in August 1912 at almost the same location below Wanless. On August 2 the engine of train 143 suddenly left the rails for no apparent reason and went into the river. Mr. Sampson was not hurt and the fireman, Ray Kincaid, suffered slight injuries. On the following Friday, the 9th, the same thing happened with the same train. This time the cause was a cow that came plunging out of the brush immediately in front of the engine. The same cow had been on the track in the morning as the train went up

river but the train was able to stop. It seemed as if the cow had lain in wait for the train to make its return trip. Mr. Sampson was again not injured but fireman McNunly suffered a broken ankle. No passengers were hurt in either accident.

Passenger train 143 and freight train 146 nearly had a head on collision on August 18, 1913, at Big Run, with the engines coming within about three rail lengths of each other before stopping. The freight engineer, new to the line, had orders to take the side track at Clawson but misunderstood and thought the orders meant Clover Lick.

Two cars of the morning train from Ronceverte, No. 142, were derailed just above Spice Run on October 20, 1914. The rails spread under the express car, derailing it and the baggage/smoking car following. Several passengers were shaken up but none seriously injured.

The luck of the Greenbrier line held in two passenger train wrecks in 1916. On the 11th of January, train 141 had its engine and tender derailed by a broken rail just north of Burnsides. The cause of the break was a large rock which slid from the hillside, struck the inside rail, bounced clear of the outside rail, and went into the river. The quick reaction of the engineer, Thomas Surber, prevented the entire train from leaving the track. Neither he, the fireman, Fred Mitchell, nor any of the passengers were injured.

On December 21, 1916, the evening train from Winterburn, No. 143, arrived at Marlinton without its three coaches. A rail had broken beneath the train about one and one-half miles north of town. At least one car went into the river but there were no serious injuries. "It shook them up good and addled their brains and curdled their blood, but beyond this it was only a question of a wrecking crew." The train continued on to Ronceverte after borrowing a car from No. 144 when it arrived on its way up river.

A wreck on the evening of April 13, 1920, resulted in the engine and baggage car of train 144 going into the river upside down and the forward coach derailed and lodged against a telephone pole. The accident, which happened just above Clawson, was caused by an immense stone slipping from the hillside and pushing the track over. Almost miraculously only the express messenger William Stone, and one passenger, Joseph Gilliam, were injured, as the train was crowded. Their injuries were minor. They were brought to the Marlinton hospital on a relief train made up of the engine from the Marlinton tannery and a box car.

Tragically, however, deaths did continue to occur due to train operations on the Greenbrier Division. The body of John Thompson, 56, was found on the track near Boyer on October 27, 1911. Drinking was given the blame for his being hit by a train. He was a foreman for the Brushy Run Lumber Company.

Deaths from the collisions of trains and road vehicles, although more common since the start of the age of the automobile, have occurred since the beginning of railroads. The Marlinton depot was the site of such an accident on July 4, 1912. Albert Shaheen, about 30, drove his carriage in front of train 142 and died soon after from head injuries. Mr. Shaheen was a peddler and had pursued his business in Marlinton for a number of years.

Drunkenness was blamed for the death of George B. Hillis on November 23, 1913. He was struck by passenger train 141 that morning at Watoga and died from the injuries he received that afternoon.

An attempt to board a moving freight train at Stony Bottom resulted in the death of Robert Burns, 24, of Highland County, Virginia, on November 13, 1914. He was thrown under the wheels of the train.

Earlier in the same month, on the 3rd, Charles Drummond, of Weston, West Virginia, was seriously injured at Durbin. He was running beside a Western Maryland passenger train when he was knocked under the slow moving train. Mr. Drummond suffered a broken arm and leg as well as facial injuries.

A Chesapeake and Ohio track worker was killed in an accident on April 13, 1915. Lewis Harding, 17, was on a motor car when it derailed a mile below Hosterman. The seven man crew was thrown off and Mr. Harding hit his head on either a rail or a tie. An angle bar falling off of the motor car was the cause of the accident. Two of the other men were injured.

One of the most tragic deaths in the history of the Greenbrier line occurred on May 24, 1915, at the Buckeye station. Maggie Higgenbotham was attempting to cross the track in front of the engine of train 142 as it was pulling into the station when she stumbled and fell. The engine ran over her, causing instant death. Miss Higgenbotham was on her way to Marlinton to visit her mother in the hospital when the accident happened.

The all too common attempt to board a moving train was the cause of another death on May 31, 1916. Frank Alderman, 22, attempted to get on a freight train at Denmar and was thrown under the wheels. It was the same story with the death of a twelve-year-old Italian boy at Deer Creek on July 23, 1918. He was trying to take a train ride and fell under the wheels.

On August 30, 1917, Fred Lightner, 22, fell under the wheels of a moving freight train at Thorny Creek. He was lucky, however, and only lost a leg instead of his life. A four-year-old son of Patsy Anastasio was seriously injured when hit by a passenger train at Big Run on November 15, 1918.

Tragedy struck on January 28, 1919, when two Chesapeake and Ohio section men were killed when their motor car collided with freight train No. 145 in a curve just above the Anthony Station. Killed were Section Foreman Bryant and James Knight with a third man badly hurt. They knew the train was approaching and it was speculated that high wind may have kept them from hearing the train in time to get their motor car off the track.

By late 1912 the effects of what must have been another period of insufficient maintenance were beginning to show. Any of the original ties still in place would have been years beyond their useful life and many of those put down during the 1907-08 period would have been approaching old age. Slides also remained a problem. In addition to the passenger train accidents already described, some twenty-three derailments and delays were mentioned in the Marlinton papers from the last part of 1912 through 1914 with the condition of the track being given as the cause in many cases. By the middle of 1914 the deteriorated condition of the Greenbrier Division seems to have come to the attention of officials at a high enough level to accelerate tie replacement and other needed maintenance. A special train brought a group of railroad officials up the Greenbrier line on June 8 on a tour of inspection.

Perhaps a complaint filed in May 1914 with the Public Service Commission by C.P. Dorr, of Marlinton, had helped to awaken the Chesapeake and Ohio to the fact that a problem existed on the Greenbrier line. The PSC report notes: "Matter given immediate attention by Railway Company."

Regardless of the reason, by April of 1915 *The Pocahontas Times* was able to report that 54,000 new ties had been installed and ballasting greatly improved. Heavier rail was also scheduled to be placed on ten more miles to complete rail replacement from Durbin to Marlinton. Chesapeake and Ohio President Stevens made an inspection trip on the Division in early April.

This repair work had the desired result of reducing the number of accidents and improving train service throughout the rest of the decade.

1921-1940

Due to the extensive maintenance and improvement work done on the Greenbrier line from the late teens until the early 1930s (see Chapter Three), train operations were relatively free from wrecks and derailments during the next twenty years of the life of the Greenbrier, even with the greatly increased traffic of the 1920s.

All was not perfect, of course. On Thursday night, August 9, 1923, what must have been a tremendous cloudburst hit the area between Renick and Anthony and put the line out of commission until the following Wednesday morning due to slides. The report on the slides gave the following:

• Mile 13—slide 60 feet long and 15 feet deep; slide 75 feet long and 20 feet deep.

• Mile 14—bridge gone; 1500 feet of track gone.

• Mile 16—Slides 60' by 2'; 60' by 5'.

• Mile 19—slides 300' by 20'; 250' by 15'; 60' by 10'; 200' by 45'; 60' by 4'; 150' by 15'; 70' by 10'; 150' by 15'; 60' by 5'; 75' by 10'; 30' by 5'; 20' by 2'; 300' by 20'; 250' by 15'; 60' by 10'.

• Mile 20—slides 100' by 3'; 130' by 5'; 200' by 10'; 200' by 5'.

• Mile 21—slides 30' by 2'; 40' by 3'; 75' by 2'; 24' by 5'; 20' by 4'; 30' by 5'.

At least four steam shovels were used to clear the slides, including one provided by the West Virginia Pulp and Paper Company at Cass.

What was certainly the most spectacular wreck in the history of the Greenbrier line occurred on May 4, 1925, when one span of the bridge across the river at Watoga collapsed. That morning an up river manifest freight, with sixty-two cars and two engines, was approaching the bridge when a boxcar loaded with brick near the middle of the train derailed. This car bounced along the ties for a short distance and then hit the edge of the bridge, causing one span to drop into the river. The car of bricks remained on the ground but four cars dropped with the bridge, three going into the river and the other hanging into the water from the bridge abutment. Two of these cars contained flour which Benton Smith remembers as being "Larabee's Best" from Kansas City, in 200 pound bags and en route to Italy. Mr. Smith also recalled to the author using his boat to ferry workmen, mail, and passengers while a temporary bridge was being built. The Western Maryland Railway also sent men and equipment to help.

Only two references have been found to wrecks involving passenger trains in this twenty year period. On

Aftermath of the wreck at the bridge across the Greenbrier River at Watoga on May 4, 1925.

PCHS

Freight cars derailed near the water tank in Renick, August 1928.   Wendell A. Scott

January 21, 1926, the morning train from Durbin (no. 141) struck a rock on the track a short distance below Sitlington. The engine and a coach were damaged and the conductor, Captain Cowherd, was injured when he was thrown across a seat.

The same train, No. 141, was partially derailed on March 11, 1930, just north of Cass due to an open switch. Although it was necessary to bring in the wreck train to get the engine back on the track, no injuries resulted from the accident.

One end of the Cass depot was damaged about 1929 when a freight car rammed into it. The car was being allowed to roll into the depot siding when its brakes failed. The result was a caved in wall on the depot freight room.

Unfortunately, deaths continued to mar train operations on the Greenbrier line. On March 30, 1926, Chester Nottingham, 18, died from injuries received the evening before. He had fallen under a freight train at Boyer and both legs were cut off about the knees.

The body of Dave T. Corbett, of Washington, D.C., was found on the morning of February 20, 1929, by the track walker below Cass, near the extract plant. He had been run over by a freight train that had passed shortly before his body was found.

Albert O'Brien, 29, of Cass, died on August 13, 1929, from injuries he suffered the day before at Durbin. He

had ridden a freight train to Durbin and fell under the wheels when he attempted to get off before the train had stopped. Both of his legs were cut off. Ironically, his father had also been killed by being run over by a train in the Cass yard about twenty-three years previously.

A train/car collision on December 26, 1930, left one person dead and another seriously injured. Victor Wood was blinded by snow and drove in front of a passenger train at Bartow. He was badly injured and his mother, Florence, 67, of Mingo, was killed in the accident.

On July 29, 1933, Zed Phillips, 14, was hit and killed by a freight train near Denmar "while asleep near the track."

Lincoln E. Spankle, 36, was killed in a similar fashion on September 1, 1934. He was lying on the track below Watoga and was hit by the down passenger train, No. 143. A Civilian Conservation Corps member, his home was in East Palatine, Ohio.

The engine of a down freight train struck and killed John W. Hayslett, Sr., on July 19, 1938. He was walking on the track near his home in Marlinton and it was thought that deafness prevented him from hearing the train approach.

In the early part of December 1940, Gordon Sanford, of Rainelle, was hit by a train near Clover Lick while deer hunting. He died from his injuries a few hours following the accident.

Carl Smith lost a leg to a train in Marlinton on October 3, 1936. He had gone to sleep on the track and a night freight, which had become rare by this time, crushed his leg.

A track walker on the Clover Lick Section, William A. Barlow, 57, was seriously injured on October 23, 1939, when his velocipede was hit by a freight train in the first curve below Clover Lick.

A confrontation between a train and a billy goat ended in a draw in March of 1937. A few miles south of Durbin the goat took offense at the passenger train coming along and tried to butt the gas/electric motor car off the track. The train was stopped and the crew expected to find the remains of the goat spread along the track. Instead, it was found caught on the front of the car by its horns. Freed, the goat took off, unharmed.

1941-1978

The last fatalities on the Greenbrier Branch occurred in 1941 and 1942.

Roland Swisher, c. 30, was hit by a train and killed near his home near Cass on December 16, 1941.

The year 1942 was a tragic one, with three deaths.

A landslide was the cause of an accident between Spice Run and Locust on Friday, May 22, in which the engineer was killed. Involved was an H Class 2-6-6-2 locomotive, No. 1486, which was traveling down river with only a caboose. The engine was 0.1 miles south of milepost 37 when it struck (or maybe was struck by) a slide in a curve at 3:30 a.m. The engine was derailed, rolled down the embankment, and came to rest on its right side, partly

H-6 Class 2-6-6-2 No. 1486 in the rain-swollen Greenbrier River after it hit a slide on the track just south of milepost 37, between Locust and Spice Run, early on the morning of May 22, 1942.   PCHS

Photograph taken during the process of removing No. 1486 from the river.   COHS

Three cranes working on wreck of H-6 No. 1486 on the Greenbrier Subdivision near Beard, W. Va., May 22, 1942.   COHS

Wrecking crane that overturned during the effort to remove engine No. 1486 from the river.   COHS

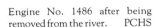

Engine No. 1486 after being removed from the river.   PCHS

submerged in the river. The tender remained coupled to the engine and went over the embankment also. The caboose was derailed and came to a stop on its left side, but did not go over the bank. The slide occurred either just before or as the engine arrived at the site, as a track patrolman passed the spot on foot only minutes before the train arrived. It was raining at the time of the accident and had been for several days. The slide covered about 101 feet of the track and its greatest depth on the track was 5½ feet.

Elba W. Lane, 51, of Hinton, the engineer, was killed. Injured were fireman George Smith, of Hinton, with burns, Conductor Robert Kincaid, of Covington, Virginia, Brakeman Brady Cales, of Hinton, and Flagman Con Murphy, of Ronceverte. The last three men all suffered cuts and bruises. The crew had taken a through freight to Durbin and were returning to Hinton when the accident occurred.

Later on the day of the accident one of the large steam wrecking cranes brought to remove the engine upset into the river. Its operator, Arthur Dolan, of Ronceverte, was severely injured.

In order to remove the locomotive, a track was laid on the embankment beside the engine. It was lifted onto this track and pulled back onto the main track. Train service on the Greenbrier line was delayed until about 1 p.m. on Sunday, May 24.

The body of George Wilson, 20, of Clover Lick, was found along the track between mileposts 59 and 60, north of Marlinton, on the morning of July 17, 1942. It was believed that he was either sitting or asleep on the track and hit by a train about 10:30 the night before.

Herman Erwin, 58, a Track Patrolman, was killed on December 3, 1942, near Anthony. His motor car was hit by the morning passenger train.

In July or August of 1943 one of the big 2-6-6-2 freight

engines derailed in the Cass yard near the water tank. The engine was coming from Durbin with only a caboose when the accident occurred at a switch. The cause of the wreck was believed to have been the improper closing of the switch by a Mower Lumber Company employee.

The last wreck of consequence on the Greenbrier line occurred on February 18, 1958. Twelve cars of the down river freight, including four cars of explosives were derailed at 12:10 p.m. near the Thorny Creek road crossing. A broken rail was the cause. Five empty hopper cars went over the embankment and were badly damaged. There were no injuries to the crew.

The Town of Marlinton was cut in two for a number of hours by a derailment at the Marlinton depot on January 19, 1977, at 6 p.m. Ice and snow had packed so tightly into the Eighth Street crossing that the engine, No. 8126,

of the weekly freight derailed as it approached the station. Both the Eighth and Ninth Streets crossings were blocked by the twenty-seven car train. A temporary crossing was constructed north of the depot until crews re-railed the engine the next morning and the train could continue on its way to Durbin.

What was probably the last derailment on the Greenbrier line happened during the last steam powered train movement on the line. As Cass Scenic Railroad Heisler No. 6 was returning with a train from 1978 Pioneer Days at Marlinton the cars derailed near milepost 76 about 4:30 p.m. on July 8. The locomotive did not leave the track. The probable cause of the accident was the track gauge being too wide in a curve. The train had over 300 passengers and some went swimming in the river as they waited for a relief train to arrive from Cass.

Believed to be a photograph of the 2-6-6-2 locomotive derailed at Cass in July or August 1943.   Clark Phillips

Engine No. 8126 derailed at the Marlinton depot on January 19, 1977, while en route to Durbin with the weekly freight train. The derailment was caused by snow and ice packed in the Eighth Street crossing.
WPM

Rerailing No. 8126 the following morning, January 20, 1977.
WPM

Chronological List of Accidents and Other Operating Problems

January 1901—100 yards of grade washed away at the Sliding Bend below Keister

January 11, 1901—slide at Renick

January 12, 1901—slides at various places due to heavy rain

January 17, 1901—freight train wreck below Locust, two cars in the river, caused by a brake beam falling off a car

April 20, 1901—slide

May 24, 1901—passenger train delayed, no reason given

May 29, 1901—slide at Droop Mountain

June 16, 1901—bridge at Stony Bottom taken out by high water.

October 24, 1901—a car of hay in a freight train was found to be on fire in Marlinton. An attempt to put the fire out at the water tank was unsuccessful.

December 13, 1901—passenger train wreck at Keister, see text

January 3, 1902—freight cars derailed below Beard

January 4, 1902—freight cars derailed in Sharps Tunnel

March 25, 1902—freight train wreck near North Caldwell, see text

April 8, 1902—Engine on Train 141 derailed near Anthony, no injuries.

June 7, 1902—freight train wreck near Beard, see text

September 15, 1902—caboose derailed a mile above Cass, three crewmen injured

December 17, 1902—freight train wreck near Sitlington

February 16, 1903—slide at Droop and freight train derailment near Sharps Tunnel

February 1903—one of ten cars of cinders for ballasting tannery side tracks at Marlinton arrived on fire and burned for several days

March 21, 1903—slide near Droop

February 24, 1904—six freight cars derailed at Droop

February 25, 1904—freight cars derailed at Stony Bottom

September 7, 1904—three freight cars derailed near Harter

December 13, 1904—freight car derailed near Droop

February 8, 1905—line blocked by snow, see text

April 25, 1905—passenger train wreck near Hosterman, see text

July 4, 1905—passenger train wreck above Marlinton, see text

July 5, 1905—freight cars derailed below Cass

July 24, 1905—nine freight cars derailed in the Droop Tunnel, caused by rotten ties. (Work on this wreck was made unpleasant by the odor from a car of spoiled hides that had not been accepted by the Marlinton tannery and ordered out of town by city officials.)

December 21, 1905—train 142 hit a rock below Seebert, but did not derail

January 6, 1906—train 143 hit a tree near Harter, but not damaged

January 1906—freight train wreck at Harter

January 22, 1906—train 141 delayed by a slide, location not given

February 8, 1906—five freight cars derailed in the Droop Tunnel

March 15, 1906—passenger train delayed by a broken rail and fallen tree two miles above Marlinton

April 14, 1906—numerous slides

May 8, 1906—freight train wreck at Boyer, see text

July 20, 1906—five or six freight cars derailed at Marlinton

November 5, 1906—last coach on train 141 derailed above Sharps Tunnel due to the rails spreading

November 20, 1906—slides and washouts

December 10, 1906—two or three freight cars derailed at MP 15

December 12, 1906—four or five freight cars derailed at Improvement Lick, rails spread due to rotten ties

December 15, 1906—passenger train derailed, location not given; also three other train derailments between December 10 and 15

January 1907—slide at Droop Mountain

January 16, 1907—slides between Hosterman and Cass, trapping two passenger trains

January 20, 1907—two box cars and caboose derailed above Marlinton

January 26, 1907—six box cars derailed at Boyer

February 20, 1907—slide above Stony Bottom

February 28, 1907—ten freight cars derailed at Hopper due to bad track

March 14, 1907—slides at Cass and Renick

March 29, 1907—train 141 derailed near Wanless by running into a slide, no injuries

April 16, 1907—freight train wreck at Hosterman

May 1, 1907—four or five freight cars derailed at Improvement Lick

May 8, 1907—freight train wreck near Wanless, see text

June 3, 1907—freight cars derailed above August

June 11, 1907—freight train wreck above Hosterman

June 13, 1907—freight train wreck near Anthony

June 5-15, 1907—seven wrecks in this period

June 15, 1907—freight train wrecks at Hosterman and August

June 27, 1907—three cars of lumber in the river at MP 66, caused by a broken axle

June 30, 1907—three box cars wrecked above Marlinton and loads dumped into the river, caused by rails spreading due to rotten ties

June 1907—the month averaged a wreck every other day

November 12, 1907—slide at August

November 24, 1907—slide at August

December 3, 1907—freight train wreck at Watoga

December 4, 1907—nine cars in the river near Droop Tunnel due to a broken axle

February 4, 1908—up freight engine into the river at Droop; down freight train derailed at Watoga; two Coal and Iron passenger trains collided near Durbin and the engines went into the river, but no one injured

March 31, 1908—slide at Anthony

April 16, 1908—seven box cars smashed in a wreck at Renick

July 15, 1908—slide at Anthony

January 26, 1909—freight wreck near Cass

January 31, 1909—train 141 hit a slide above Sitlington, no one injured

February 26, 1909—two railroad camps cars smashed in a wreck at Improvement Lick

September 4, 1909—train 144 hit by a falling tree at Clover Lick, damaging the coaches but causing no injuries

September 10, 1909—freight engine damaged at Boyer by striking a freight car that was on the siding but not clear of the main line, engineer and fireman injured

November 1, 1909—engine derailed at Droop Mountain due to broken rail

January 26, 1910—freight train wreck at Sixty

February 8, 1910—train 141 wrecked at Frank, see text

April 7, 1910—slide at Woodman, see text

September 26, 1910—freight train hit slide at MP 59, engine went into the river and seven cars derailed

January 21, 1911—train 141 wrecked near Stony Bottom, see text

January 29, 1911—train 144 wrecked at Spice Run, see text

February 2, 1911—freight train wrecked near Renick

April 26, 1911—freight engine derailed in Marlinton

June 5, 1911—slide at Anthony

July 1911—freight engine derailed in Marlinton

May 30, 1912—four freight cars derailed 1½ miles below Marlinton

July 4, 1912—train/carriage accident in Marinton, see text

August 2, 1912—engine of train 143 derailed below Wanless, see text

August 9, 1912—engine of train 143 derailed below Wanless, see text

August 31, 1912—five loaded freight cars derailed at the Kennison Curve due to bad track

September 3, 1912—several freight cars derailed above Marlinton

November 22, 1912—five freight cars derailed at the Kennison Curve

January 25, 1913—freight train wreck a mile below Hosterman

February 5, 1913—freight train wreck at Burnsides

March 5, 1913—passenger train engine derailed below Hosterman

April 26, 1913—two freight cars derailed at Sixty

May 1913—freight train wreck at Clawson

May 18, 1913—seven freight cars derailed at Buckeye

May 24, 1913—six box cars derailed at Droop Mountain

August 18, 1913—near collision at Big Run, see text; slide at Anthony

September 8, 1913—five freight cars derailed just above Renick due to bad track

November 29, 1913—thirteen freight cars derailed at Denmar

February 24, 1914—six freight cars derailed at Droop

February 25, 1914—freight car derailed at Stony Bottom, caused by broken flange

March 28, 1914—slide at MP 19.

March 30, 1914—engine on Train 142 blew its flues at Sixty.

April 1914—freight train wreck near Hosterman

May 20, 1914—four freight cars derailed below Marlinton; passenger engine derailed at Clover Lick

June 15, 1914—four freight cars derailed at Beard

July 14, 1914—slide at MP 13

October 4, 1914—slide above Anthony

October 13, 1914—five box cars derailed below Seebert

October 20, 1914—passenger train wreck at Spice Run, see text

November 20, 1914—freight train wreck near Harter

December 31, 1914—two freight cars in the river at Anthony

February 4, 1915—wreck near Stony Bottom

February 15, 1915—train 143 delayed by boulder on track below Bowes

January 11, 1916—train 141 wrecked at Burnsides, see text

February 2, 1916—three freight cars derailed in Droop Tunnel

February 29, 1916—freight train wreck between Anthony and Spring Creek

December 21, 1916—train 143 wrecked above Marlinton, see text

January 6, 1917—freight train wreck near Pine Flats

March 4, 1917—slides above Marlinton and near Anthony

January 1, 1919—slide at Droop

April 13, 1920—passenger train wreck above Clawson, see text

August 16, 1921—freight car derailed at Marlinton, caused by rails spreading

September 26, 1922—train 141 hit a truck at Bartow, driver and passenger in truck slightly injured, truck demolished

January 1923—four freight cars derailed below Seebert, some going into the river

July 22, 1923—ten freight cars derailed near Stillwell

August 9, 1923—slides between Renick and Anthony, see text

June 7, 1924—freight engine hit a car in Marlinton at the Ninth Street crossing, driver and passenger slightly injured

November 30, 1924—freight engine hit a car in Marlinton near the turntable, no injuries

March 3, 1925—freight train wreck at Watoga

May 4, 1925—freight train wreck at Watoga bridge, see text

January 21, 1926—train 141 wrecked below Sitlington, see text

January 25, 1926—seven or eight cars of a freight train derailed above Cass due to the track being damaged by a car in an earlier freight train that jumped the track, bounced along the ties for ¼ mile, and then re-railed when it hit a switch

March 30, 1926—freight train wreck near Boyer

June 19, 1928—slide near Sitlington

August 1928—freight cars derailed at Renick

About 1929—Cass depot damaged by freight car, see text

March 11, 1930—train 141 derailed near Cass, see text

December 26, 1930—train/car accident at Bartow, see text

January 22, 1933—slide at Trout Run

February 18, 1936—slide a mile above Anthony

May 26, 1939—washout near Raywood

May 22, 1942—freight engine wrecked near Locust, see text

July or August, 1943—freight engine wrecked at Cass, see text

July 28, 1945—track washed out near Seebert

February 18, 1958—freight train wreck at Thorny Creek, see text

January 19, 1977—freight engine derailed at Marlinton, see text

July 8, 1978—Cass Scenic Railroad train derailed at MP 76, see text

*Note: The information for the above list came from news stories in *The Pocahontas Times* and other newspapers and not railroad records. Thus it is not to be considered a definative listing of mishaps on the Greenbrier line.

G-5 Class 2-8-0 No. 328 and its engineer and fireman with a freight train at the Durbin depot about 1905. The 2-8-0 locomotives were the most common freight power on the Greenbrier Division until the H Class 2-6-6-2 engines appeared on the line in 1929.   COHS

CHAPTER VII
Other Railroads

AS THE CHESAPEAKE AND OHIO RAILWAY AND THE Coal and Iron Railroad were actually building and then operating their lines into the Upper Greenbrier Valley, other railroad companies were planned and in some cases survey crews employed to lay off projected railroads into the area.

In May of 1900 the Cherry Valley Railroad was chartered with a group of men from Richwood as incorporators. The charter called for a line between Richwood and the Chesapeake and Ohio in Pocahontas County. The company soon had an engineering force in the field and had a route surveyed by September 1900. A tunnel through Droop Mountain was considered at one point but was not part of the final route. The route was a tortuous one, starting on the Chesapeake and Ohio near Kennison, climbing across Droop Mountain into the Bruffey and Hills Creeks area, crossing from Hills Creek to the North Fork of the Cherry River, and then down the Cherry to Richwood. Looking at the plat and profile of this railroad today, it is not surprising that the line was not built.

A group of Little Levels men incorporated the Marble Mountain Railroad in April 1901 for the purpose of building a railroad from the mouth of Stamping Creek to the "Marble Field" near the head of the creek. This proposal was one of a number over the years to develop the marble deposits in the Little Levels.

In July of 1901 the charter was issued for the Iron Mountain and Greenbrier Railroad to a group of men from Greenbrier County and Baltimore, Maryland. According to the charter, the railroad was to begin near the mouth of Beaver Creek in Pocahontas County, go up the North Fork of Beaver Creek, and then by the most practicable route go to White Sulphur Springs. Construction on the new railroad began the same month, on the Greenbrier County end. By November of 1902 the line was in operation for a total of fifteen miles from White Sulphur Springs up Howard Creek and Anthony Creek. A plat filed at this time shows that the terminus had been changed to Huntersville. The proposed route went up the North Fork of Anthony Creek from Neola, down Douthards Creek to Knapps Creek, and on to Huntersville. It was being speculated by the next year that the line would be built on to Durbin to connect with the Chesapeake and Ohio and the Coal and Iron. From

Neola the line was built up the North Fork of Anthony Creek as far as the Dock on the divide between the North Fork and Douthards Creek. At the Dock the railroad received loads of lumber form the narrow gauge railroad of the J.E. Moore Lumber Company at Mountain Grove, Virginia.

Predictions of the extension of this railroad were made several times, mainly based on hopes of providing access to the Pittsburgh market for the rich iron ores believed to be present in Greenbrier and Pocahontas Counties. However, the line remained basically a lumber railroad, supplying the St. Lawrence mill at Ronceverte with logs as well as serving several sawmills on its route. The Dock was as far as the railroad went and it never reached Huntersville, much less Durbin.

The Iron Mountain and Greenbrier Railroad was sold under foreclosure of its first mortgage bonds in April 1912 and a new company organized, the White Sulphur and Huntersville Railroad. However, even with the name change it still did not reach Huntersville. The line from Neola to the Dock was abandoned about 1922. The West Virginia Public Service Commission granted permission for the railroad to discontinue all service in November 1927.

In the 1901-1906 period there was a big flurry of activity, both by surveying crews and news reporters, on possible railroads into and through the Upper Greenbrier Valley.

In early 1901 there were news reports of a railroad survey being made east from Durbin. This survey may have been part of the plans for the Greenbrier, Monongahela and Pittsburgh Railroad mentioned in Chapter Two.

At least two surveys were run from Marlinton up Stony Creek and down the Williams River in 1901 and 1902. One was done by the Chesapeake and Ohio and filed at the Pocahontas County Court House in March 1902 as the Williams River Branch of the Greenbrier Railway. It was speculated that this line was to make a connection between the Chesapeake and Ohio and the West Virginia and Pittsburgh Railroad.

The other survey up Stony Creek was done by engineers for the Chesapeake and Western Railroad as part of a projected line through Pocahontas County. Bringing the line into the county from Virginia by way of the gap in the Allegheny Mountain near Frost, the Chesapeake and Western surveyors ran two lines to the Greenbrier River. One came to the river at Sitlington and the other at Marlinton.

This work by the Chesapeake and Western engineers may have produced the maps and profiles that were filed in November 1902 at the Pocahontas County Court House under the name of the Midland Railway. The Midland maps show a proposed railroad from Durbin to Frost by way of the East Fork of the Greenbrier, Laurel Run, Brush Run, Deer Creek, Sitlington Creek, and Knapps Creek. From Frost the survey went down Knapps Creek to Marlinton and then up Stony Creek. At Marlinton the railroad was to go through a 450 foot tunnel to avoid the loop in Knapps Creek. The Midland Company had already obtained rights-of-way on Stony Creek in February and March and through the Huntersville and Green Bank Districts in July and August. No further mention is found of the Midland Railway in any source after early 1903.

Some of the most intense media speculation about new railroads into the Upper Greenbrier Valley in this period came from the efforts of George J. Gould to expand the Wabash Railroad into a transcontinental railroad running from Baltimore, Maryland, to San Francisco, California. In 1902 Gould acquired the Western Maryland Railway as well as the West Virginia Central and Pittsburgh of Senators Davis and Elkins. The Western Maryland was planned as the eastern outlet for the transcontinental and the connection with the Wabash was to be made through West Virginia; or at least a number of West Virginians thought so at the time. The details of all of Gould's plans and maneuvers are beyond the scope of this history, but the manipulations of men elsewhere did give rise to the hope that a line of the new transcontinental would go through Pocahontas County.

In early 1903 local promoters were encouraged by reports that the Wabash also controlled several railroads in central West Virginia as well as the Chesapeake Western Railroad in Virginia. It seemed to them that the only logical way to connect these lines was by way of the Stony Creek Gap on the west and the Frost Gap on the east. In March 1903 a writer in *The Pocahontas Times* was convinced enough of this to write.

> The Wabash is evidently going to build through Pocahontas very shortly. We believe work will commence this summer. This will make Pocahontas the best and richest county of the two Virginias, and we again voice our standing invitation to every young man that wishes a chance to make something of himself to come early and avoid the rush.

Nothing happened in 1903 but in the spring and summer of 1904 a survey was made through Pocahontas County by engineers reported to be in the employ of the Wabash. This survey started at Sitlington on the Greenbrier Railway, worked its way along Clover Lick Mountain, around Elk Mountain, through the Stony Creek Gap, down the Williams River to the Gauley River, and finally down that stream to Gauley Bridge. This survey was filed at the Pocahontas County Court House in the name of the Atlantic and Western Railroad.

The Wabash never came through the Greenbrier Valley, of course. George Gould's plans to develop a transcontinental railroad also never came to pass, a victim of resistance from competing railroad barons, overspending by Gould on acquiring and extending existing railroad, and the Panic of 1907.

In August 1905 the West Virginia Midland Railroad was incorporated by John T. McGraw and others to build a railroad from Sutton, up the Elk River to Webster Springs, and then by the most practicable route on up the Elk and over to the Greenbrier River and Marlinton. The Midland was actually a reorganization of McGraw's existing Holly River and Addison Railroad which was built from Holly Junction on the Baltimore and Ohio Railroad to Webster Springs. The new company officially took over the other company in early 1906. Work on the line from Webster Springs up the Elk River towards Pocahontas County was underway in 1906 and the line eventually got as far as Bergoo but never to the Greenbrier Valley. The track from Bergoo to Webster Springs is now part of the Western Maryland, having been acquired by that company in 1929.

Some other railroads that were planned, but never built, to tap the resources of the Upper Greenbrier Valley were:

West Virginia, Pittsburgh, and Atlantic Railroad. Incorporated in 1905 to build a line from Rowlesburg in Preston County by the most practicable route to Durbin. R.F. Whitmer was an incorporator, so the Dry Fork Railroad may have been included in the plans for this line.

Parsons and Marlinton Railroad. Its 1905 charter describes a line beginning at Parsons and going by the most practicable route to Marlinton. The incorporators were men from Tucker County.

Little Kanawha Railroad. This line was incorporated in 1896 by men from Parkersburg. In 1905 there was a report that it was to be built as far as Durbin to connect with the Chesapeake and Ohio.

Hampshire Southern Railroad. Incorporated in 1906 to build a railroad beginning in Hampshire County and to run through Grant and Hardy Counties and on to Durbin.

Trans Appalachian Railway. H.M. Lockridge, of Huntersville, was one of the incorporators of this line which was chartered in 1913 to run from Parkersburg to Covington, Virginia. The main goal of the incorporators seems to have been, however, to build a railroad from Marlinton to Minnehaha Springs to "open up an immense acreage of well timbered lands, large deposits of fine iron ore, and a fine agricultural and grazing section." Although it was hoped to have the line completed at least to Huntersville by the next winter, running a survey up Knapps Creek seems to have been the extent of its activities.

Lumber Company Railroads

A number of the lumber companies along the Greenbrier Division incorporated their logging railroads as separate companies.

Pocahontas Railroad was the name given by the M.P. Bock Lumber Company to the railroad for its lumber operation on Deer Creek. Incorporated in August 1901, the line was chartered to build from the mouth of Brushy Run to the head of the North Fork of Deer Creek. Having a more modest charter than most of the lumber company incorporated railroads, the Pocahontas Railroad was the only one along the Greenbrier Division actually to build to its full authorized length. The Pocahontas Railroad remained a separate company through the several different ownerships of the lumber company until it was dissolved in March 1926, a little more than a year before the mill closed.

In the early 1900s the Warn Lumber Company planned to harvest timer on the Cranberry River and incorporated the Greenbrier and Gauley Railroad. The charter was issued in November 1901 and authorized the company to build from Stamping Creek to the mouth of the Gauley River. Before the Warn mill at Mill Point went into operation in 1905, a new railroad, the Cranberry Railroad, was incorporated in June 1903. Its charter gave it authority to build from Seebert, up Stamping Creek, and down either Cranberry, Cherry, or Williams Rivers to the Gauley River, and then on to Gauley Bridge. Not surprisingly, the railroad never carried out the full measure of the charter and got only as far as the head of the Cranberry River and the head of Hills Creek. The Cranberry Railroad was dissolved in December 1913 following the closing of the mill.

The Campbell Lumber Company at Campbelltown incorporated their railroad under the name Marlinton and Camden Railroad to build a line from Marlinton to Camden-on-Gauley. The charter was issued in March 1904. The line only got to the head of the Williams River and never on to Camden-on-Gauley, but perhaps the company had hopes of acquiring the timber down the Williams that was later cut by the Cherry River Boom and Lumber Company. The Marlinton and Camden Railroad was dissolved in October 1918, several years after the mill closed. This was the only railroad to actually use the oft-time surveyed Stony Creek Gap.

Harter Brothers Lumber Company filled the sides of the tank on their diminutive Climax locomotive with "Pocahontas Central Railroad of W. Va." However, no record has been found of the actual incorporation of a railroad with that name.

The West Virginia Pulp and Paper Company incorporated a number of railroads while conducting their lumber operations in the Upper Greenbrier Valley. In November 1899 the company incorporated the Greenbrier and Cheat River Railroad. This line was chartered to build from the Forks of the Greenbrier, by the most practicable route, to Rowlesburg in Preston County. This railroad was never constructed and also seems to have had no connection with the Cass operation of the paper company. The reason for this proposed railroad may have been some timber acquired by the company in the Durbin area in the late 1890s. Although the company got this timber to Covington by floating it down the Greenbrier River to the railroad at Ronceverte, they may have considered taking it out by rail to the north.

Several West Virginia Pulp and Paper Company incorporated railroads involved the logging operation on Cheat Mountain. The first was the Greenbrier and Elk River Railroad, incorporated in August 1905 to build from Cass to Fishing Hawk (Bemis) on the Coal and Iron Railway. At this time the logging railroad had been built from Cass, up the mountain to Spruce, and branches up to the head of the Shavers Fork, up Black Run, and down Shavers Fork for several miles.

In January 1909 a new company was chartered, the Greenbrier, Elk and Valley Railroad. This line was authorized to begin at Cass, run to the Elk and Tygarts Valley Rivers, and on to Huttonsville. It is doubtful if this name ever appeared on any railroad equipment.

Finally in 1910 the West Virginia Pulp and Paper Company found the railroad corporate structure it wanted with the Greenbrier, Cheat and Elk Railroad, incorporated in September. The charter outlined an extensive system beginning at Bemis, going by way of Shavers Fork to the Big Spring Fork of Elk River, and down the Elk to Webster Springs. Branches were authorized up the Old Field Fork of Elk to join the Marlinton and Camden Railroad; up the Slaty Fork of Elk to the Chesapeake and Ohio near Clover Lick; and up the Valley Fork of Elk to join the Valley River Railroad on the Tygarts Valley River.

At the time of the incorporation of the Greenbrier, Cheat and Elk, the paper company's railroad went from Cass to Spruce and from there down to Shavers Fork to about Cheat Bridge. Work had also begun on the line from Spruce to the Elk River at Slaty Fork, through the Big Cut.

In December 1913 the charter of the Greenbrier, Cheat and Elk Railroad was amended. The charter now called for the line to begin at Cass, go to Spruce, and from Spruce to Bemis and Webster Springs, as in the previous charter. In the new charter authority was given to continue on from Webster Springs to the Baltimore and Ohio Railroad at Centralia. The branches up the Slaty Fork and Valley Fork are given again as well as a line from the Valley Fork over to the Back Fork of Elk and on to Webster Springs.

In 1918 a connection was made near Bemis between the Greenbrier, Cheat and Elk and the Western Maryland Railway line to Durbin. This, however, was the only part of either charter to be carried out. On the Elk River the line got out as far as Bergoo. Logging lines did go up Old Field Fork, Slaty Fork, and Valley Fork but never as far as proposed in the charters.

In March 1927 the West Virginia Pulp and Paper Company sold the Western Maryland all the stock in the Greenbrier, Cheat and Elk. The line from Spruce to Cass and various logging branches were transferred to the paper company and the Western Maryland took over the operation of the line from Cheat Junction to Bergoo

on March 15, 1928. After this the paper company continued to operate trains over its former railroad, but by paying the Western Maryland for the privilege.

The line remained in the Greenbrier, Cheat and Elk name until deeded over to the Western Maryland on January 20, 1950.

Polar axis for the 140-foot telescope at the National Radio Astronomy Observatory ready at the Westinghouse plant in East Pittsburgh, Pennsylvania, for shipment to Bartow. This piece weighs 215 tons and arrived in Bartow in December 1963. *National Radio Astronomy Observatory*

Preparations underway at Bartow to unload the 150-ton spherical journal for the 140-foot telescope at the National Radio Astronomy Observatory at Green Bank, April 24, 1964.

National Radio Astronomy Observatory

CHAPTER VIII
Structures, Engineering, and Station List

THE MOST IMPORTANT SOURCES OF DATA FOR THIS chapter are the Greenbrier Division right-of-way and track maps and engineering notes produced in 1916-1917 by the survey teams employed by the Interstate Commerce Commission as part of the nation-wide inventory of all the property owned by the country's railroads.

Information prior to 1916 comes mainly from newspaper accounts, a few employee timetables, photographs, and a right-of-way map prepared in early 1901 (with some revisions to about 1906). The ICC surveyors fortunately also included abandoned sidings and some other pre-1916 facilities on their maps.

For the years following 1916-1917 the sources of information are more numerous and include a revised edition (to 1977) of the ICC track maps, Chesapeake and Ohio Roadway Completion Reports, employee timetables newspaper articles, West Virginia Public Service Commission records, photographs, recollections by former railroad employees, and on the ground inspection by the author.

In this chapter the author will use the east-west direction used by the railroad on the Greenbrier Branch. For railroad purposes east was the direction towards Winterburn (up river) and west the direction towards Whitcomb (down river). Geographically this fits the line only between Durbin and Winterburn, but the Chesapeake and Ohio based its branch line directions on its east-west main line.

Passenger and Freight Facilities

At the time of the construction of the Greenbrier Division, the Chesapeake and Ohio Railway had standardized the design for the depots that were being located along its growing system. One writer has referred to the design as "Standard C. and O. Victorian." The design was used during the period of the railroad's greatest period of expansion and depots of the style were built in great numbers in Virginia, West Virginia, and Kentucky on main and branch lines.

The depots varied in size depending upon the needs of the communities they served. On the inside the buildings were divided into at least three rooms. There was an office with a bay window on track side for the agent, a waiting room for passengers on one side of the office, and a freight/baggage/express room on the other side of the office. The freight rooms had one or two sliding doors on each side, depending upon the size of the depot. In depots serving large towns there were often two waiting rooms, one on each side of the office. One of the waiting rooms was for men and the other for women, although in some localities one was designated "White" and the other "Colored."

The outside features of the Chesapeake and Ohio standard depot included a board and batten siding with wainscoting of diagonal or vertical slats about two feet high. Overhanging eves were supported by 4" by 4" braces. One of the distinctive features of these buildings was the "gingerbread" at each gable and above the bay window made from 4" by 4" timbers. The roofs originally were covered with slate shingles.

As a variation on the theme the standard depots occasionally had two stories or had a switching tower built on the roof. The shelters used at flag stops also followed the same general pattern. Some had a small room for the protection of freight and passengers while others were merely three sided shelters.

On the newly constructed Greenbrier Division all the depots were of the standard design and were located at North Caldwell, Anthony, Spring Creek, Renick, Beard, Seebert, Marlinton, Clover Lick, Sitlington, Cass, Hosterman, Durbin, Bartow, and Winterburn. Details on these station buildings are given in the Station List.

An agency station was established at Raywood in 1915 following the building of the sawmill there. A photo has not been located of this station so it is not known how closely the building followed the standard design. It is known that it did not have the bay window. Although it was not an agency station, Watoga had a depot building which was similar in style to the standard depot. In a photograph, it does not appear to have the bay window. Completed in early 1907, it was probably built by the lumber company rather than the railroad. The Raywood depot may have also been built by the lumber company.

The original color of the Greenbrier stations was green. In early 1911 the Marlinton depot was repainted yellow and it is assumed the other stations on the line were also repainted in the new color. The next Chesapeake and Ohio paint scheme involved several shades of gray. The body of the depot buildings was a medium gray with light and dark grays used as trim. This paint scheme was adopted by the railroad at least by 1931 and perhaps earlier. The final paint scheme used on the Greenbrier structures was white with gray around the doors and baseboard.

The only major structure to be used strictly for freight was the freight station built at Marlinton in 1905. There were a few small buildings along the line that were identified as freight stations.

Water and Fuel Facilities

In the days of the steam locomotive the location of adequate supplies of boiler water was of the utmost importance along a new line of railroad. On the Greenbrier Division, following its namesake river as it did, the Chesapeake and Ohio had no problem as to the source of good water for its engines. The only decisions to be made were the sites of the tanks.

Water tanks were in place at Anthony by early November 1900, Marlinton by early January 1901, Sitlington in February 1901, and Cass by early March 1901. It is probably also safe to assume that a tank was in place at Durbin by soon after the time the railroad was completed to that point. Droop Mountain was also the site of one of the original water tanks on the line.

In 1906 it was reported that the tanks at Droop Mountain and Sitlington would be removed and tanks built at Renick, Beard, and Clover Lick.

The locations of these tanks were as follows:
• Anthony—on the north side of the track about 1000 feet west of the depot.
• Renick—about 3500 feet east of the depot on the north side of the track.
• Droop Mountain—north side of the track and about 500 feet east of MP 32.
• Beard—about 85 feet east of the depot on the north side of the track.
• Marlinton—on the south side of the track about 250 feet west of the depot, between Eighth and Ninth Streets. The pump house was located at the east end of the Knapps Creek bridge and the water was taken from the creek.
• Clover Lick—at the west end of the depot.
• Sitlington—north side of the track, west of the road crossing.
• Cass—about 1600 feet east of the depot on the north side of the track. This tank served the engines of both the railroad and lumber company. The water was pumped from the mill to the tank.
• Durbin—on the north side of the track about 165 feet east of the depot.

These tanks were of wooden construction, 50,000 gallon capacity, 24 feet in diameter, and 16 feet in height.

During the construction of the Marlinton tank at least one accident occurred, but fortunately the results were more humorous than serious. As reported in *The Pocahontas Times*:

A man fell into the water tank last week and was hurt. He was at work on the top of it and fell to the bottom bruising himself considerably. To add to his discomfort, no sooner had he landed and hurt himself because there was no water to break his fall, the water came pouring in from the pumps and came near drowning him.

During the 1920s several of the tanks were replaced by new structures. In early 1923 a new wooden tank was built at Marlinton. The new tank was located at the upper end of the Marlinton yard, about 2230 feet east of the depot and on the south side of the track. The source of water for the tank was changed with a new pump house being built on the river. In March of 1925 the installing of new steel tanks of 50,000 gallon capacity was completed at Anthony and Renick. In late 1927 Clover Lick also got a 50,000 gallon steel tank. The tank at Durbin was rebuilt, as a wooden tank, in late 1928 and hooked onto town water to save pumping. The tank at Cass was rebuilt about 1933, also as a wooden tank. An electric pump replaced the steam pump at Renick in the summer of 1934 and the same was done at Clover Lick in early 1948. The Marlinton pump house was retired in February 1941 and the tank hooked onto town water.

Two tanks were taken out of service in the 1930s. The tank at Beard was retired in June 1935 and the Anthony tank in August 1937.

The remaining tanks were in service until the end of the use of steam locomotives on the Greenbrier line. The Renick and Clover Lick tanks were retired in November of 1953. The tank at Clover Lick was donated by the Chesapeake and Ohio for use at the new Boy Scout camp being built at Dilleys Mill and was moved there in September 1959. The Cass tank was donated to the West Virginia Department of Natural Resources in November 1961 for use of the locomotives on the proposed Cass Scenic Railroad. This tank remains in use today. The Durbin tank was retired in May 1965. The tank at Marlinton contained water into the 1970s and remains in place in 1984.

Facilities to coal locomotives were located at Beard, Marlinton, Cass, and Durbin.

The major coaling structure was at Marlinton where a 44 foot by 100 foot coaling trestle was located. The trestle was on the main track 3600 feet east of the depot. The trestle was reduced in length by 36 feet in May 1938. A sandhouse was located at the coaling trestle.

At Beard a coaling platform was located on the passing siding just east of the road crossing.

The coaling platform at Cass was a 16 foot by 51 foot structure and located west of the road crossing on the spur leading into the mill yard.

At Durbin an 11 foot by 50 foot coaling platform was located on the passing siding about 175 feet west of the depot.

The Marlinton structure was in use until the end of the use of steam locomotives on the line. The others were out of service by the 1940s; probably much earlier.

At Durbin the coaling platform was replaced by a side track raised on an earth embankment. From this track coal was shoveled from a gondola car into engine tenders on an adjacent siding. These two sidings were located across from the depot. The date the raised siding was laid is not known, but it may have been in place by 1924.

The Clifton Forge Grocery Company had a commercial coal trestle at Marlinton, 174 feet long. It was located along the railroad just east of Fifth Street and was served by a short side track.

Other engine facilities included a turntable at Marlinton, an inspection pit at Durbin, and ash pits at Marlinton, Cass, and Winterburn. The turntable, 60 feet long, was installed in the latter part of 1920 in the upper part of the Marlinton yard, adjacent to the second water tank. It was removed in early 1939.

A wye track for turning engines was located between Deer Creek and Cass. It was most likely built as soon as the railroad reached Cass and was removed in June 1934. The brief existence of a wye track at Marlinton is related in Chapter Two. At Durbin there would have been the need for a way to turn locomotives prior to the formation of a wye track by the junction of the two railroads. There is evidence that a wye track was located across from the Durbin depot.

Other Facilities

Dwellings used by section foremen and their families were located at North Caldwell, Keister, Anthony, Spring Creek, Renick, Droop Mountain, Beard, Seebert, Buckeye, Marlinton, Clawson, Clover Lick, Sitlington, Cass, Hosterman, Durbin, and Bartow.

With one exception these houses were frame structures, 16.5 feet by 46 feet with a 16.5 feet by 25 feet addition, give or take a foot or two at some locations. The section house at Clawson is described as being two story, 18 feet by 30 feet.

Bunk houses for use by laborers and train crews were located at North Caldwell, Keister, Anthony, Woodman, Spring Creek, Renick, Beard (four), Seebert, Marlinton (three), Clawson, Clover Lick (two), Sitlington (three), Cass, Hosterman, Durbin (five, not all in use at one time), and Bartow.

These structures varied in size as might be expected. About half were 15.5 feet by 30.5 feet, although some this size had additions. The only modern bunk house on the Greenbrier Branch was the existing block buiding constructed at Durbin in late 1967.

Standard 10.5 feet by 15.5 feet tool houses for the section crews were located at North Caldwell, Keister, Anthony, Spring Creek, Renick, Droop Mountain, Beard, Seebert, Buckeye, Marlinton, Clawson, Clover Lick, Cass, Hosterman, and Durbin.

Stock pens to hold farm animals being sent to market were located at North Caldwell, Renick, Beard, Seebert, Marlinton, Clover Lick, Durbin, and Bartow. The Durbin pens were retired in 1928, North Caldwell in 1940, and the others in the late 1950s or early 1960s.

A 100-ton track scale was installed at Durbin in late 1917 to weigh cars being transferred to the Western

Maryland. It was removed in 1942.

Bridges

Some fifty-three structures crossing streams were large enough to be counted as bridges on the Greenbrier Division. Of these, twenty-six were steel bridges of various styles while the rest were of wood construction

The largest bridge made of wood was the trestle over the East Fork of the Greenbrier River at Winterburn, 168 feet long. The others were generally wood stringers on masonry piers, most of one span and a few consisting of two spans.

The inventory of steel bridges originally consisted of bridges built new for the Greenbrier line and bridges moved from other locations.

All but one of the bridges built new for the line are of the through plate girder design and were built by the A.P. Roberts Company at the Pencoyd Iron Works in Pencoyd, Pennsylvania, in 1900. The location of these bridges is as follows:

• Bridges No. 17, Little Sulphur Creek; 296, Garners Run; 409, Mill Run; 550, Stillhouse Run; 608, Thorny Creek; 743, Elk Creek; 780, Moses Run; 801, Cold Run; 843, Wanless Run; 864, Trout Run; and 926, Elk Creek, consist of a single span 30'6" in length.

• Bridge No. 609, Thorny Creek, and No. 670, Big Run, consist of a single span 55' in length.

• Bridge No. 810, Leatherbark Creek, consists of a single span 60' in length.

• Bridge No. 881, Allegheny Run, consists of two 30'6" spans side by side for the main and passing tracks.

• Bridge No. 653, the bridge over the Greenbrier River at Sharps Tunnel, was also built at the Pencoyd Iron Works in 1900. It is of the deck plate girder design and consists off four spans, 55' 2½", two 57' 5", and 59'.

The other steel bridges were moved from several locations as follows:

• Bridge No. 216, Spring Creek, three span through truss with spans 75' and 80', built by the Phoenix Bridge Company in 1887. It was originally on the Maysville and Big Sandy Railroad.

• Bridge No. 376, Locust Creek, Bridge No. 464, Stamping Creek, and Bridge No. 714, Clover Creek, through lattice girder bridges of two spans, each 55', built by the Phoenix Bridge Company in 1887. They were originally on the Chesapeake and Ohio's Cincinnati Division.

• Bridge No. 470, Steven Hole Run, through lattice girder of one span, 55', built by the Phoenix Bridge Company in 1887. Originally on the Cincinnati Division.

• Bridge No. 479, Greenbrier River at Watoga, through pin truss of two spans built by the Phoenix Bridge Company in 1886. Originally over the Little Sandy River on the Maysville and Big Sandy Railroad. Both spans were 149' 11" but one was shortened to 128' 6" when moved.

• Bridge No. 493, Beaver Creek, through pin truss of one 86' span, built by the Louisville Bridge and Iron company in 1890. Originally on the Chesapeake and Ohio's Loup Creek Branch.

• Bridge No. 557, Knapps Creek, through pin truss of two spans, each 132', built by the Passaic Rolling Mill Company in 1889. Originally over the Jackson River in Virginia.

• Bridge No. 949, West Fork of the Greenbrier River, through pin truss of one span, 132', built by the Edge Moor Iron Company in 1888. Originally on the main line at Dunlap, Virginia.

The west span of the Greenbrier River bridge at Watoga had to be replaced following the accident in May 1925. The new span, 151' 3" long, was built by the American Bridge Company. The installation work began in September 1925 and was completed in January 1926.

All of the "used" steel bridges were replaced in the major bridge strengthening program of 1929. The bridges over Spring Creek, Locust Creek, Stamping Creek, Steven Hole Run, Beaver Creek, and Clover Creek were replaced with through plate girder structures of the same number of spans as the original bridges. The bridge over the West Fork was replaced with a through plate girder bridge of two spans, each 68' 7½". The Knapps Creek bridge and the Greenbrier River bridge at Watoga remained truss bridges (only the east span, 129' 3" long, on the latter was replaced at this time, of course). The replacement bridges were all built by the Bethlehem Steel Company. The work of replacing the bridges began in March 1929 and was completed in February 1930.

Rail

The author has found two references giving information on the weight of the rail originally laid on the Greenbrier Division. One states that it was 56 pound rail and the other gives 62 pound rail. Judging by the amount of 62 pound rail on the line in 1917, the author assumes the line was initially laid with mainly 62 pound rail.

The first date for which definitive rail data are available is 1917. By then the Greenbrier main track was made up of the following rail weights:

100 pound—0.05 miles	62 pound—59.13 miles
75 pound—17.54 miles	56 pound—2.50 miles
70 pounds—21.56 miles	

All of this rail was originally used elsewhere before being placed on the Greenbrier line; the Greenbrier Division, like most branch lines, probably never had the luxury of new rail.

By 1930 the upgrading work done during the 1920s to allow heavier engines to be used on the Greenbrier line had eliminated all of the 56 pound rail and all but a very short section of 62 pound rail. That year the rail on the main track was as follows:

130 pound—0.70 miles	85 pound—27.5 miles
100 pound—47.8 miles	75 pound—3.1 miles
90 pound—18.6 miles	62 pound—3.2 miles

The 62 pound rail was located from Bartow to Winter-

burn and was mostly eliminated in 1933 when that track was taken up.

By 1960 the main track was made up of the following weights:

130 pound—5.1 miles	85 pound—10.9 miles
100 pound—64.8 miles	62 pound—0.3 miles
90 pound—16.8 miles	

The last rail replacement program of any size on the Greenbrier line was in 1965 when 10,027 feet of rail was laid on the main track, 9,955 feet of 100 pound rail and 72 feet of 112 pound.

Curvature and Gradient

Any railroad built in West Virginia is anything but straight and the Greenbrier Division was no exception. Tangents of any length were few and none was even a mile in length. The longest stretches of straight track (one-half mile or more) were at North Caldwell, Kennison, Thorny Creek, Big Run, Cup Run, Durbin, and Thornwood.

As the Greenbrier River curved, so curved the railroad to the extent that 64% of the line was in curves. The sharpest curves were four of 14 degrees located at MP 68.5, MP 85.5, MP 86, and Nida. Of these, the first one was the longest and a train made a 180 degree change in direction as it went through this curve. Other curves of greater than 10 degrees were east of Anthony, through the Droop Tunnel, east of Kennison, west of the Watoga bridge, at Sitlington, east of Raywood, west of Nida, at MP 89, Boyer, Houchins, and Winterburn. The railroad followed an 8 degree curve across the river bridge and through the tunnel north of Marlinton.

From Whitcomb to Winterburn the gradient of the line was ascending as the railroad followed its namesake river towards its head. Stretches of level track were rare and none were as much as a mile in length. The steepest grades were at the end of the line, short distances of 1.30% grade at Houchins and Thornwood. Otherwise the gradient remained under 1%.

Between Whitcomb and Marlinton the stiffest grade was about two and a half miles of 0.30% from Golden to the east side of the Droop Tunnel, as well as short distances of 0.30% approaching Camp Allegheny and the Watoga bridge. The grade through Marlinton was 0.20%.

Between Marlinton and Cass the maximum grade was in the Cass yard, east of the station, at 0.63%. Most of this section of the line had gradient 0.20% or above, particularly east of Clawson. The grade was 0.46% through Harter, across the river bridge, and through the tunnel; 0.35% at Clover Lick; 0.40% east of MP 75; 0.45% through Sitlington; 0.50% at Raywood; and 0.60%, 0.59% and 0.40% between MP 79 and Cass.

With only minor exceptions, the gradient from Cass to Winterburn was above 0.30%. The steepest sections were 0.42% west of Cup Run; 0.46% approaching Wanless; 0.55%, 0.70%, and 0.64% between Wanless and

Trout Run; 0.58% and 0.43% east of Hosterman; 0.40% between Boyer and Whiting; 0.50% approaching the West Fork bridge; 0.60% through Bartow; 0.66% between Houchins and Thornwood; and the 1.30% already mentioned.

Station List

In the following list of stations along the Greenbrier Division the agency stations and passenger train flag-stops have their names in bold, capital letters. These stations all appear on at least one of the passenger time-tables the author has for the line.

The locations that the author lists only as "siding" would have had names of some sort, even if only being referred to by the nearest milepost. However, names have not been determined for certain for these locations.

At agency stations the mileposts given are for the depots. At flagstops the mileposts are the location of the passenger shelter, if there was one, or the station sign, unless otherwise indicated. At the unnamed sidings, the mileposts are for the switches. The milepost figures used by the author are the distances from Whitcomb based on the Valuation Stations surveyed in 1916 by the Interstate Commerce Commission crews. They may vary slightly at some stations from the mileposts that appear on time-tables.

Passing sidings are on the south side of the main track unless otherwise indicated. Passing sidings were, of course, connected to the main track at both ends. For sidings with only one switch the author has used the expression "stub siding." The term "spur" is used to indicate a track that switches from the main track and leaves the Chesapeake and Ohio right-of-way.

WHITCOMB: Milepost 0, elevation 1701. Whitcomb is the junction of the Greenbrier line with the main line. The 1901 right-of-way maps for the Greenbrier Railway show a proposed location for the Greenbrier line not joining the main track at Whitcomb, but running parallel to it; presumably to Ronceverte.

A standard style depot with a switch tower built on its roof was located at the junction.

A passing siding 3158 feet in length was located a short distance east of the junction (west switch at MP 0.33). It was probably used mainly during the construction period and was removed before 1916.

NORTH CALDWELL (LITTLE SULPHUR): Milepost 1.82, elevation 1693. Agency station and telegraph office with call NH. The standard depot still exists and measures 16.5×61.5 feet. Its original position was on the north side of the track just west of the existing road crossing. The agency was closed in 1967 and the building has been moved a short distance and is now used commercially.

Other facilities here included a section foreman's house, bunkhouse, section tool house, and stock pens.

The Little Sulphur name was used only for a short period of time.

A passing siding 3282 feet long was located here. It was reduced in length on the east end at two different times, leaving an existing siding of 1896 feet. The date of the first reduction of 391 feet is not known. The second reduction was done in November 1940.

North Caldwell was the site briefly considered by the West Virginia Pulp and Paper Company for its new paper mill. A map dated May 1899 shows the mill located in the large field east of present Rt. 60. To serve the mill a yard complex of five tracks was proposed. One track was to be north of the main track and the others to the south. Several spurs left the yard tracks to serve the mill.

Interstate Amiesite Plant (Stone House): Milepost 2.82 (west switch). Two sidings to serve the asphalt plant of the Interstate Amiesite Company (now owned by Anderson Paving, Inc.) were installed in the summer of 1948. Located on the south side of the main track, one is a 957 foot siding connected at both ends. The second was a 340 foot stub siding from the first siding. It was retired in July 1976.

An earlier stub siding of about 200 feet was located here to the south of the main track and connected on the west end. Removed before 1916, it may have served a brick factory.

Beginning point for 1978 abandonment: Milepost 3.06. The track is removed east of this point.

CAMP ALLEGHENY (TOTTENS): Milepost 3.54. A shelter shed, 10×10 feet, was built here in July 1922. The name was changed to Camp Alleghany in December 1940. A summer youth camp is located across the river from the site of this station.

A 642 foot stub siding was located south of the main track, connected on the west end. It was retired by late 1939.

HOPPER: Milepost 5.55. A 490 foot stub siding was located here to the south of the main track, connected on the west end. It was retired in January 1938.

BOWES: Milepost 7.29.

Siding: Milepost unknown. By the fall of 1923 a siding was installed for W.O. Slusser between MP 7 and 9 but neither its exact location nor date of removal has been determined.

LOOPEMOUNT: Milepost 8.71. A shelter shed, 10×9 feet, was erected here in the summer of 1925. A summer camp was located across the river from this station.

BRINK: Milepost 9.32. A 549 foot stub siding was located here for the Clear Creek Lumber Company. It was south of the main track and connected on the west end. The siding was retired in April 1926.

KEISTER: Milepost 11.08. A station building, 10×18.5 feet, was provided here, probably of the type with an open passenger shelter and freight room. Other facilities here included a section foreman's house, bunkhouse, section tool house, and mail crane.

A passing siding of 2430 feet was located at Keister. In February 1935 the east end of the siding was removed, reducing it to a stub siding of 398.5 feet. This siding was

North Caldwell depot.
    Glema Auldridge

The North Caldwell depot has been moved a short distance from its trackside location, had a basement added, and is now used as a warehouse.   WPM

Anthony depot about 1915.
    COHS

Renick depot in the early 1940s.   Wendell A. Scott

Stockpens at Renick, 1930. Similar facilities were located at North Caldwell, Beard, Seebert, Marlinton, Clover Lick, Durbin, and Bartow. Note the lack of water in the Greenbrier River.   Wendell A. Scott

Depot at Spring Creek. The agent is Charles Holliday.   Glema Auldridge

removed in October 1963.

Siding: Milepost 13.74. Location of a spur track of unknown length, leaving the railroad right-of-way after 225 feet. It was on the south side of the main track and connected on the east end. It was abandoned before 1916.

ANTHONY: Milepost 14.12, elevation 1796. Agency station and telegraph office with call HY. The standard depot building here was 15.5×58.5 feet located north of the track just west of a private road crossing. The agency was closed in 1928 and the depot replaced with a shelter shed in May 1939. Due to increased traffic during World War II the railroad re-established a telegraph office at Anthony and replaced the shed with a small building.

Other facilities here included a water tank, section foreman's house, bunkhouse, a section tool house.

A passing siding of 2997 feet (later shortened slightly to 2854 feet) was located here. A 797 foot stub siding switched off of the passing siding to serve the mill of the Henderson Lumber Company (c. 1903-?). This siding was retired in December 1936. By early 1943 a 471 foot stub siding was located on the site of the previous siding. This second stub siding was removed in July 1976. Both were connected on the west end.

WOODMAN: Milepost 16.12. A structure, 12.5 by 28.5 feet, described as a freight house was located here. The only other railroad company facility at Woodman was a bunkhouse.

A 2240 foot stub siding, connected on the west end, served the Donaldson Lumber Company's mill (c. 1906-?). The lumber company railroad was narrow gauge and the siding had a third rail for part of its length to allow equipment of both gauges to operate over it. The siding was retired in October 1931.

Siding: Milepost 16.83. A siding of about 350 feet was located here, connected on the west end and on the south side of the main track. It was abandoned by 1916.

DEETER: Milepost 17.01 (switch). A stub siding of about 500 feet was located here to serve the mill of the Kendall Deeter Lumber Company (c. 1906-?) on the south side of the main track. The siding had a third rail for most of its length and was connected on the east end. It was removed by 1916.

SPRING CREEK: Milepost 21.53, elevation 1858. An agency station with a standard depot building 16.5×46 feet. The depot was located about 450 feet west of the bridge over Spring Creek and north of the main track. It was closed in 1955 and replaced by a shelter shed in April 1959.

Other facilities here included a section foreman's house, bunkhouse, and section tool house.

In 1916 a passing siding 2941 feet in length was located here (the length of this siding was given as 3211 feet on the 1901 map and 2131 feet on a 1912 employee timetable). After the building of the mill of the Spring Creek Lumber Company (1921-1934), two sidings to the mill were laid at the end of 1921, both connected on the east end. Also at this time the passing siding was reduced

in length on the east end to 2816 feet. This shortening was probably done because of the need for the lumber company's logging railroad from Spring Creek to cross the Chesapeake and Ohio line to reach the mill. The exact arrangement of this crossing, which was east of the depot, is not known to the author. Automatic signals were installed to protect this crossing.

After the closing of the Spring Creek Lumber Company's mill, the site was occupied by the mill of the S.J. Neathawk Lumber Company (later Greenbrier Lumber Company). The passing siding was reduced to a stub siding of 652 feet, connected on the west end, in the spring of 1937.

RENICK: Milepost 24.77, elevation 1873. Agency station and telegraph office with call RN, later RW. A standard station building, 16.5×71 feet, was located west of the road crossing and north of the tracks. The Renick agency was closed in 1966 and the building removed the same year.

Other facilities here included a section foreman's house, bunkhouse, section tool house, water tank, and stock pens.

A passing siding of 3510 feet (given as 3416 feet in 1912) and a loading siding of 2188 feet (north of the main track) were located at Renick. Both of these tracks were reduced in length on the east end in November 1940 to 2507 and 1284 feet respectively. The passing siding was retired in July 1976.

A stub siding serving a Standard Oil Company bulk plant was located south of the passing siding, probably connected on the east end. The siding was probably installed in the early 1920s. It was removed by early 1933.

The Horrocks Desk Company (1904-c. 1925) had a factory in Renick, located along the loading siding just east of MP 25.

Renick Stone Company: Milepost 25.81 (tipple). The tipple of the Renick Stone Company (1907-1940s) was served by three tracks. Two, stub sidings of 361 and 1331 feet, were connected to the main track at their east ends. The third siding, 343 feet long, came off of the longer of the other two tracks and was connected at both ends. A short stub siding, about 125 feet long, ran east from the longer siding, but was removed by 1916. All the tracks were retired in February 1955.

Siding: Milepost 26.2 (approximate). Probable location of a siding installed in the early 1920s for S.D. DeHart. It was on the south side of the main track. Date of removal is not known.

GOLDEN: Milepost 28.18. A stub siding to serve the mill was located south of the main track, connected on the west end.

HORROCK: Milepost 29.64. A 10.5×16.5 foot station building was provided here. It was removed in early 1937.

A stub siding of 435 feet was located here for the Horrocks Desk Company. It was north of the main track and connected on the west end. The siding was retired in

November 1935.

RORER: Milepost 30.62 (originally 30.82). A 32 foot boxcar body was provided here to shelter freight and passengers. It was removed in October 1957. A mail crane was also at this site.

A 279 foot stub siding was located at Rorer, south of the main track and connected on the east end. It was retired in the late summer of 1976.

Droop Mountain Tunnel: Milepost 30.91 (west portal). This tunnel is 402 feet long.

Just west of the tunnel, a spur track left the main track to serve the mill of the Grove City Lumber Company (c. 1903-?).

DROOP MOUNTAIN: Milepost 32.10. Railroad facilities here included a water tank, section foreman's house, and section tool house.

A passing siding was located at this station. Its length is given as 3200 feet in 1901, 2841 feet in 1912, and 3240 feet in 1916 and at the time of its removal in January 1937.

Siding: Milepost 35.13. A 328 foot stub siding was located here north of the main track, connected on the east end. It was abandoned before 1916.

SPICE RUN: Milepost 36.03. While the Spice Run Lumber Company (1913-c. 1926) was in operation, the Chesapeake and Ohio ticket office was in the lumber company's store which was located along the track. A shelter shed was provided in later years.

A 1651 foot passing siding was located here, probably after the mill was built. Two stub sidings switched from the passing siding to serve the mill. One, 922 feet long and connected on the west end, went to the mill and pond. The other, 594 feet long and connected on the east end, provided access to the mill yard and the lumber company's track across the river. The mill sidings were no doubt removed soon after the mill closed. The passing siding was retired in February 1935.

A stub siding of about 300 feet was located north of the main track and connected on the west end. It was abandoned before 1916.

The Vulcan Last Company had a plant across the river from Spice Run, served by the lumber company railroad.

Siding: Milepost 36.66. Stub siding of about 190 feet on the north side of the main track, connected on the west end. It was abandoned by 1916.

LOCUST (BREAKNECK): Milepost 37.40. A 12×12 foot building described as a freight house was located here.

Two stub sidings were located at Locust, both on the north side of the main track and connected on the west end. To the west of the Locust Creek bridge a 400 foot siding was built about 1904 under a contract between the railroad and local landowners. During the years the mill of the Kidd, Kirby, and Lilly Lumber Company was in operation on Trump Run (1907-c. 1918), this siding may have extended to the mill. The siding was retired in April 1935.

To the east of the bridge a siding about 300 feet long was located. It was abandoned by 1916. It may have been the loading track for the J.E. Moore Lumber Company's mill on Locust Creek (1911-c. 1913).

BEARD (BEARDS): Milepost 38.48, elevation 2010. An agency station and telegraph office with call BA. The standard depot building here was two stories high and 16.5×53.5 feet in size. It was on the north side of the track and just west of the road crossing. The second story served as a residence for the agent and his family. The agency was closed in 1928 and the building removed in April 1937.

Other facilities at Beard included a water tank, coaling platform, stock pens, section foreman's house, section tool house, and, for some reason, four bunkhouses.

A 2998 foot passing siding (length was given as 3150 feet on the 1901 map and 3299 feet in 1912) and a 355 foot stub siding were located here. The stub siding was on the south side of the passing siding and connected on the west end. It was laid about 1927 with rail taken from Denmar. The track was retired in December 1936. The passing siding was retired in the late summer of 1976.

DENMAR (DEN MAR): Milepost 39.33. The Maryland Lumber Company's store building was located at the railroad with the platform in front, so it no doubt

View at Beard showing the depot, water tank, and coaling platform. The Beard depot building was the only two-story structure on the line. The second floor was used as a residence by the agent and his family.   PCHS

Beard, December 1978. The two-story depot, water tank, coaling platform, and passing track have all been removed, the last train will soon pass by the faded station sign, and within a year all that will remain will be the roadbed. WPM

served as a passenger station.

To serve the mill of the Maryland Lumber Company (c. 1910-1918), a 1246 foot siding was installed, connected at both ends. A track switched off from this siding to connect with the mill tracks. The siding was reduced by 355 feet on the east end and changed into a stub siding by early 1927. In early 1933 the siding was again shortened. The remaining 309 foot siding was retired in September 1968.

MILL RUN: Milepost 40.89. A 16×24 foot building described as a freight house was located here.

Mill Run was the junction with the logging railroad of the Spice Run Lumber Company to Hills Creek (1915-c. 1920).

BURNSIDES: Milepost 41.70. A 8.5×10.5 foot shelter shed was provided for passengers.

A 342 foot stub siding was located here. Retired in April 1935, it was on the north side of the main track and connected on the west end.

Siding: Milepost 42.46. Stub siding of about 275 feet in length, located north of the main track and connected on the west end. It was removed by 1916.

KENNISON: Milepost 42.96. Site of a small sawmill operated by F.P. Kidd (1918- c. 1921). It is assumed that a siding was installed for the mill but no evidence of it has been found.

Siding: Milepost 44.57. Stub siding 300+ feet long, connected on the east end, and north of the main track. It was abandoned by 1916.

SEEBERT: Milepost 45.77, elevation 2059. Agency station and telegraph office with call SB. The standard depot building here was originally 16.5×55 feet. In 1907 the freight room was lengthened by 25 feet. The building

was located about 1000 feet east of the road crossing, north of the track. The Seebert agency was closed in 1965 and the depot sold.

Other facilities here included stock pens, section foreman's house, bunkhouse and section tool house.

The passing siding at Seebert was originally 2997 feet in length. In June 1938 it was reduced in length on the east end to slightly over 1700 feet. It was extended eastward 250 feet in the spring of 1946, making its final length 1974 feet.

Two stub sidings were located on the north side of the main track, west of the depot. One switched from the main track and ran to the depot, 1419 feet in length (later 1408 feet). The second switched from the first and was 581 feet long (later 609 feet). This second siding was built to serve the Farmers Implement and Supply Company and the Seebert Milling Company. After World War II coal mined in the Briery Knob area was loaded on this track.

To the east of the depot a 553 foot stub siding switched from the main track and ran to the depot, serving the store of S.J. Payne. It was retired in June 1938.

WARNS: Milepost 46.32. Junction with the spur to the Warn Lumber Company mill on Stamping Creek (1905-1913). A 1316 foot siding, connected on both ends, was located on the Warn spur, a short distance from the Chesapeake and Ohio.

Greenbrier River Bridge: Milepost 47.87 (west pier).

WATOGA: Milepost 48.10. A passenger station, 16.5×30.5 feet, was located here in the "S" curve south of the main track and lumber company siding. It was similar in appearance to a standard depot but had no bay window. The building was probably built by the lumber company. A shelter shed was provided later.

Watoga was the location of a sawmill owned in succession, by the J.R. Droney, Tomb, and Watoga Lumber Companies (1906-c. 1920). The Empire Kindling Wood Company also had a plant here (1908-?). The track connecting the railroad to the mill tracks left the main line east of the depot. A logging line switched from this siding at the depot, ran parallel to the Chesapeake and Ohio to Violet, and then went up Beaver Creek

VIOLET (DAN): Milepost 49.23. Two sidings were located here. One was on the north side of the main track, connected on the west end, and 564 feet long. It was retired in February 1938.

The other siding was on the south side of the main track, connected on the west end, and 225 or more feet in length. It was removed before 1916.

A telegraph office may have been located here for a brief period of time right after the railroad was constructed.

Improvement Lick: Mileposts 50.23 and 50.32 (switches). Two stub sidings were located here, one on each side of the bridge. The one west of the bridge was 579 feet in length and owned by the Marlin Lumber Company. It was south of the main track and connected on the east end. The Marlin Lumber Company logging

Seebert depot as originally constructed. PCHS

Seebert depot after the freight room was lengthened in 1907. PCHS

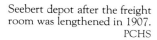

railroad came down Improvement Lick to this point and probably connected with the siding. The date the siding was removed is not known.

To the east of the bridge there was a siding about 400 feet long, south of the main track, and connected on the east end. It was probably installed to serve a small sawmill operated by Judson Howard prior to 1910. The siding was removed before 1916.

Siding: Milepost 51.48. Stub siding about 300 feet long on the south side of the main track and connected on the east end. It was abandoned by 1916.

BUCKEYE: Milepost 52.18. A 10.5 × 19.5 foot waiting shelter/freight room building was provided here. It was reduced to just a shelter shed by 1943.

Other facilities here included a section foreman's house and a section tool house.

Buckeye was the location of a 2528 foot passing siding (length given as 2009 feet in 1912), built on the north side of the main track instead of the more usual south side. At the east end of the passing track an abandoned (in 1916)

track continued about 350 feet to a former switch. Whether this indicates the passing siding was longer at one time or this was a separate side track has not been determined. The passing siding was retired in late 1936.

A 929 foot spur switched off from the passing siding to serve the mill of the American Column and Lumber Company (1914-1917).

Siding: Milepost 52.65. stub siding of about 200 feet on the south side of the main track, connected on the west end. It was removed by 1916.

MUNDAY LICK: Milepost 53.93 (switch). This flagstop (with Monday spelled Munday) appeared on only a few early schedules. A stub siding of about 450 feet was located here on the south side of the main track. Connected east of the stream, the siding crossed Monday Lick on its own bridge. This siding was no doubt used by the Greenbrier River Lumber Company as that company has a camp at Monday Lick. It was removed before 1916.

Flagstop shelter at Buckeye, about 1912.　　　PCHS

2432

Note: A number of the other early sidings along this section of the railroad were probably also put in for the Greenbrier River Lumber Company.

Between Monday Lick and Stillwell a logging railroad of the Marlin Lumber Company parallelled the Chesapeake and Ohio.

Siding: Milepost 54.21. Stub siding on the north side of the main track, about 225 feet long, and connected on the east end. It was removed by 1916.

Burrus Lumber Company Siding: Milepost 54.79. Stub siding of 501 feet to serve the mill of the R.S. Burrus Lumber Company (now the Kramer Lumber Company) (1963 to date). Built in April 1964, the siding was connected on the east end and on the north side of the main track.

STILLWELL: Milepost 55.06. Site of the mill of the Marlin Lumber Company (1921-1932). A spur from the main track served the mill, which was on Stillhouse Run.

Knapps Creek Bridge: Milepost 55.71 (west pier).

MARLINTON: Milepost 56.13, elevation 2128. Agency station and telegraph office with call MO. The still existing standard depot building here measures 16.5×76 feet and is located just east of the Eighth Street crossing. As originally constructed, it had three rooms— waiting room, 15.5 feet, agent's office, 12 feet, and freight room, 48.5 feet. The freight room had two doors on each side. A loading platform was built across the back side of the depot and connected with the trackside platform at least on the waiting room end of the building.

In late 1905 a separate freight station, 20.5×80.5 feet, was built east of the depot. At some date after 1917, the freight room in the depot was shortened by 22 feet to provide for a second waiting room, 19 feet, and enlarge the office by 3 feet.

The Marlinton depot was in use until the Greenbrier line closed at the end of 1978. The building has been donated to a local preservation group and renovated for use as a craft shop, information center, and museum.

The freight station was closed about 1955 and the building was removed in late 1976.

Sharing the depot platform is an 18.5×30.5 foot building that was originally a warehouse located across the tracks from the depot. It was moved to its present location in 1913 and converted to an office building. It housed the Greenbrier Division dispatcher for a few years. It was also used as the office for the Greenbrier maintenance supervisor as well as a Western Union telegraph office.

Other facilities at Marlinton included water tank, turntable, coaling trestle, section foreman's house, three bunkhouses, section tool house, stock pens, blacksmith shop, store house, and ashpit.

As might be expected there were a number of tracks in the Marlinton yard and variation in their arrangement over the years. The two major sidings were a loading siding north of the main track and a passing siding south of the main line. The loading siding's length was 2807.5 feet in 1916 and later extended to 3020 feet. The length of the passing siding was 2637 feet in 1916 with its length later increased slightly to 2701 feet.

For details on tracks in Marlinton see the maps.

Marlinton and Camden Railroad Junction: Milepost 56.96 (west switch). A 1530 foot siding on the north side of the main track, connected at both ends, served as the interchange track between the Marlinton and Camden Railroad and the Greenbrier Division. The Marlinton and Camden was the railroad of the Campbell Lumber Company (1905-1914) which had its mill at Campbelltown.

Greenbrier River Lumber Company Siding: Milepost 57.44. Spur serving the mill of the Greenbrier River Lumber Company (1900-1904), connected at the east end.

KNAPP (SIXTY): Milepost 59.36. A stub siding of about 570 feet in length was located here to the south of the main track and connected on the west end. Aban-

Depot at Marlinton as originally constructed.   PCHS

The Marlinton depot dozes in the summer sun on August 6, 1962, a far less busy place than when the above photo was taken. Note the physical changes in the building. One freight door has been eliminated and replaced with a window and door for what was originally a second waiting room. With the elimination of passenger service on the line, a train schedule board is no longer needed. The ramp on the platform was installed after the freight depot was closed in the mid 1950s.   A.D. Mastrogiuseppe, Jr.

Original bridge across Knapps Creek. It was replaced in 1929. The identity of the woman in the photograph is not known.
PCHS/NRP

Completing the new bridge across Knapps Creek in 1929 as part of a major bridge improvement program on the Greenbrier line so heavier freight engines could be used. PCHS/NRP

doned by 1916, the siding probably was for the small sawmill operated by the firm of Brown, Depp, and Swanson (c. 1909-c. 1911).

A second siding may have been laid on the same location in the early 1920s.

AUGUST: Milepost 60.25. A spur track, connected on the east end, served a small sawmill operated by a number of owners from 1899 to 1909.

A mail crane was located on the August platform.

THORNY CREEK: Milepost 61.02. A 15×24 foot building described as a freight house for the Kendall Lumber Company was located here.

Junction with the Kendall Lumber Company's railroad up Thorny Creek (1914-?).

Milepost 61.28. At some point the flagstop location was removed. A shelter shed was provided for passengers at the new location.

Two stub sidings were at this location, on the same grade south of the main track and connected on the east end. The first was about 380 feet long and out of service by 1916. The second siding was slightly shorter, 364 feet. It was in place by the summer of 1923 and retired in October 1963.

CLAWSON: Milepost 62.11 (later 62.40). A shelter shed was provided for passengers. Other facilities here included a section foreman's house, bunkhouse, and section tool house.

Edray was considered by the railroad as a name for this station but never used to the author's knowledge.

A 1501 foot passing siding was located at Clawson on the north side of the main track (the length was given as 2062 feet in 1912). It was retired in early 1977.

Double Culvert Hollow: Milepost 63.64 (stream). Location of a siding (or sidings) for the Kendall Lumber Company, south of the main track. Whether there was a single siding connected at both ends or two sidings, one on each side of the stream, is not clear at this writing. A logging spur track switched off from the siding on the west side of the stream. The siding or sidings were retired by the middle of 1921.

HARTER: Milepost 64.55. A station building, 10.5×20.5 feet, was provided here; probably of the passenger shelter/freight room arrangement.

A spur track served the mill of the Harter Brothers Lumber Company (1903-c. 1911).

Greenbrier River Bridge: Milepost 65.22 (west pier).

Just west of the bridge a logging spur track switched off to the south. It was built by A.D. Neill about 1920. Date of removal is not known.

Sharps Tunnel: Milepost 65.28 (west portal). This tunnel is 511 feet long.

Siding: Milepost 65.86. Stub siding to the north of the main track, about 220 feet in length and connected on the west end. It was abandoned by 1916.

BIG RUN (Lombardy): Milepost 66.74. At least three stub sidings were located here over the years, two on about the same grade.

One was on the north side of the main track, about 700 feet long, and connected on the west end. It served the small sawmill of W.W. Dempsey and was removed by 1916.

A second siding on this grade was installed in May 1920, also connected on the west end. Originally it was 465 feet long and later extended to 520 feet. Installed for P. Anastasio, it was also used by Williams and Pifer Lumber Company. The siding was retired in October 1963.

The third siding at Big Run was on the south side of the main track and also connected on the west end. It was about 530 feet long. Part of the siding was abandoned by 1916 and the remainder at an unknown date.

CAMPER: Milepost 70.11 (switch). Location of a short stub siding about 200 feet long. It was on the north side of the main track and connected on the west end. The siding was removed by 1916 and the flagstop did not appear in the schedule for many years.

CLOVER LICK: Milepost 71.17, elevation 2292. Agency station and telegraph office with call KC. The standard depot building here was west of the road crossing and north of the track. As built, it was about 40 feet

long. By 1907 however, the freight room was lengthened and the building became 65.5 feet long (16.5 feet wide). A second freight door was added. The next change in the Clover Lick building was a reduction in size, a dubious distinction that only this depot on the Greenbrier received. In October 1940, the freight room was removed, reducing the length of the depot to 29 feet. The waiting room was converted into a freight room with a freight door on each side. This station closed in 1952. The building still exists and is located in a field not far from its original trackside position.

Other facilities here included a water tank, section foreman's house, two bunkhouses, section tool house, and stock pens.

Ligon was briefly considered by the railroad as the name for this station (Dr. John Ligon was the postmaster), but never used.

A passing siding 1778 feet was located here. (Its length was given as 1500 feet in 1901 and 1461 feet in 1908.) It was retired in early 1977.

The track arrangement on the north side of the main track varied over the years. A stave mill was located at Clover Lick in 1901 by the National Cooperage Company and a spur track to it switched off from the main track near the bridge. By 1908 the track layout had been altered; probably at the time the DeRan Lumber Company built its mill on Clover Creek in 1906. The spur to the now out of business stave mill is gone and an 881 foot stub siding installed. It switched from the main track just

Clover Lick depot and original water tank, about 1907. When this photograph was taken the building was longer than originally built; note the change in shade of paint behind the man to the left.
PCHS

east of the depot. A spur to the DeRan mill switched from this siding. By 1911 the stub siding had been altered. The switch was moved to just west of the bridge and the siding lengthened to 949 feet, ending behind the depot. The spur to the Deran mill still switched from the siding. The DeRan mill closed in 1911. In November 1936 the siding was reduced in length on the west end, to 755 feet. It was removed in the summer of 1967.

A band mill was built across the river from Clover Lick by F.S. Wise and Sons in 1913 and a 2910 foot spur line built to it. This spur switched off from the passing siding near the depot. After being sold to A.D. Neill and then to the Raine Lumber Company, the mill finally closed in 1929. The date the spur track was removed has not been determined.

A short stub siding was on the north side of the main track just east of the bridge over Clover Creek. It was removed at an early date.

Final form of the depot building at Clover Lick. It was originally about 40 feet in length, later increased to 65.5 feet, and finally reduced to 29 feet. The building is now located in a field about a quarter mile from its trackside site.   WPM

STONY BOTTOM: Milepost 74.37. An 11×30 foot building described as a freight house was located here as well as a mail crane.

Two sidings were located at Stony Bottom to serve small sawmills on the north side of the main track. A spur to the Stony Bottom Lumber Company's mill (1906-?) left the main track west of Elk Creek. This spur was removed by 1916.

The other siding served the Buena Vista Hardwood Company (1901-middle 1920s) and was 618 feet long. It was connected on the west end. It remained in place following the closing of the mill but was reduced in length on the west end, to 500 feet, by the summer of 1933. It was retired in December 1966.

SITLINGTON (FORREST): Milepost 76.79 (second depot), elevation 2364. Agency station. The first depot here was of standard design and 61 feet long. It was located on the north side of the track and east of the road crossing. This building burned in October 1908. The replacement building, 16.5×32.5 feet, was of a different style from the standard depots as can be seen from its photo. The new depot was on the south side of the track about 475 feet west of the road crossing. The agency was closed in 1928. The depot building was removed in July 1947 and replaced with a 10.5×21 foot passenger shelter/freight room structure.

Other facilities here included a water tank, section foreman's house, agent's house, three bunkhouses, and another dwelling.

A passing siding, 2467 feet in length, was at Sitlington, on the north side of the main track rather than the more usual south side. It was retired in late 1936.

The name change from Forrest to Sitlington was made in 1903 or 1904.

Track remaining in place: Milepost 78.0. From this point to Durbin the track was purchased by the State of West Virginia and remains in place.

RAYWOOD: Milepost 78.46, elevation 2392. Agency station and telegraph office with call RW. This was the only agency station established after the early years of the Greenbrier Division. It served the mill and town of the Warn Lumber Corporation (1914-1928). A 16.5×50 foot freight and passenger station was built here but as no photograph of the building has been located it is not known if it was of the standard style. The building did not have the usual bay window of the standard depot. The agency was closed in 1929 but the building was not removed until October 1957.

A passing siding 1579 feet in length was located here. The spur track to the mill, which was across the river from the railroad, switched from the passing tracks. The passing siding was retired in late 1936.

An abandoned 700 foot westward extension from the passing siding is shown on the 1916 map. This is probably a portion of a previous siding as this is the probable site of a sawmill operated by Mohn and Braucher for a few years, beginning in 1901. A station called Moses Run (the stream just west of Raywood) appears on records of freight loadings in the early 1900s.

DEER CREEK: Milepost 79.55. The store of the Range Lumber Company was located at the platform and no doubt served as a depot. A mail crane was located adjacent to the platform.

Tracks were located here to serve the mill of the Range Lumber Company (originally Deer Creek Lumber Company) (1909-c. 1922) and an extract plant owned by the West Virginia Pulp and Paper Company (1914-1928). A spur to the sawmill yard left the main track 1400 feet west of the platform.

The extract plant was served by a 2326.5 foot siding that was connected at both ends. A number of sidings switched from this track to the plant area. At some date

Original depot building at Forrest (Sitlington). This building burned in October 1908. PCHS

Second depot building at Sitlington. Note the change in architecture between this building and the original depot. The photograph was taken on July 29, 1911, while the passengers are waiting for the arrival of Train No. 143.
PCHS

Section foreman's residence at Sitlington. PCHS

between the closing of the extract plant and 1937 the siding was reduced to stub siding of 1305 feet, connected on the west end. It was removed at a date not yet determined.

There was also a stub siding on the north side of the main track, about 200 feet long. It was connected on the west end and abandoned by 1916.

Wye track: Milepost 80.21 (west switch). A wye track for turning locomotives was located east of Cold Run. It was retired in June 1934.

CASS: Milepost 80.68 (original depot), elevation 2446. Agency station and telegraph office with call CS. The original depot was a standard style, measured 16.5×78 feet, and located east of the road crossing on the north side of the tracks. In the summer of 1923 the original station was replaced with a larger structure, 20.5×92.5 feet, located a few feet east of the first building. The new building was a modified form of the standard depot without a peaked roof over the agent's bay window and less gingerbread at the gables. The agency at Cass was closed in 1965 but the station continued to be used by the Cass Scenic Railroad. The building was destroyed by fire on May 5, 1975. The state built a new depot based on the 1923 structure but with a peaked roof over the bay window. The new building was completed in the spring of 1979.

Other facilities at Cass included a water tank, coaling platform, ash pit, section foreman's house, bunkhouse, and section tool house.

Given the size of the Cass lumber operation and the number of years it was in existence, 1900-1960, it is not surprising that there was a variation in track arrangement at Cass over the years. Prior to the opening of the sawmill in January 1902 a long siding switched from the main track west of the depot and eventually became the logging railroad up Leatherbark Creek. From this track a loading siding ran in behind the depot from the east. To complete the track layout in 1901, a siding which no doubt served as a passing siding was located south of the main track with a spur to the site of the mill construction.

With the completion of the mill the amount of track in the Cass yard expanded rapidly, coming to over 14,000 feet of track (not counting the main line). The track north of the main track became the passing siding and was 4496 feet in 1916. It was later split into two sidings, 1930 feet and 2533 feet in length. The track south of the main line became the major siding serving the mill complex, varying in length over the years, but in excess of

Part of Business Section, Cass, W.

POCAHONTAS SUPPLY CO

2440

Original depot at Cass. This building was replaced in 1923.   PCHS

A Shay locomotive poses for railfan photographers in front of the second Cass depot in 1961. The Shay is No. 1, built in 1905 and acquired by the West Virginia Pulp and Paper Company in 1915. At the time the photo was taken, the tank was lettered Greenbrier, Cheat and Bald Knob Scenic Railroad. After finishing its active career pulling trains on the Cass Scenic Railroad, No. 1 was sent to the Baltimore and Ohio Museum in Baltimore, Maryland, where it is now on display. This depot was built in 1923 and destroyed by fire in 1975.   John Killoran

2200 feet. The line of the logging railroad (the Greenbrier, Cheat and Elk Railroad after 1910) joined the passing siding. Various cross-over tracks, loading sidings near the depot and in the lumber yard, and a track to the mill pond completed the complex. The lumber company had its shops and engine facilities on Leatherbark Creek. (See map for details.)

Deever Run and CUP RUN: Milepost 82.49 (bridge over Deever Run). Although the flagstop was called Cup Run, Deever Run may have been the more appropriate name.

A stub siding of about 400 feet was located on the east side of Deever Run on the north side of the main track and connected on the west end. The siding was removed before 1916. A.V. Miller had a small sawmill at the mouth of Deever Run (c 1909-c. 1911) and this siding may have served the mill.

The West Virginia Pulp and Paper Company had a railroad up Deever Run in the late 1910s. It left the Greenbrier line west of Deever Run.

PINE FLATS: Milepost 83.33. Location of another sawmill operated by A.V. Miller (c. 1911-c. 1916). A spur track ran to the mill, connected on the west end. It was abandoned about 1916.

WANLESS: Milepost 84.40. A passenger shelter shed, 8×10 feet, was provided here.

In 1913 the Monroe Lumber Company located a mill here and installed a 300 foot stub siding north of the main track, connected on the west end. This siding was purchased by the railroad in December 1919. It was removed by early 1943 and rebuilt at Anthony. This siding was probably the second one at Wanless as the Coyner Brothers had a small sawmill here in the early 1900s.

Trout Run: Milepost 86.44 (switch). Junction with the West Virginia Pulp and Paper Company's logging railroad up Trout Run.

Note: Beginning with Milepost 87 the actual distance from Whitcomb is 0.1 of a mile or more than the mile of the milepost. The author has been using the actual distance as the station mileposts and will continue to do so. However, since the mileposts are still in existence as far as Durbin, a second figure will be given in parentheses based on the nearest milepost in case anyone is actually standing on the track with this book in hand. The author has found no explanation for this large variation between the mileposts and the actual distance; surveyor error, perhaps.

NIDA: Milepost 87.01 (86.92). A mail crane was located on the Nida platform.

Location of a third small sawmill operated by A.V. Miller (1916-1920). The mill was served by a spur track 696 feet long, connected on the west end. The spur had a third rail for most of its length to accommodate Miller's narrow gauge equipment.

About 0.2 of a mile east of Nida there was a stub siding

of 190 feet. It was on the north side of the main track and connected on the west end. In existence in 1916, it was removed at a date not yet determined.

HOSTERMAN (COLLINS): Milepost 88.17 (88.05), elevation 2584. Agency station and telegraph office with call CN. A standard depot, 20.5×60 feet, was located here on the north side of the track about 200 feet west of the bridge over Allegheny Run. This agency was one of the first on the Greenbrier to be closed although the exact date has not been found. The depot building was replaced by a 10×12 foot shelter shed in July 1928.

Other facilities here included a section foreman's house, two bunkhouses, and section tool house.

The name was changed from Collins to Hosterman about 1902 when the Hosterman Lumber Company erected a mill near here (1902-c. 1912).

Hosterman had a passing siding 2514 feet in length. It was reduced to a stub siding of 680 feet in November 1939 by removing the west end. The siding was retired in October 1963.

A logging railroad of the West Virginia Pulp and Paper Company was built from here up Allegheny Run in 1916.

No evidence has been found of a siding to the Hosterman mill; the mill was located close to the tracks, so the passing siding may have served the mill.

BOYER: Milepost 92.21 (92.02). This station was often referred to by local people as Boyer Siding to distinguish it from the community of Boyer on present day Routes 28/92.

Boyer served as the station for the long-lived lumber operation begun by M.P. Bock in 1900 and not finished until 1927 by the North Fork Lumber Company, with several other corporate names in between.

As the lumber company commissary was located trackside, it no doubt served as a depot. A shelter shed was provided in later years. A separate freight house for the lumber company was located here also.

A passing siding of 1451 feet was located at Boyer. It was retired in February 1935. From the passing siding a spur track went across the river to the mill. The mill was originally located at (highway) Boyer but later moved to a site at the mouth of Brush Run.

WHITING: Milepost 92.80 (92.61). A shelter shed was provided for passengers.

Whiting was the site of a small sawmill operated by Smith and Whiting (c. 1903-?). A stub siding, 599 feet long, was located here on the north side of the main track, connected on the east end. It was retired in November 1937.

Spillman Bottom: Milepost 93.8 (approximate). Site of a small sawmill operated by A.G. Miller and A.V. Miller (c. 1905-c. 1909). There may have also been a logging railroad switching from the Chesapeake and Ohio at this location to reach timber on the other side of the river, operated by Clark and McCullough (1909-?).

The author assumes that while the Miller mill was in operation a siding was located here and that it was a flagstop. However, no details on a siding have been found

nor has the flagstop name used by the railroad been determined.

West Fork Greenbrier River: Milepost 95.07 (94.90) (west pier).

End of 1978 Abandonment: Milepost 95.10 (94.93). The 1978 abandonment of the Greenbrier Branch ended at the east end of the bridge over the West Fork of the Greenbrier River.

DURBIN: Milepost 95.55 (95.38), elevation 2723. Agency station and telegraph office with call DR. The Durbin depot still exists but has been considerably altered from its original configuration. As originally built, it was a standard style building, 16.5 feet wide, and from photos looks to have been about 75 feet long. By 1917 the building had been lengthened to 109 feet. Although the freight room may have been enlarged some, most of the additional space was used for a larger office. At some later date the bay window was moved about 25 feet and the peaked roof above it removed. The Durbin depot, as related before, handled the business of both the Chesapeake and Ohio and Western Maryland. The depot remained open until the closing of the Greenbrier line in 1978. It was not used by the Western Maryland during the final years of freight service on that railroad's Durbin Branch. Now owned by the State of West Virginia, the building has been leased for use as a senior citizens center and also contains a craft shop.

Other facilities at Durbin included a water tank, coaling platform, engine inspection pit, track scale, office building, section foreman's house, five bunkhouses, section tool house, and stock pens.

At Durbin the junction between the Chesapeake and Ohio and the Western Maryland is in the form of a wye track, west of the depot. A 2104 foot passing siding is located east of the wye. In 1916 the other tracks at Durbin were two stub sidings north of the main track. One, 624 feet long, was built from the east leg of the wye to the depot. The other was a 662.5 foot siding on the east side of the depot, connected at the east end.

Little change was made at Durbin as the years went by. In the summer of 1923 a 435 foot stub siding, west connected, was laid from the passing siding to serve a Standard Oil Company bulk plant, located south of the main track. This siding was also used as an engine track. A 190 foot stub siding was built from bulk plant siding and raised by an earth embankment to provide a coal loading facility for the locomotives. By early 1928 the siding east of the depot was changed from being connected on the east end to have the switch at its west end. It was also shortened to 568 feet. As a guess, this change was made in connection with using this track for the passenger train to lay up over night after the cutback in passenger service to Durbin from Winterburn. These three sidings were retired in late 1976 and early 1977. (The stub siding west of the depot remains in place in 1984.)

A siding to serve the mill of the J.B. Belcher Lumber Company was laid in September of 1962, east of the West Fork bridge. It is 651 feet long, on the south side of the

Durbin depot as originally constructed and passenger train pulled by Class A-4-4-0 No. 29. Photograph taken in May 1907. PCHS

View of Durbin showing the depot after it was lengthened. The building to the right of the water tank is the pump house. Note the grade for what must have been a wye track south of the tracks.

PCHS

Durbin depot, November 1982. The weeds around the building, the vacant operator's desk in the bay window, and the calendar still showing December 1978 tell the story of a once busy facility no longer needed. However, for this particular depot the story has a happy ending. Since this photo was taken, the building has been renovated for a senior citizens center and for use by the Cass Scenic Railroad.   WPM

track, and west connected. Although the mill has been closed for a number of years, the siding remains in place in 1984.

End of Track, 1984: Milepost 96.03. In October 1984 the Chessie System donated the track material from this point to Bartow to the Cass Scenic Railroad. Removal work began the same month.

FRANK: Milepost 96.48. Site of the still operating tannery which was built by the Pocahontas Tanning

Company in 1904 and now owned by the Howes Leather Company. The tannery was served by a complex of tracks connected to the main line on both sides of the tannery.

Hoover Siding: Milepost 96.79. Spur track serving the mill operated by Hoover Brothers (1902-?) located across the East Fork from the tannery. The spur was gone by 1916.

BARTOW: Milepost 97.88, elevation 2774. Agency station and telegraph office with call BR. The standard depot here was a 20×81 foot structure located on the south side of the track about 1200 feet east of the road crossing. The agency was closed in 1928. In early 1935 the depot building was replaced by a 10×20.5 foot passenger shelter/freight room structure.

Other facilities here included stock pens, section foreman's house, and bunkhouse.

A total of three stub sidings have been located at Bartow. The original siding was a depot track south of the main track. Connected on the west end, it was 627 feet long.

An east connected siding of 309 feet was located on the north side of the main track to serve the bulk plant of the Marlinton Electric Company. Neither the date of installation or retirement have been determined.

A siding was installed in the summer of 1963 on the south side of the main track to serve the sawmill of Green Bank Mills, Inc. (now Interstate Lumber Company). Connected on the west end, it was 499 feet long.

Coming from the west, these sidings were located in reverse order from the way described.

End of Track, 1939-1984: Milepost 97.94. In 1933 the Chesapeake and Ohio received permission from the Interstate Commerce Commission to abandon the track between Bartow and Winterburn. The track from Milepost 98.08 was taken up in December 1933 and January 1934. In September 1939 another 742 feet of track was removed.

HOUCHINS: Milepost 99.2 (approximate). The exact location of the flagstop is not known. Several sidings and spurs were located here; one or more of them no doubt in connection with the mill of the Hoover and Yeager Lumber Company (later Bartow Lumber Company) (1907-c. 1913 or 1914).

Coming from the west, a west connected spur switched off to the south. In 1916, 335 feet were still in place and were removed in August 1917.

Next, a logging line of the George Craig and Sons Lumber Company joined the Chesapeake and Ohio from the north. It was built about 1915.

Then there was a stub siding, about 950 feet long, on the south side of the main track, connected on the east end. It was abandoned before 1916.

Finally a spur track of unknown length, connected on the east end, switched off to the south. No doubt serving the Hoover and Yeager mill, it was removed by 1916.

THORNWOOD (DUNLEVIE): Milepost 100.46. Location of a large sawmill started by E.V. Dunlevie in

Depot at Bartow.   PCHS

End of the line—Winterburn. This depot served the adjacent towns of Thornwood and Winterburn. The photograph shows the original depot building at this station.
                                                                                    PCHS

1905. The mill operated until 1920 under several different corporate names. The lumber company store was located at the platform and no doubt served as a depot.

Three sidings switched from the main track to serve the mill complex. One switched off some 2100 feet west of the bridge to the mill yard. The other two switches were just west of the bridge over the East Fork.

East Fork Greenbrier River: Milepost 100.64 (west pier).

WINTERBURN: Milepost 100.72 (second depot), elevation 2868. Agency station and telegraph office with call WN. The original depot was a standard building about 40 feet long, located north of the main track and about 100 feet east of the bridge. By 1916 a larger building had been constructed south of the main track within the wye. This building was 16.5×61.5 feet and had two bay windows. The station platform extended along both the main track and the west leg of the wye. The date the Winterburn agency was closed is unknown but the depot was removed in July 1926.

Winterburn was the location of the mill of the George Craig and Sons Lumber Company (1905-1918).

The Chesapeake and Ohio main track, after crossing the East Fork, formed the top of the wye track. The legs and tail track of the wye were formed by the Craig logging railroad up the Little River (also used by the Thornwood mill). The main track continued on Chesapeake and Ohio right-of-way until Milepost 100.79 and then on Craig land to an ending at Milepost 100.96. The last 730 feet of the track were the "laying up track" for Train 141/144 when it ran as far as Winterburn. An ash pit was located on this part of the track.

Mock-up of the spherical journal for the 140-foot telescope at the National Radio Astronomy Observatory at Green Bank being checked for clearance in Sharps Tunnel, September 1, 1961.
National Radio Astronomy Observatory

Epilogue

AS THE PLANS WERE BEING DEVELOPED FOR THE BUILD-
ing of one or more railroads into the Upper Greenbrier
Valley, numerous predictions were made as to the long
term prosperity such a project would bring both to the
region and the railroad company itself. Some of these
predictions have already been quoted in Chapters One
and Two.

To encourage the construction of the proposed Greenbrier Railroad along the river south of Marlinton, a
writer in *The Pocahontas Times* in February 1898
predicted:

> . . . Large towns would spring up in both the Little Levels of
> Pocahontas and the Big Levels of Greenbrier, both of which
> sections would be forever patrons of the Greenbrier Railroad.

A similar prediction had been made in the same
publication almost two years earlier:

> . . . When the timber is removed a rich farming country would
> be left, peopled as thickly as the most populous sections of the
> state, and who would forever support a railroad.

Those commenting on the future should, of course
never use the word "forever." As the history of the
Greenbrier Division unfolded, it was abandoned before
even reaching its eightieth birthday. Eighty years is but a
split second in the course of history and far from forever.

In defense of the writers in the *Times* in the late nineteenth century, however, it must be said that no one
could have predicted the rapid economic and technolog-
ical changes that have occurred throughout the twentieth century. The automobile in the 1890s was little more
than a toy for the idle rich, the motor truck was yet in the
future, and the first airplane had not yet flown. The
nation's economy has changed from one based on heavy
industry and resource extraction to the production of
high technology and providing services.

The effect that these changes would have on the
almost totally dominant form of transportation at the
turn of the century—the railroad—in less than a person's
lifetime could not have been foreseen by the most per-
ceptive person, much less the promoters of a railroad
into the Greenbrier Valley. Also impossible to predict
would have been the way the railroad industry has
acquiesced in its decline and often seemed to have co-
operated with its executioners. The loss of business due
to competition has generally brought from the railroads

a reaction of reducing service, in both quantity and quality, and cutbacks in trackage instead of fighting back with
new ideas, aggressive marketing, and improved service.

To a certain extent this was true on the Greenbrier
Division. Although the closing of most of the major
industries on the line by 1970 probably made the future
of the branch extremely doubtful, the author can't help
but wonder what might have been the results of a determined effort by the Chesapeake and Ohio to increase
business and improve service to existing customers. It
might have only delayed the inevitable, but we will now
never know for sure.

One can also speculate on whether the choice of routes
may have ensured the closure of the Greenbrier line at a
relatively early time. As related in Chapter Two, Chesapeake and Ohio Vice-president Decatur Axtell argued
for a route from Covington using the already existing
line to Hot Springs, going by way of Mountain Grove,
through the Ryder Gap and on to the Greenbrier River
north of Marlinton. The advantages of this route, in his
opinion, over the all-river route were a shorter distance
and better gradients for traffic en route to Covington. Mr.
Axtell also had a low opinion of the potential for traffic of
the region south of Marlinton. Perhaps if the Greenbrier
line had gone the way Mr. Axtell urged, this combination
of the Greenbrier and Hot Springs Branches into one line
might have meant that trains would still be running to
Hot Springs and into the Upper Greenbrier Valley instead of both lines now being abandoned.

However, this alternate routing of the Greenbrier
Division would have no doubt prevented the heavy use
of the division for through traffic that occurred in the
1920s and during World War II. This was because the cars
making up the through traffic came from the west and
would have had to climb the Allegheny Mountain twice
if the line to Durbin began at Covington. Mr. Axtell
died in 1922 before this use of the Greenbrier line began.
If he had lived to have seen the manifest trains traveling
on "The Durbin Route," he might have changed his
mind about the river route for the Greenbrier Division.

With the ever increasing costs of building and maintaining our nation's highway system and the inevitable
depletion of the oil supplies that will occur in the future,
the abandonment of the Greenbrier Branch and similar
rail lines may come to be regretted by people other than

just rail buffs. The future may see the re-laying of track on some abandoned rail lines as the nation finds the need to return to a more fuel efficient transportation system. Unfortunately, the cost of restoring the one hundred miles of track along the Greenbrier River may preclude the returning of rail service to the Upper Greenbrier Valley. Our future in this region may be a return to the isolation that created the desire for the construction for the Greenbrier Division in the first place.

All of the above is speculation, of course. So as we consider the history of the Greenbrier line, we should not dwell on its relatively early demise, but that it provided the service for which it was constructed. That the line fell victim to technical, economic, and social change and corporate decision making after less than eighty years of operation is no reflection upon the men who dreamed the necessary dreams, did the construction work, manned the depots and maintenance forces, and operated the trains. They and the Greenbrier Division did what they were called upon to do and though the Greenbrier line may be gone, it will live on in the memories of those of us who knew it.

Droop Tunnel, 1980s.   Photograph by Ron Snow

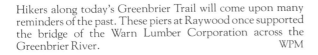

Hikers along today's Greenbrier Trail will come upon many reminders of the past. These piers at Raywood once supported the bridge of the Warn Lumber Corporation across the Greenbrier River.   WPM

Bibliography

Arritt, Gay, *Historical Sketches of the Allegheny Highlands*, Allegheny Historical Society, Covington, Virginia, 1982.

Callahan, James M., *History of West Virginia*, The American Historical Society, Inc., Chicago and New York, 1923.

Chesapeake and Ohio Railway (C. and O. Ry. material on the Greenbrier Division used by the author is located in a number of places including the Chessie System office in Baltimore, Md., Interstate Commerce Commission, Washington, D.C., and the collections of the Chesapeake and Ohio Historical Society and the Marlinton Railroad Depot, Inc.):

Agreement No. 10361, September 1, 1925, between the Chesapeake and Ohio and the Western Maryland Railways concerning joint facilities at Durbin.

Annual Reports, 1899-1939.

Axtell, Decatur, "Greenbrier Railway," from an unpublished manuscript history of the Chesapeake and Ohio, written in 1920, pp. 47-49.

Bridge List, Greenbrier Sub-division, revised to 1977.

Comparative Statement of Passengers, Freight Tonnage, and Revenue for the years ending June 30, 1903, 1904, 1905, 1906, 1913, 1914, 1915, and 1916.

Employee Timetables for June 4, 1905; June 2, 1912; May 24, 1914; April 3, 1927; July 24, 1932; March 21, 1937; April 27, 1941; September 26, 1948; April 27, 1952; and October 28, 1956.

Freight Bills, Receipts for LCL Freight, and Through Bills of Lading, Marlinton Depot, 1903 and 1904.

List of Force Code Numbers, Clifton Forge Division, August 1, 1953, and January 1, 1963.

Map of Greenbrier Branch (Alternative Routes) and Contemplated Connections, May 19, 1899.

Map of Located Line, White Sulphur to Marlington (sic) and Projected Line North, to Forks of Greenbrier, Office of Chief Engineer, July 29, 1897.

Map of Greenbrier, West Va. (North Caldwell), May 1899.

"On Time Circular," September 3, 1927, giving the schedule of manifest time freight trains.

Public Timetables for June 20, 1911; June 2, 1912; _____, 1914; September 15, 1922; April 4, 1925; February 10, 1928; April 30, 1930; July 15, 1930; December 12, 1937; April 28, 1940; and October 27, 1957.

Rail Chart, 1930.

Roadway Completion Reports, Greenbrier Branch, 1917-1976.

Side Track Records, 1937, revised to 1943.

Sketch of Chesapeake and Ohio Ry. from Boyer, West Va., to Winterburn, West Va., Office of Engineer Maintenance of Way, September, 10, 1909.

Telegraph messages, 1901, from employees on the Greenbrier Division to various officials.

Track Chart and Profile, Greenbrier Branch, revised to 1960.

Valuation maps and engineering notes produced in 1916 and 1917 by the survey teams under the direction of the Interstate Commerce Commission; in particular:

Accounting Report on the Chesapeake and Ohio Railway Company, as of June 30, 1916.

Engineering notes on the physical aspects of the Greenbrier Division (buildings, bridges, rail, etc.)

Right-of-way and Track Maps, Greenbrier Branch (V-12), June 30, 1916, and a revised (to 1977) set of the same.

Clemons, Thomas E., unpublished manuscript of notes on his years of work on Chesapeake and Ohio maintenance forces.

Deike, Dr. George H., III, *Logging South Cheat, The History of the Snowshoe Lands*, Cass, West Virginia, 1978.

Dixon, Thomas W., Jr., "Parlor Car to Durbin, A History of Passenger Service on the Greenbrier Subdivision of the C&O," *Chesapeake and Ohio Historical Newsletter*, Chesapeake and Ohio Historical Society, January 1973 (Vol. V, No. 1), pp. 10-14.

Dixon, Thomas W., Jr., "Doodlebugs, A History of the C&O Gas-electric Cars and RDCs," *Chesapeake and Ohio Historical Newsletter*, Chesapeake and Ohio Historical Society, October 1975 (Vol. VII, No. 10), pp. 11-14.

Dixon, Thomas W., Jr., "The 'Standard C&O Victorian' depot," *Railroad Model Craftsman*, July 1979 (Vol. 48, No. 2), pp. 76-84.

Fansler, Homer F., *History of Tucker County, West Virginia*, McClain Printing Company, Parsons, West Virginia, 1962.

Greenbrier County:

County Court Book No. 6.

Deed Books, various ones between 1881 and 1966.

Greenbrier Scenic Railway, various items including correspondence, newspaper articles, scenic railroad proposals, and trip brochures.

Greenbrier Railway, Right-of-Way Maps, February 1901, with some revisions to 1906.

Interstate Commerce Commission:

Investigation No. 2588 on the accident on May 22, 1942.

Various documents and orders relating to the abandonment of the Chesapeake and Ohio Greenbrier Branch, Docket No. AB-18 (Sub-No. 17).

Various documents and orders relating to the abandonment of the Western Maryland Durbin Branch, Docket Nos. AB-18 (Sub-No. 48F), AB-69 (Sub-No. 10F), and AB-19 (Sub-No. 60F).

McKee, Leo A., and Lewis, Alfred L., *Railroad Post Office History*, Mobile Post Office Society, Pleasantville, New York, 1972.

Newspapers:

The major newspaper source was *The Pocahontas Times*, which began publishing at Huntersville, W. Va., in 1883, moved to Marlinton, W. Va., in 1892, and continues today. File copies exist from 1889 to the present and the complete file was researched.

Other newspapers which were important sources of information were the *Greenbrier Independent* (Lewisburg, W. Va.,), *The Marlinton Journal*, the *Marlinton Messenger*, and *The Republican News* (Marlinton).

Pocahontas County:

County Court Order Books 5, 7, and 8.

County Court Docket Book

Deed Books, various ones between 1875 and 1980.

Railroad maps and profiles on file at the Courthouse, Atlantic and Western RR, Cherry Valley RR, Chicago, Parkersburg, and Norfolk Ry., Greenbrier Ry., Greenbrier, Monongahela, and Pittsburgh RR, Iron Mountain and Greenbrier RR, Kanawha and Chesapeake RR, Midland Ry., and Williams River Branch of the Chesapeake and Ohio Ry.

Release of Liens Book 25.

Trust Deed Book 1

Price, Paul H., *Pocahontas County*, West Virginia Geological Survey, Morgantown, 1929.

Price, Paul H., and Heck, E.T., *Greenbrier County*, West Virginia Geological Survey, Morgantown, 1939.

Small, Maxwell M., "The New 140-foot Radio Telescope," *Sky and Telescope*, November 1965 (Vol. XXX, No. 5).

Staufer, Alvin, Shuster, Philip, and Huddleston, Eugene L., *C&O Power*, Alvin Staufer, Publisher, 1965.

Summers, Festus P., *John Newlon Camden, A Study in Individualism*, G.P. Putnam's Sons, New York, 1937.

Turner, Charles W., *Chessie's Road*, Garrett and Massie, Richmond, Virginia, 1956.

Turner, William P., Jr., *From Bourbon to Liberal, The Life and Times of John T. McGraw, 1856-1920*. PhD dissertation, West Virginia University, 1960.

Western Maryland Railway, Public Timetable, January 6, 1958.

West Virginia, State of:

Acts of the Legislature, 1867-1907.

Public Service Commission, Annual Reports 1 to 61, Order Book 22.

Secretary of State, Annual Reports 1902-1907.

West Virginia State Gazetteer and Business Directory, 1908-1909, R.L. Polk Company, Pittsburgh, 1908.

West Virginia University Library, West Virginia and Regional History Collection:

Johnson N. Camden Papers

Henry G. Davis Papers

John T. McGraw Papers

Westvaco Corporation, Covington, Virginia, various articles and unpublished notes on the history of the company.

Wickline, W.W., Jr., "The Iron Mountain and Greenbrier Railroad," *The Journal of the Greenbrier Historical Society*, September 1965 (Vol. I, No. 3), pp. 11-23.

Williams, John A., *West Virginia and the Captains of Industry*, West Virginia University Library, Morgantown, 1976.

Appendix

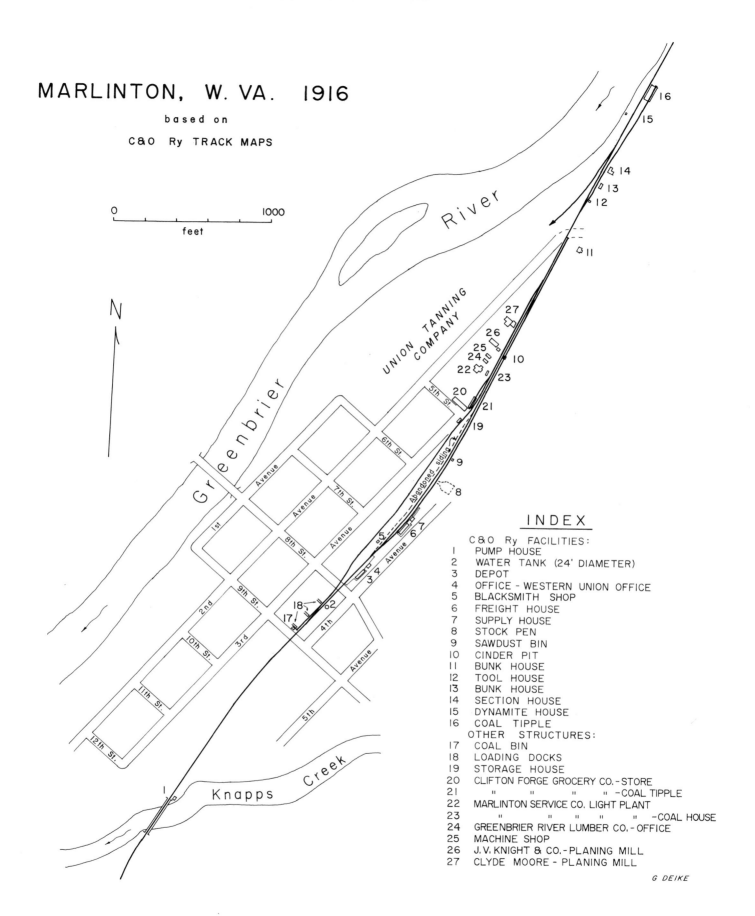

MARLINTON, W. VA. 1916

based on

C&O Ry TRACK MAPS

0 _____ 1000
feet

N

River

Greenbrier

UNION TANNING COMPANY

Abandoned siding

Knapps Creek

1st Avenue
2nd Avenue
3rd Avenue
4th Avenue
5th

5th St.
6th St.
7th St.
8th St.
9th St.
10th St.
11th St.
12th St.

INDEX

C&O Ry FACILITIES:
1 PUMP HOUSE
2 WATER TANK (24' DIAMETER)
3 DEPOT
4 OFFICE - WESTERN UNION OFFICE
5 BLACKSMITH SHOP
6 FREIGHT HOUSE
7 SUPPLY HOUSE
8 STOCK PEN
9 SAWDUST BIN
10 CINDER PIT
11 BUNK HOUSE
12 TOOL HOUSE
13 BUNK HOUSE
14 SECTION HOUSE
15 DYNAMITE HOUSE
16 COAL TIPPLE
OTHER STRUCTURES:
17 COAL BIN
18 LOADING DOCKS
19 STORAGE HOUSE
20 CLIFTON FORGE GROCERY CO.-STORE
21   "   "   "   " -COAL TIPPLE
22 MARLINTON SERVICE CO. LIGHT PLANT
23   "   "   "   " -COAL HOUSE
24 GREENBRIER RIVER LUMBER CO.-OFFICE
25 MACHINE SHOP
26 J. V. KNIGHT & CO.-PLANING MILL
27 CLYDE MOORE - PLANING MILL

G DEIKE

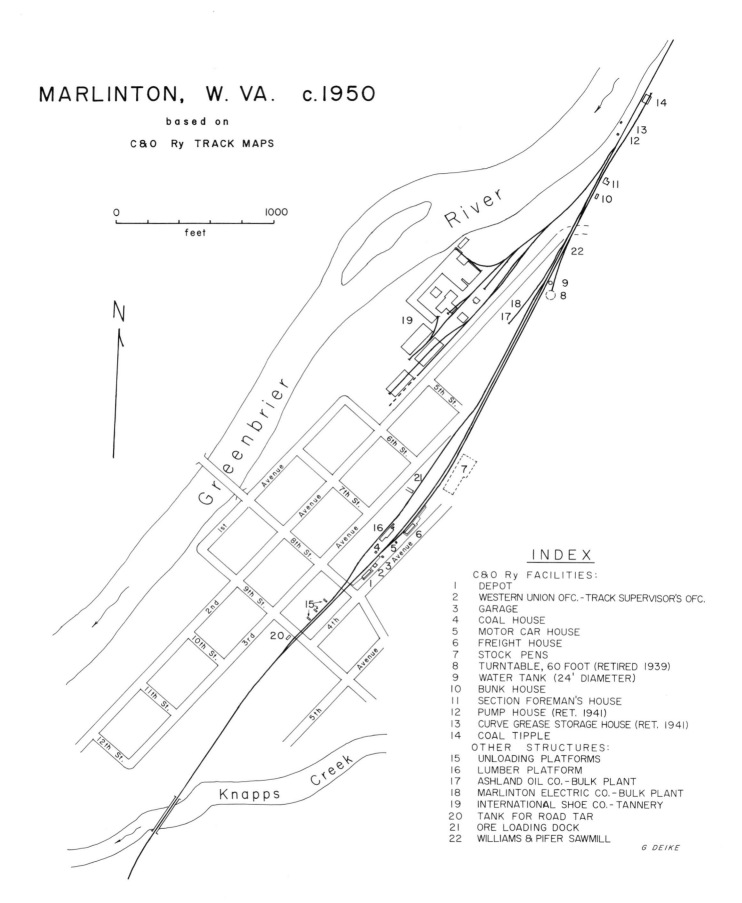

MARLINTON, W. VA. c.1950

based on

C&O Ry TRACK MAPS

0 _____ 1000
feet

N

River

Greenbrier

Knapps Creek

1st Avenue
2nd Avenue
3rd Avenue
4th Avenue
5th Avenue

5th St.
6th St.
7th St.
8th St.
9th St.
10th St.
11th St.
12th St.

INDEX

C&O Ry FACILITIES:
1 DEPOT
2 WESTERN UNION OFC. - TRACK SUPERVISOR'S OFC.
3 GARAGE
4 COAL HOUSE
5 MOTOR CAR HOUSE
6 FREIGHT HOUSE
7 STOCK PENS
8 TURNTABLE, 60 FOOT (RETIRED 1939)
9 WATER TANK (24' DIAMETER)
10 BUNK HOUSE
11 SECTION FOREMAN'S HOUSE
12 PUMP HOUSE (RET. 1941)
13 CURVE GREASE STORAGE HOUSE (RET. 1941)
14 COAL TIPPLE
OTHER STRUCTURES:
15 UNLOADING PLATFORMS
16 LUMBER PLATFORM
17 ASHLAND OIL CO. - BULK PLANT
18 MARLINTON ELECTRIC CO. - BULK PLANT
19 INTERNATIONAL SHOE CO. - TANNERY
20 TANK FOR ROAD TAR
21 ORE LOADING DOCK
22 WILLIAMS & PIFER SAWMILL

G DEIKE

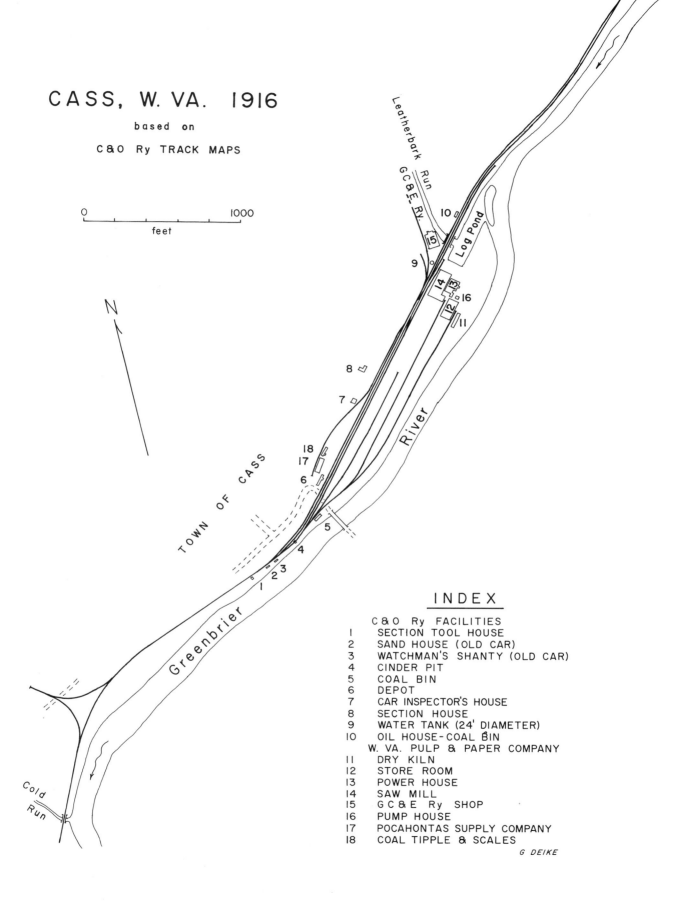

CASS, W. VA. 1916

based on

C & O Ry TRACK MAPS

0 _____ 1000
feet

N

Leatherbark Run

GC&E Ry.

Log Pond

River

Town of Cass

Greenbrier

Cold Run

INDEX

C & O Ry FACILITIES
1   SECTION TOOL HOUSE
2   SAND HOUSE (OLD CAR)
3   WATCHMAN'S SHANTY (OLD CAR)
4   CINDER PIT
5   COAL BIN
6   DEPOT
7   CAR INSPECTOR'S HOUSE
8   SECTION HOUSE
9   WATER TANK (24' DIAMETER)
10 OIL HOUSE-COAL BIN
W. VA. PULP & PAPER COMPANY
11 DRY KILN
12 STORE ROOM
13 POWER HOUSE
14 SAW MILL
15 GC&E Ry SHOP
16 PUMP HOUSE
17 POCAHONTAS SUPPLY COMPANY
18 COAL TIPPLE & SCALES

G DEIKE

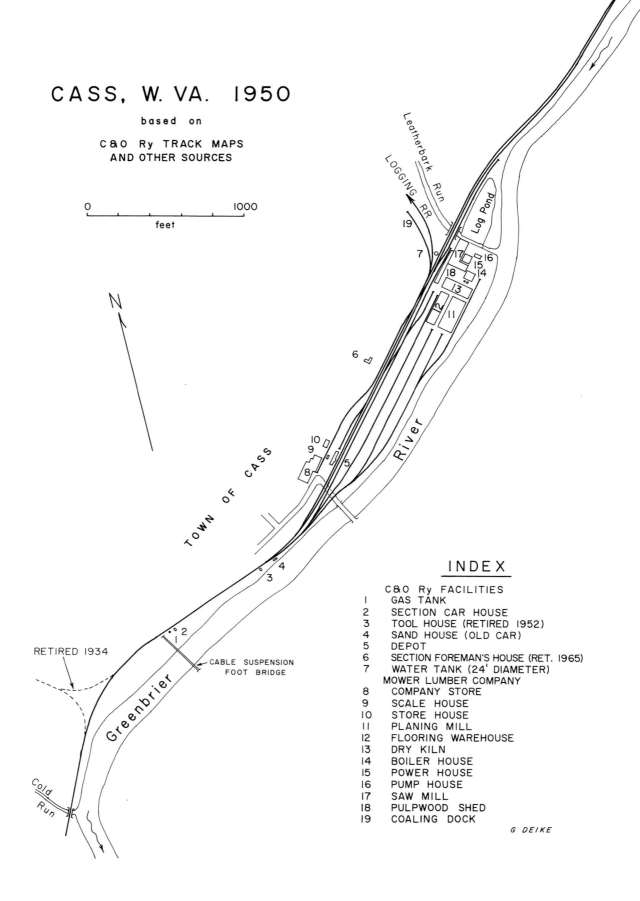

CASS, W. VA. 1950

based on

C & O Ry TRACK MAPS
AND OTHER SOURCES

0   1000
feet

N

Leatherbark Run

LOGGING RR

Log Pond

River

TOWN OF CASS

Greenbrier

RETIRED 1934

CABLE SUSPENSION
FOOT BRIDGE

Cold Run

INDEX

C&O Ry FACILITIES
1   GAS TANK
2   SECTION CAR HOUSE
3   TOOL HOUSE (RETIRED 1952)
4   SAND HOUSE (OLD CAR)
5   DEPOT
6   SECTION FOREMAN'S HOUSE (RET. 1965)
7   WATER TANK (24' DIAMETER)
MOWER LUMBER COMPANY
8   COMPANY STORE
9   SCALE HOUSE
10   STORE HOUSE
11   PLANING MILL
12   FLOORING WAREHOUSE
13   DRY KILN
14   BOILER HOUSE
15   POWER HOUSE
16   PUMP HOUSE
17   SAW MILL
18   PULPWOOD SHED
19   COALING DOCK

G DEIKE

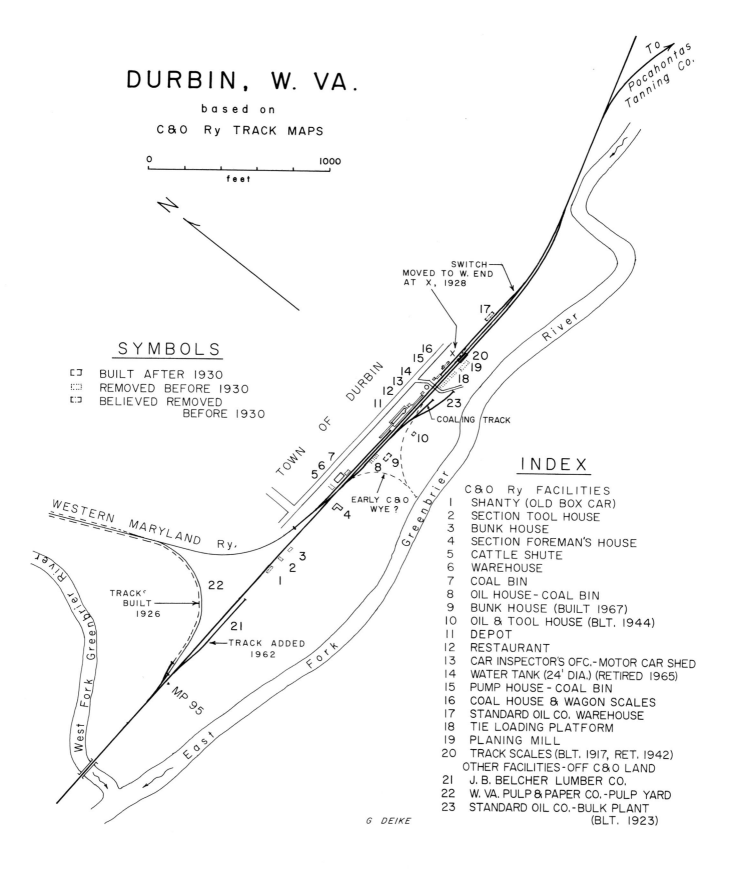

DURBIN, W. VA.

based on

C&O Ry TRACK MAPS

0 —————————————— 1000
feet

N

SYMBOLS

⊏⊐ BUILT AFTER 1930
⊏⊐ REMOVED BEFORE 1930
⊏⊐ BELIEVED REMOVED
            BEFORE 1930

To Pocahontas Tanning Co.

River

SWITCH
MOVED TO W. END
AT X, 1928

TOWN OF DURBIN

COALING TRACK

EARLY C&O
WYE ?

Greenbrier

WESTERN MARYLAND Ry.

TRACK
BUILT
1926

West Fork Greenbrier River

TRACK ADDED
1962

MP 95

East Fork

INDEX

C&O Ry FACILITIES
1   SHANTY (OLD BOX CAR)
2   SECTION TOOL HOUSE
3   BUNK HOUSE
4   SECTION FOREMAN'S HOUSE
5   CATTLE SHUTE
6   WAREHOUSE
7   COAL BIN
8   OIL HOUSE - COAL BIN
9   BUNK HOUSE (BUILT 1967)
10 OIL & TOOL HOUSE (BLT. 1944)
11 DEPOT
12 RESTAURANT
13 CAR INSPECTOR'S OFC.-MOTOR CAR SHED
14 WATER TANK (24' DIA.) (RETIRED 1965)
15 PUMP HOUSE - COAL BIN
16 COAL HOUSE & WAGON SCALES
17 STANDARD OIL CO. WAREHOUSE
18 TIE LOADING PLATFORM
19 PLANING MILL
20 TRACK SCALES (BLT. 1917, RET. 1942)
    OTHER FACILITIES-OFF C&O LAND
21 J. B. BELCHER LUMBER CO.
22 W. VA. PULP & PAPER CO.-PULP YARD
23 STANDARD OIL CO.-BULK PLANT
                        (BLT. 1923)

G DEIKE

From 1942 until the end of Western Maryland Railway passenger service to Durbin, the service was provided by a mixed train. On June 13, 1952, WM train No. 153 is photographed at Glady en route to Durbin. The engine is H7b class 2-8-0 No. 752.   William P. Price

C. and O. motor car 9055 and WM 2-8-0 752 rest at the Durbin water tank before beginning their trips back to Ronceverte and Elkins respectively. June 13, 1952.   William P. Price

Gas-electric No. 9055 pulling a wooden combination coach/baggage car at Durbin on July 24, 1936. Note the track scale on the passing siding that was used to weigh the cars interchanged between the Western Maryland and the Chesapeake and Ohio. Robert G. Lewis

Original water tank in Durbin, photographed on December 21, 1917. This tank was replaced in 1928.

Western Maryland Historical Society
courtesy of Ed Palaszynski

Addendum

Page 47

In August of 1926 the office of the Chesapeake and Ohio's Chief Engineer prepared a series of drawings showing proposed extensions of most of the passing sidings along the Greenbrier Subdivision. The sidings would then be able to hold trains of 100 cars. Also proposed at this time were extensions of the yard tracks at Ronceverte to hold 100-car trains and a new 100-car passing siding between Whitcomb and Ronceverte. The passing sidings to be extended were those at North Caldwell, Anthony, Renick, Droop Mountain, Beard, Seebert, Clawson, Cass, Hosterman, and Durbin. At Marlinton the loading siding was to be extended rather than the existing passing siding. The lengths of the extended sidings were to range from 5600 feet to almost 6600 feet.

None of the proposed extensions were constructed, possibly indicating that the traffic on "The Durbin Route" manifest freight trains never grew to the extent the Chesapeake and Ohio expected.

Page 50

In the late 1920s thought was given to extending both the Greenbrier and Warm Springs Valley Subdivisions northward. This planning went at least as far as the preparation of a preliminary map in June 1929. In both cases the tapping of new timber lands seems to have been the motivation behind the proposed extensions.

On the Greenbrier line a thirty-mile extension was proposed from Winterburn into Pendleton County. The map shows the extension going up the East Fork of the Greenbrier River to Poca Lick Run; up that stream and Walderman Run to the top of Allegheny Mountain; crossing into Pendleton County near the point where Pocahontas, Pendleton, and Highland counties join; down the mountain to the North Fork of the Potomac River; and finally down the North Fork almost to Macksville.

The proposed extension of the Warm Springs Branch was longer, 43½ miles. It was to leave the existing line at Bacova; cross to the Jackson River; continue up the Jackson River to its head; cross to the South Branch of the Potomac; and end about two miles into Pendleton County, at Harper.

Neither extension was built, of course, victims of the Depression, if not of other factors.

Page 57

Diesel locomotives were used at least twice on the Greenbrier Branch before the July, 1953 runs of No. 5882. In either 1949 or 1950, ALCO RS-2 diesel switcher 5500 or 5501 made about two runs on the Greenbrier line as part of the testing of these two units on the Chesapeake and Ohio. About 1951, two other ALCO diesel engines, probably S-2s, were used on two consecutive coal trains over the line. No. 5882 and the other diesels that ended the era of steam power on the Greenbrier Branch were EMD GP-7 class road switchers.

Page 70

Since the first printing of this book, the history of the Greenbrier line has proceeded as follows as of early 1986:

—The disastrous flooding that hit the Greenbrier Valley and other parts of eastern West Virginia on November 4-5, 1985, heavily damaged the track between Cass and Durbin as well as the Greenbrier River Trail below Cass. The Marlinton depot had about four feet of water inside but, fortunately, structural damage to the building was slight. As the Cass to Durbin track is state owned, it is eligible for federal funding for repair. Plans are now underway for the rebuilding of the line and hopefully the work will be underway in the summer of 1986.

—On December 18, 1985, the Chesapeake and Ohio applied to the Interstate Commerce Commission for authority to abandon the portion of the Greenbrier Branch that remained in commercial use after the 1978 abandonment, the 3.06 miles from Whitcomb to just beyond North Caldwell. The railroad had retained this section of track due to traffic inbound to a lumber warehouse and cement plants and outbound traffic from a scrap yard. However, since 1978 this traffic declined. The investigation by the West Virginia Railroad Maintenance Authority following the railroad's request to abandon found the traffic on this section of track had consisted of only four cars in the past year.

No protests against the abandonment were filed and the ICC approved the ending of service to North Caldwell in a decision dated January 23, 1986.

—No progress has been made in making the Old Spruce to Spruce connection for use by the Cass Scenic Railroad.

—An agreement between the state and the Chessie System concerning the track into the Durbin depot has several times been reported to be nearly finalized, but as of this writing there has been no public announcement of any such agreement.

—Providing any type of rail service for the tannery at Frank seems to no longer be under consideration by anyone involved.

—The Western Maryland line into Durbin remains in place at this writing. The Chessie System and the U.S. Forest Service are moving toward the sale of the right-of-way to the Forest Service and this should be completed by the summer of 1986. The Forest Service has no interest in the track but is willing to consider the track remaining in place if another agency is willing to buy the rail. This is not likely to happen and the track will probably be sold by the railroad for scrap as soon as the land is transferred to the Forest Service.

What will very likely be the final train to operate on this line was run on October 28, 1985, by the Cass Scenic Railroad. Shay No. 6 ran to Greenbrier Junction and returned to Cass with a train of rolling stock that were surplus from the state-owned South Branch Railroad.

Page 77

In time for the beginning of the school year in the fall of 1915 the Chesapeake and Ohio granted a special rate of 1½ cents per mile to pupils attending school in Marlinton.

Page 78

Wendell A. Scott was at Renick when Nos. 141 and 144 made their last runs and recalls the event as follows:

"I was there" when the last A-10 pulling the evening "up" train deadheaded back to Ronceverte. It was after dark—a rare occasion for us to see the headlight and the coaches lit—when he came down the river. He really whistled for the crossings as the little train went down the river and around the mountain—into history. We could even hear the whistle faintly as he went through Spring Creek.

Mr. Scott shared some other memories of Greenbrier Branch with the author:

The "up train" would be on the ready track at Ronceverte, the coaches on a siding, until after 16* arrived. The engine would then run east to get on the siding, pick up the coaches, east again to get onto the main, then back down to the depot. In the very early 20s, they still had the yellow (wooden?) coaches—the seats were woven-wicker upholstery. I remember stopping at Whitcomb and whistling for permission to cross over the west main to go up the Greenbrier. Pictures that stay in your mind—I remember meeting the "down" train at about Anthony—it passed us on our left—I can see it coming toward us, the exhaust gleaming white in the summer morning sun.

In the later years, the quality of the roadbed was apparent after you left the branch to the mainline to Ronceverte—very smooth on the main "high iron."

One time, at least, they used a G-5 freight engine on the morning "up" train. Heard the low pitch "hoot" whistle, and ran out in the yard. Those little drivers and rods were really flashing. For whatever reason, made me think of "The Little Engine That Could." In the late afternoon, the sunlight would bounce off the counterweights of the G-5s westbound.

The A-10s had Stephenson valve gear and an incredibly sharp exhaust working eastbound out of the Renick station—almost like the "pop pop pop" of a gas engine.

*Note: No. 16 was an eastbound local passenger train on the main line due in Ronceverte before the morning Greenbrier train was scheduled to leave.

Page 111 under NORTH CALDWELL

In September 1901 the depot was completed and the name of the station changed from Little Sulphur to Hunter. In August 1902 the name was changed again, to North Caldwell, due to confusion with a station called Hunter on the Norfolk and Western Railway.

Page 116

revised details on Siding and KENNISON

Siding: Milepost 42.46. Stub siding about 275 feet long that served a small sawmill operated by A.R. Kennison. Removed by 1916, it was located north of the main track and connected on the west end. This siding may have gone by the name of Andrew.

KENNISON: Milepost 42.5 (approximate). Site of sawmill operated by F.P. Kidd (1918-c. 1921). A siding of unknown length served the mill, which was south of the main track. A mail crane was located here for the Kennison Post Office.

Milepost 42.96. After the Kidd mill closed, the flagstop location was changed. A shelter shed was provided for passengers.

Eugene Burner shared with the author some of his memories as a boy in Durbin growing up around the railroad as follows:

Although I never worked for the R.R., reading the book brings back many memories—playing baseball in the wye, putting pennies on the tracks, walking up the Western Maryland tracks and down the C & O to go fishing and waving at the section crews as they bumped by on their motor cars. At night I remember lying in bed listening to the freights shifting in the yard and the locomotives blowing off down by the water tank.

During 1944 and 1945 I worked at the Durbin post office under the postmaster, Harper Hudson. The mail was brought to the office by car (Luther Peck) but the clerk on the train always threw off the first class mail sack opposite the post office (at the lower edge of town) and we went over after it. Almost every day especially during the summer, a lady from Hosterman got off the train with a basket of eggs, did her shopping at our metropolis and then rode the train home.

In reference to your section on accidents I wonder how many incidents were indirectly cause by trains, etc. I know that my great uncle, Lee Burner, was killed at Durbin in 1905 when his horse, scared by the train, ran away at the crossing just north of the water tank. We had a horse, Myrtle, which ordinarily was as slow as molasses, but the sight of a train brought her to life. We were careful to time our crossings of the Western Maryland tracks in West Durbin so they wouldn't coincide with the train's appearances.

The accident in which Lee Burner was fatally injured occurred on August 14, 1905. Mr. Burner, 69, was thrown from his buggy when his horse started to run as a train pulled into the Durbin depot. He died in about two hours from injuries. The news accounts of the accident do not say which railroad's train was involved.

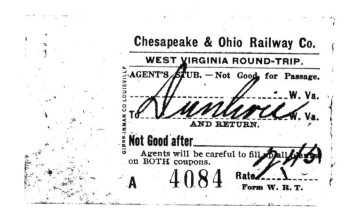

Durbin Depot, Sta. 2465+74 (47.04) E.D.

By the date of this photo, December 21, 1917, the Durbin depot had been lengthened from its original size to handle the business of the two busy branch lines that joined at this location. The milepost on the photo, 47.04, is the Western Maryland milepost for the Durbin depot and is the miles from Elkins.

Western Maryland Historical Society, courtesy of Ed Palaszynski

The Durbin depot in its final form shown in a photo taken on May 22, 1963. By this date the only train activity was tri-weekly freights of the Chesapeake and Ohio and the Western Maryland.

Photo by Ray Hicks, courtesy of Ed Palaszynski

At several locations along the Greenbrier Division, lumber company buildings served as unofficial or semi-official depots. This photo shows the Range Lumber Company store at Deer Creek near Cass.
PCHS

Western Maryland Railway passenger train at Burner, on the West Fork of the Greenbrier River above Durbin.   PCHS

About the Author

William Price McNeel has deep roots in the Greenbrier Valley of West Virginia, with his father's family having lived in Pocahontas County since before the Revolutionary War. His mother's family came into the area in the early 1800s. He grew up in Charleston, W. Va., but came to his parents' home country to teach at Marlinton High School following graduation from Marietta College, Ohio. He also taught at Pocahontas County High School and earned a MS degree from the University of Oregon. After teaching in Australia for two years, he returned and went to work at *The Pocahontas Times*, which has been owned by the Price Family since 1892. He is presently the editor of the paper.

The author has had a lifelong interest in railroads and the history of the Pocahontas County area. He is a founding member of both the Pocahontas County Historical Society and the Mountain State Railroad and Logging Historical Association and serves on the boards of each. *The Durbin Route* is the author's first book and the result of a number of years of information gathering.

He and his wife, Denise, have one son, James.